Praise for Previous Edition of *Joomla!: A User*

"A complete guide to the powerful features of Joomla! 1.5 ... ... a holistic approach to building a Joomla!-powered website—from th... ...tself to its many extensions, search engine optimization, and even building your own tableless template. The novice reader is eased into the subject and confidently guided through the basic principles and on to the more advanced features. This guide empowers the user not only to build a professional website but to also to make it a success."

—Russell Walker, CEO, Netshine Software Limited
(Joomla! Development Consultancy)

"If you've been using or following Joomla! in the past years, you've most likely seen the name Barrie North or Joomlashack. Barrie has been a member of the community for a long time and, as such, my expectations for this book were pretty high. Besides explaining how Joomla! works from a usability point of view, there is valuable information for people who want to learn serious template building, and readers can stand out of the crowd by using Barrie's steps to make their (X)HTML and CSS optimized for accessibility and SEO. All in all, this book is a great guide that comes at the right time for newcomers and more experienced Joomla! users and developers alike. Well done, Barrie!"

—Arno Zijlstra, Joomla! cofounder, custom template specialist,
www.alvaana.com

"In a time when solid, real-life Joomla! 1.5 information is rarely available, this book is a thirst-quenching oasis of knowledge. The abundant and clear examples in the book make Joomla! 1.5 websites within anyone's reach. I heartily recommend *Joomla! 1.5: A User's Guide* by Barrie North."

—Tom Canavan, author of *Dodging the Bullets:
A Disaster Preparation Guide for Joomla! Based Web Sites*

"Refreshing! After reading many how-to books, this one is a step beyond the rest because of its focus on examples based on live sites. This book is well crafted for beginners to advanced users with a well-organized overview that walks you through the entire Joomla! CMS."

—Steven Pignataro, corePHP, www.corephp.com

"As a long-time Joomla! end-user and developer, I had low expectations for anything new I might learn from this book. However, I was pleasantly surprised to find it a great refresher course, especially since the book is logically organized, leading beginners from the most basic Joomla! concepts and continuing through to more complex ones, such as tableless template design and how to write a template for Joomla! 1.5. In summary, Barrie North has produced the gold-standard print reference for Joomla! 1.5. I highly recommend this book for novice and intermediate users if you want to make the most of Joomla!"

—Vicor Drover, http://dev.anything-digital.com

Joomla!™ 1.6:
A User's Guide

Building a Successful Joomla! Powered Website

Barrie M. North

PRENTICE
HALL

Prentice Hall
Upper Saddle River, NJ · Boston · Indianapolis · San Francisco
New York · Toronto · Montreal · London · Munich · Paris · Madrid
Cape Town · Sydney · Tokyo · Singapore · Mexico City

Joomla!™ 1.6:
A User's Guide

Building a Successful Joomla! Powered Website

Barrie M. North

PRENTICE
HALL

Prentice Hall
Upper Saddle River, NJ · Boston · Indianapolis · San Francisco
New York · Toronto · Montreal · London · Munich · Paris · Madrid
Cape Town · Sydney · Tokyo · Singapore · Mexico City

Many of the designations used by manufacturers and sellers to distinguish their products are claimed as trademarks. Where those designations appear in this book, and the publisher was aware of a trademark claim, the designations have been printed with initial capital letters or in all capitals.

The author and publisher have taken care in the preparation of this book, but make no expressed or implied warranty of any kind and assume no responsibility for errors or omissions. No liability is assumed for incidental or consequential damages in connection with or arising out of the use of the information or programs contained herein.

The publisher offers excellent discounts on this book when ordered in quantity for bulk purchases or special sales, which may include electronic versions and/or custom covers and content particular to your business, training goals, marketing focus, and branding interests. For more information, please contact:

U.S. Corporate and Government Sales
(800) 382-3419
corpsales@pearsontechgroup.com

For sales outside the United States please contact:

International Sales
international@pearson.com

Visit us on the Web: informit.com/ph

Library of Congress Cataloging-in-Publication Data:

North, Barrie M.
  Joomla! 1.6 : a user's guide : building a successful Joomla! powered website / Barrie M. North.
    p. cm.
  ISBN 978-0-13-248706-1 (pbk. : alk. paper)
  1. Joomla! (Computer file) 2. Web sites--Authoring programs. 3. Web site development.
I. Title.
  TK5105.8885.J86N67 2011
  006.7'8--dc22
                                                                          2010051011

ISBN-13: 978-0-132-48706-1
ISBN-10: 0-132-48706-3

Text printed in the United States on recycled paper at RR Donnelley in Crawfordsville, IN.

First printing February 2011

Editor-in-Chief
Mark Taub

Executive Editor
Debra Williams Cauley

Development Editor
Songlin Qiu

Marketing Manager
Stephane Nakib

Managing Editor
Kristy Hart

Project Editor
Anne Goebel

Copy Editor
Geneil Breeze

Indexer
Heather McNeill

Proofreader
Kathy Ruiz

Technical Reviewers
Robert P. J. Day
Torah Bontrager

Publishing Coordinator
Kim Boedigheimer

Cover Designer
Chuti Prasertsith

Compositor
Nonie Ratcliff

For Sarah

Contents

Preface

Joomla is an open source content management system (CMS) that anyone can download for free (see forge.joomla.org/sf/go/projects.joomla/frs). This makes it an ideal choice for small businesses. Don't let the price tag fool you, though; Joomla is powerful and robust, and more big organizations are choosing to use open source software solutions all the time. Its universal appeal has made Joomla hugely popular as a CMS.

As Joomla matures, it is being adopted by more and more organizations, from corporations to schools and universities to government organizations to newspapers and magazines to small businesses. Its greatest advantage is its flexibility. You can see it on a huge variety of sites.

The Purpose of This Book

This book is about Joomla, a popular and award-winning ("Best Linux/Open Source Project" for 2005) open source CMS. This book walks, step-by-step, through everything you need to develop a successful website powered by Joomla. The book gives a general overview of management of a CMS and teaches you key concepts regarding content organization, editing, and templates. Finally, this book examines some more general topics, such as how to maximize search engine optimization (SEO) with Joomla and what resources are available in the Joomla web community.

This book focuses on the most current release of Joomla—version 1.6. This release is an important update that includes some key new features such as better Access Control Levels (ACL).

This Book's Target Audience

This book primarily targets people using Joomla to create a website, either for themselves or their clients. It's easy to read and low on technical jargon. It doesn't assume that you know PHP or CSS.

All the concepts in this book are explained with step-by-step contextual examples. If you follow all the steps in all the chapters, you will build seven separate Joomla websites!

How to Use This Book

You can use this book in several ways. You can start at the beginning and go chapter-by-chapter, as you develop your own site. The book is carefully laid out so that introductory ideas in the earlier chapters are developed and built on to help you understand more advanced concepts later. You can also use the book as a reference. If you need some quick ideas of what newsletter extensions are available, for example, head to Chapter 6, "Extending Joomla!" Finally, the appendixes contain valuable information about various aspects of Joomla.

Chapter 1: Content Management Systems and an Introduction to Joomla!

In today's fast moving web, if you have a website that doesn't have rich functionality or fresh content, you will find yourself at a disadvantage to those that do. The idea of powering websites with a CMS has been around for some time, but only recently with the advent of high-quality open source CMS scripts like Joomla have we seen these powerful CMS tools coming into the hands of you and me.

In this chapter, I explain in detail the difference between a "traditional" website and one using a CMS. We also look at the history of Joomla and an overview of some of its features.

Chapter 2: Downloading and Installing Joomla!

Joomla is one of the most popular open source CMSs on the planet. The first step in becoming part of the "Joomlasphere," the vibrant community that exists around the Joomla Project, is to download Joomla and install it on your web server.

This chapter shows you how to get up and running with a Joomla site. The two steps are to find and download the latest files and to install them on a web server. This chapter describes both a local installation—your home computer to use as you read this book (if you don't have a hosting account or have a slow Internet connection)—and a real web server installation.

Chapter 3: Joomla! Administration Basics

The term "site administration" usually means the day-to-day tasks of adding content, managing users, and making sure installed components and modules are running correctly. With a properly configured Joomla site, the administration burden is relatively low. Most of the effort can be dedicated to generating that all-important content.

In this chapter, we go on a whirlwind tour of the core administrative functions you need. I won't be going step-by-step explaining every last button in the admin backend, but rather picking out key functions, tips, and tricks that you need to know to keep your site humming.

Chapter 4: Content Is King: Organizing Your Content

As a CMS, Joomla's primary function is to organize and present all the content in your site. It does this through content articles. These discrete pieces of content must be organized into a hierarchy of categories.

This chapter provides an in-depth tutorial that explains how Joomla displays its content articles and how you can organize the hierarchical structure of them. It details how to plan and organize the content and user experience for the site. It also explains how to best structure content into them for small and large sites.

Chapter 5: Creating Menus and Navigation

Menus are perhaps the core of a Joomla site. In a static HTML site, they merely serve as navigation. In a Joomla site, they serve that purpose, but also determine the layout of what a dynamic page looks like and what content appears on that page when you navigate to it. The relationship between menus, menu items, pages, and modules is perhaps one of the most confusing in Joomla. This chapter explains this relationship so that you can create a navigation scheme that works for your site.

Chapter 5 examines how the navigation (menus and links) is built for a Joomla website and how the different aspects interact to produce a coherent navigation structure.

Chapter 6: Extending Joomla!

It's hard to find a Joomla powered website that has not added functionality beyond the basics with some sort of extension. The word "extension" collectively describes components, modules, plug-ins, and languages. Many hundreds of extensions are available both free and commercially from third-party providers.

In this chapter, we look at some examples of core and third-party Joomla extensions. We also examine how they are installed and managed in Joomla.

Chapter 7: Expanding Your Content: Articles and Editors

There are two main ways to add and manage content in a Joomla site: through the frontend or backend. Part of the attraction of Joomla is the ability to easily add and edit content through a What You See Is What You Get (WYSIWYG) editor.

In this chapter, we look at WYSIWYG and how it functions in the backend with managers, administrators, and super administrators. We then examine how authors, editors, and publishers manage content through the frontend.

Chapter 8: Getting Traffic to Your Site

Search Engine Optimization (SEO) might be one of the most maligned subjects on the Web. From black hat SEO—people who use unethical methods to gain rank in search engines—to their counterparts white hat SEO—the good guys—how best to get traffic to your site is loaded with opinion and myth.

Trying to learn about SEO is difficult, to say the least. In this chapter, I emphasize *Search Engine Marketing* (SEM). I point out some obvious SEO tips and how they apply to Joomla, but I also discuss a more holistic marketing plan including such strategies as Pay Per Click and blogging.

Chapter 9: Creating Pure CSS Templates

In this chapter, we go through the steps of creating a Joomla template. Specifically, we create a template that uses Cascading Style Sheets (CSS) to produce a layout without use of tables. This is a desirable goal as it means that the template code is easier to validate to World Wide Web Consortium (W3C) standards. It also tends to load faster, be easier to maintain, and perform better in search engines. We discuss these issues in detail later in the chapter.

Chapter 10: Creating a School Site with Joomla!

School websites tend to be medium to large in size. Two of Joomla's defining characteristics are its power and flexibility, but it can be time intensive to set up. This leads us to this chapter—an extensive guide to creating and setting up a school website using the Joomla CMS.

Chapter 11: Creating a Restaurant Site with Joomla!

This chapter looks at the entire process of creating a small business website, in this case a restaurant website, from scratch. Starting from an analysis of needs, this chapter shows you how to organize possible content all the way through to adding photos and considering further extensions.

Chapter 12: Creating a Blog with Joomla!

It seems like everyone has a blog these days. Many people still think of blogs as personal diaries, but more and more organizations and companies are using blogs as a way to shape perception of who they are and what they do. Chances are, if you go to a company's website today, you will find a link to its blog somewhere on the site. What is becoming more common on websites now, is a section of the site that is dedicated to the blog.

This chapter talks about blogs in a more general sense: a dynamic communication medium for a person or organization to interact with stakeholders. We look at creating a blog from scratch using Joomla.

Appendix A: Getting Help

Stuck with Joomla? A tremendous amount of information is available on the Web, as well as many active communities to ask for help.

Appendix B: A Guide to Joomla! 1.6 ACL

Access Control Levels dictate what users can perform what tasks in your Joomla website. This brief guide helps you understand how ACL has been changed and improved in Joomla 1.6.

Appendix C: A Quick Introduction to SEO

Need some quick tips to help your search engine ranking? Implement the tips in this appendix.

Appendix D: Installing WampServer

This appendix provides a quick guide to installing WampServer on your home computer. This package is important, so you can follow along with all the site examples in the book.

What Is a Content Management System?

A CMS is a collection of scripts that separate content from its presentation. Its main features are the ease of creation and editing of content and dynamic web pages. CMSs are usually sophisticated and can have newsfeeds, forums, and online stores. They are also easily edited. More and more websites are moving toward being powered by CMSs.

Most CMSs are expensive—in the range of $50,000 to $300,000—but an increasing number of open source alternatives are becoming available. Open source CMSs have become increasingly more reliable and are now being used for important projects in many companies, nonprofits, and other organizations.

A CMS separates the responsibilities involved in developing a website. A web designer can be concerned with the design, and nontechnical people can be responsible for the content.

A modern CMS is usually defined by its capability to manage and publish content. Most CMSs do far more, taking advantage of a wide range of extensions and add-ons that add functionality.

What Is Open Source Software?

Joomla is an example of open source software; its nonprofit copyright holder is Open Source Matters (see www.opensourcematters.org). An open source project is developed by a community of developers around the world, all volunteering their time. Some examples of open source software you might have heard of are Firefox, Apache, Wiki, Linux, and OpenOffice. All these projects have challenged and even surpassed their commercial equivalents. If you are curious about how and why people should create powerful software for free, look for more information on these sites:

- en.wikipedia.org/wiki/Open_source
- www.opensource.org

Things to Look For

The following are specific elements to look for when reading:

TIP
The tip boxes give more advanced ideas about an aspect of Joomla. You usually can find more details about the tip at compassdesigns.net.

NOTE
The note boxes denote cautions about an aspect of the topic. They are not applicable to all situations, but you should check whether a note applies to your site.

THE LEAST YOU NEED TO KNOW
Explanations of key critical concepts can be found in the Least You Need to Know boxes. These are worth circling in a big red pen or writing out for yourself on a cheat sheet.

CAUTION
Cautions provide critical information.

Joomla!

The full and proper name of the Joomla CMS includes an exclamation point, as shown here. For the sake of readability, and a tree or two, I've kept the exclamation point in heads but dropped it in the text.

www.joomlabook.com

You can find more information about this book, including complete browsable and downloadable versions of all the sites created in the chapters, at www.joomlabook.com.

Writing About Open Source Products

As with many open source products, Joomla changes on a very short release cycle. New maintenance releases with slight changes can often be released in as little as six weeks, and usually the changes are difficult to find out about. This makes writing for open source challenging. If you find minor inconsistencies in this book, chances are it is because of these minor updates. To stay informed of recent changes to Joomla, consult the forum at www.joomlabook.com where you can find discussions of Joomla versions.

Acknowledgments

Without the continuing support of my wife, Sarah, this book would not have been possible. Sarah let me frequently slip off to work on the manuscript. Part of my thanks also goes to the three boys who (mostly) managed not to bug me while I was writing.

I'd also like to thank the third-party developers I frequently annoyed on Skype with questions about this or that.

Finally, many thanks to the guys who live on the trunk—the many developers who selflessly contribute code to the Joomla project on a daily basis.

About the Author

Barrie M. North has more than 20 years of experience with the Internet as a user, designer, and teacher. He has spent more than 8 years in the education field, becoming steadily more involved in web technology, teaching web design classes to students and technology integration to teachers. Most recently, he worked as an IT consultant for two new schools pioneering the use of technology. As well as web design, he has provided web marketing/SEO, usability, and standards compliance expertise to his clients.

He is a founder of Joomlashack.com, one of the oldest and most popular Joomla template providers, and SimplWeb.com, a service that provides easy-to-use, turnkey Joomla hosting for those new to Joomla. He also maintains a blog about all things Joomla at CompassDesigns.net. When not working, he can frequently be found on the Joomla community boards, and he has written many free tutorials for using Joomla. His combination of Joomla expertise, educational skills, and engaging writing has produced a book accessible to everyone. Barrie lives in South Strafford, Vermont.

Chapter 1

Content Management Systems and an Introduction to Joomla!

In This Chapter

On today's Internet, if your website doesn't have rich functionality or fresh content, you will find yourself at a disadvantage. The idea of powering websites with content management systems (CMSs) has been around for some time, but it is only recently—thanks to high-quality open source CMS scripts such as Joomla—that you and I can now use these powerful CMS tools.

In this chapter, I explain in detail the difference between a traditional website and one that uses a CMS. I also provide a look at the history of Joomla and give an overview of some of its features. This chapter answers the following questions:

- What is a CMS, and how is it different from a traditional website?
- What is Joomla, and where did it come from?
- What can Joomla do?
- What are the basic elements of a Joomla web page?

What Is a Content Management System?

What exactly is a content management system (CMS)? To better understand the power of a CMS, you need to understand a few things about traditional web pages. Conceptually, there are two aspects to a web page: its content and the presentation of that content. Over the past decade, there has been an evolution in how these two pieces interact:

- **Static web pages**—The content and presentation are in the same file.
- **Web pages with Cascading Style Sheets (CSS)**—The content and presentation are separated.
- **Dynamic web pages**—Both content and presentation are separated from the web page itself.

Static Web Pages

A web page is made up of a set of instructions written in Hypertext Markup Language (HTML) that tells your browser how to present the content of a web page. For example, the code might say, "Take this title 'This is a web page,' make it large, and make it bold." The results will look something like the page shown in Figure 1.1.

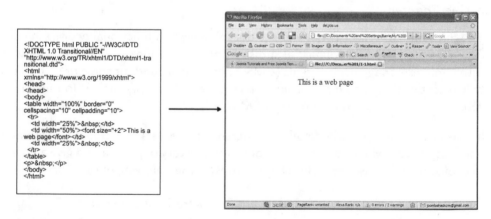

FIGURE 1.1   Results of code on a web page.

This way of creating a web page is outdated, but an astonishing number of designers still create sites using this method. Pages created using this method have two main drawbacks:

- **Difficult to edit and maintain**—All the content shown on the page ("This is a web page") and the presentation (big and bold) are tied together. If you want to change the color of all your titles, you have to make changes to all the pages in your site to do so.
- **Large file sizes**—Because each bit of content is individually styled, the pages are big, which means they take a long time to load. Most experts agree that large file sizes hurt your search engine optimization efforts because most search engines tend not to completely index large pages.

Web Pages with CSS

In an effort to overcome the drawbacks of static web pages, over the past four or five years, more comprehensive web standards have been developed. Web standards are industrywide "rules" that web browsers such as Internet Explorer and Mozilla Firefox follow (to different degrees, some better than others) to consistently output web pages onto your screen. One of these standards involves using Cascading Style Sheets (CSS) to control the visual presentation of a web page. CSS is a simple mechanism for adding style (for example, fonts, colors, spacing) to web documents. All this presentation information is usually contained in files that are separate from the content and reusable across many pages of a site.

Using CSS, the generated web page from Figure 1.1 might look as shown in Figure 1.2.

Now the file containing the content is much smaller because it does not contain presentation or style information. All the styling has been placed in a separate file that the browser reads and applies to the content to produce the final result.

Using CSS to control the presentation of the content has big advantages:

- Maintaining and revising the page is much easier. If you need to change all the title colors, you can just change one line in the CSS file.
- Both files are much smaller, which allows the data to load much more quickly than when you create web pages using HTML.

- The CSS file will be cached (saved) on a viewer's local computer so that it won't need to be downloaded from the Web each time the viewer visits a different page that uses the same styling rules.

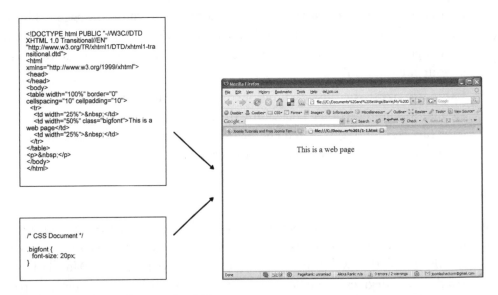

. **FIGURE 1.2**   A modern web page using CSS.

NOTE

Take a look at www.csszengarden.com. Every page on this classic CSS site has identical content but has a different CSS applied. You can browse through the designs and see the same content styled in hundreds of different ways.

THE LEAST YOU NEED TO KNOW

Modern websites separate content from presentation by using CSS. CSS files contain presentation rules that determine how content should look when it's displayed. The same CSS file can be used with many different pages of content to maintain a consistent appearance and style across a site.

Dynamic Web Pages

A CMS further simplifies web pages by creating dynamic web pages. Whereas CSS separates presentation from content, a CMS separates the content from the page. Therefore, *a CMS does for content what CSS does for presentation.* It seems that between

CSS and a CMS, there's nothing left of a web page, but in reality what is left can be thought of as insertion points, or placeholders, in a structural template or layout. For example, see Figure 1.3.

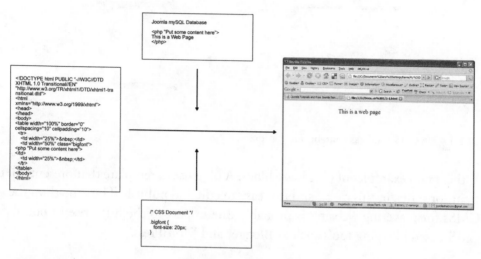

FIGURE 1.3   The structure of a CMS web page.

The "put some content here" instruction tells the CMS to take some content from a database, the "pure content," and place it in a designated place on the page. So what's so useful about that trick? It's actually very powerful: It separates out the responsibilities for developing a website. A web designer can be concerned with the presentation or style and the placement of content within the design layout—the placeholders. This means that nontechnical people can be responsible for the content—the words and pictures of a website—without having to know any code languages, such as HTML and CSS, or worry about the aesthetics of how the content will be displayed. Most CMSs have built-in tools to manage the publication of content.

It's possible to imagine a workflow for content management that involves both designers and content authors (see Figure 1.4).

A CMS makes the pages dynamic. A page doesn't really exist until you follow a link to view it, and the content might be different each time you view it. This means a page's content can be updated and customized based on the viewer's interactions with the page. For example, if you place an item in a shopping cart, that item shows up on the shopping cart page. It was stored in a database and now gets inserted into the "shopping cart placeholder." Many complex web applications—for example, forums, shopping carts, and guest books, to name a few—are in fact mini CMSs (by this definition).

FIGURE 1.4   A CMS manages content publication.

Other good examples of CMSs are blogs. A blog uses a template that presents all the content (or posts, in this case), and it is easy to edit and publish. The growth in the use of CMSs for powering websites is probably due in part to the huge rise in popularity of CMS-based blogging tools such as Blogger and WordPress.

THE LEAST YOU NEED TO KNOW
A CMS totally separates the content of the pages from their graphical design and layout. This makes it easy to keep the sitewide design coherent and easy to change. It also makes adding content easy for nontechnical people.

The range of available CMSs is extensive—from enterprise-scale versions that cost $300,000 to open source versions, such as Joomla, that are free. Modern CMSs are usually defined by their capability to manage and publish content. They typically have workflow processes that start at content creation and move through editing or approval stages to publishing. Most do far more: They have the capability to use a wide range of extensions or add-ons to give the site more functionality. Joomla has more than 4,000 extensions available through various forums and newsletters; many of them are free and are created by volunteer developers around the world. The official repository is at extensions.joomla.org. Since 2009, this now lists only GPL licensed extensions. For non-GPL extensions, you will have to resort to Google searching.

> **NOTE**
>
> extensions.joomla.org has a rating and review systems. Be careful about relying too heavily on the ratings. The highest-rated extensions are shown at the top level of the site, so they continue to get more traffic and then tend to get rated even more. There are often great extensions, especially newer ones, hidden away in the categories. It's worth taking an hour or two to browse all of them to find extensions that might be of use to you.
>
> The quality of the available extensions varies widely. If you are using an extension on an important site, do the due diligence to check out the developer and visit his or her site, as well as test the extension thoroughly before using it on a production site.

There is one large drawback to using a CMS: From a technical viewpoint, a CMS can become extremely complex, containing thousands of files and scripts that work together in concert with databases to present a comprehensive and feature-rich website. Normally, this means that a CMS site will be designed and created by technical staff and managed and run by nontechnical users. Joomla is probably the easiest to set up among currently available CMSs, allowing users with modest technical skill to harness its power. The purpose of this book is to guide nontechnical users, step-by-step, through learning how to create and manage websites powered by Joomla.

Table 1.1 sums up this concept of "difficult to set up but easy to grow."

TABLE 1.1   Comparison of Static Websites and CMSs

Static Website	Content Management System
Creating initial web pages is easy.	Creating initial pages is time-consuming because a large infrastructure must be installed, databases must be set up, and templates must be created before the first page can be created.
Content is static; changing it requires technical expertise, and multiple instances of content have to be edited individually on each page.	Content is dynamic; it can be changed with no technical knowledge, and a single change can appear or take effect sitewide.
Adding new functions is difficult and often requires custom code.	Most CMSs have many extensions that "plug in" easily.

Open Source Software

One factor that has contributed to the rise in the popularity and ease of use of CMSs is the growth of the open source software movement.

In 1998, Netscape bucked the universal wisdom of how to develop software by making the source code for its browser, Netscape, freely available to anyone and everyone. This milestone was key in creating a philosophical movement among code developers in which software is created by large communities of developers and released openly to the world. (Hence, the term *open source*.)

As the Web has grown explosively, we have seen open source software grow and mature to power the Web. The most significant open source software is collectively referred to as LAMP:

- **Linux**—An operating system
- **Apache**—Software to run a web server
- **MySQL**—Powerful database software
- **PHP**—A programming language used to write both simple and complex scripts that create interactive functionality with databases

LAMP has allowed developers to create powerful applications using the PHP programming language. One specific area of growth has been the development of CMSs that are written in PHP, such as XOOPS, PostNuke, WordPress, Drupal, and Joomla.

 THE LEAST YOU NEED TO KNOW
Joomla is an example of open source software. It's created and maintained by a worldwide community of developers and distributed at no charge.

History of Joomla!

Joomla is a powerful open source CMS that has grown in popularity since its rebranding from Mambo in 2006. Its two key features—ease of administration and flexibility of using templates—have made it useful for powering everything from corporate intranets to school district sites.

Late 2007 saw the release of Joomla 1.5, which signified a major rewrite of the software. The changes included a simplification and streamlining of the processes for users to contribute content, add extensions, and manage sites. It was a significant enough change that extensions had to be rewritten to operate efficiently in the new version. That is why you see extensions listed at extensions.joomla.org (for example, 1.0 Native, 1.5 Legacy, 1.5 Native).

This third edition of this book covers the latest release of Joomla—1.6. The change for extensions is even more than that from 1.0 to 1.5. At the time of writing, we can anticipate that the extensions directory will show a new flag for 1.6 rated extensions.

The Joomla! Community

A large and active community is an important factor in the success of an open source project. The Joomla community is both big and active. The official forum at forum. joomla.org is perhaps one of the biggest forum communities on the Web. In addition, there are many forums on Joomla's international sites and the respective sites of its third-party extension developers.

Third-Party Extensions Development

Joomla is unique among open source CMSs in the number and nature of the nonofficial developers who create extensions for it. It's hard to find a Joomla site that doesn't use at least one extension. The true power of Joomla lies in the astonishing range of extensions that are available.

The nature of Joomla developers is interesting. There are an unusually high proportion of commercial developers and companies creating professional extensions for Joomla. Although open source and commercial development might seem unlikely bedfellows, many commentators have pointed to this characteristic of the Joomla project as a significant contributor to its growth.

Joomla!'s Features

Joomla has a number of "out of the box" features. When you download Joomla from www.joomlacode.org, you get a zip file about 5MB that needs to be installed on a web server. Running an installation extracts all the files and enters some "filler" content into the database. In no particular order, the following are some of the features of the base installation:

- Simple creation and revision of content using a text editor from the main front-end website or through a nonpublic, back-end administration site
- User registration and the ability to restrict viewing of pages based on user level
- Control of editing and publishing of content based on various admin user levels

- Simple contact forms
- Public site statistics
- Private detailed site traffic statistics
- Built-in sitewide content search functionality
- Email, PDF, and print capability
- RSS (and other) syndication
- Simple content rating system
- Display of newsfeeds from other sites

As you can see, Joomla has some tremendous features. To have a web designer create all these features for a static site would cost tens of thousands of dollars, but it doesn't stop there. Joomla has a massive community of developers worldwide (more than 30,000) who have contributed more than 5,000 extensions for Joomla, most of which are free. The following are some of the most popular extension types:

- Forums
- Shopping carts
- Email newsletters
- Calendars
- Document and media download managers
- Photo galleries
- Forms
- User directories and profiles

Each extension can be installed into Joomla to extend its functionality in some manner. Joomla has been very popular partly because of the availability of the huge and diverse range of extensions.

To customize your site further, you can easily find highly specialized extensions, such as the following:

- Recipe managers
- Help/support desk management
- Fishing tournament tracking
- AdSense placement

- Multiple site management
- Real estate listings
- Hotel room bookings

You get the idea!

 THE LEAST YOU NEED TO KNVOW
Joomla provides rich functionality in its default package. It can be further extended to almost any niche application through the availability of both free and low-cost commercial extensions.

Elements of a Joomla! Website

A Joomla website has several elements that work together to produce a web page. The three main elements are content, templates, and modules. The *content* is the core aspect of the website; the *template* controls how the website's content is presented; and the *modules* add dynamic functionality around the edges of the main page content. Think of these three elements as three legs holding up a stool. Without any one of them, the page (the stool) would topple.

Figure 1.5 shows a page of www.compassdesigns.net, my own Joomla-powered blog.

Figure 1.6 highlights two of the three elements of a Joomla page—the content and the modules. The third, the template, is evident in the color, graphics, layout, and font (which are all part of the template).

On this Joomla web page, the main page content is a large column on the left with a blog post. Various modules are shown in the right-side column and at the top and bottom. The layout and positioning of the content is managed by the template, together with any CSS content styling files it references.

Content

The most important part of a website is the content—the meat and potatoes of your web page, the important stuff in the middle of the page that the viewer is looking at; you have probably heard the phrase "Content is king." Joomla, as a CMS, helps you efficiently create, publish, and manage your content. Content is organized into manageable chunks called *articles*.

FIGURE 1.5   A Joomla website, www.compassdesigns.net.

Joomla actually has a specific name for the core of the page: the mainbody of the page. This is usually the biggest column and is placed in the middle.

The content in the mainbody is generated by what Joomla calls a *component*. The biggest and most important component in Joomla is the one that handles all your articles, the individual content items in the site. In fact, it's so important that often you find these referred to as *content articles*. In the default Joomla installation, there are also a few other components that generate the content that appears in the main body, such as Weblinks and Contacts.

You can take advantage of the many available third-party components that can generate content in the main body. Examples include forums and shopping carts.

> **THE LEAST YOU NEED TO KNOW**
> The *mainbody* of a Joomla web page displays content produced by a component. The most important component within Joomla is the one that manages and displays one or more pieces of content, stored in the database as articles.

FIGURE 1.6   The elements of a Joomla web page.

Templates

A *template* is a set of rules about the presentation of components and modules within a page and their placement on the screen. A template determines the layout or positioning of a web page. A template, along with its CSS files, also determines how many columns to use and what color to make titles, for example. A template acts as a filter (or lens) that controls the presentation aspects of a web page. It does not have any content, but it can include logos.

> **NOTE**
> You will find that templates are also often referred to as a type of extension, along with components and modules. The template concept is shown in Figure 1.7. Here you can see the raw content from the database that is presented through the template to the final viewed web page.

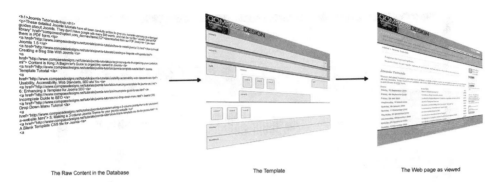

The Raw Content in the Database   The Template   The Web page as viewed

FIGURE 1.7   How a web page is built from a CMS database.

Modules

Modules are small functional blocks that are usually shown around the main part of the page, such as a poll/survey, a login form, or a newsflash. Modules may display other content from the database that may or may not be related to the mainbody content (such as related stories), implement features of the site such as manage your login status, provide navigation to other pages, or provide a search capability.

The example shown previously in Figure 1.6 has modules at the top: a search and a menu. The right column contains an RSS feed module and some banners/ads.

Components and modules are usually both referred to as *extensions* because they extend the functionality of a site.

> **THE LEAST YOU NEED TO KNOW**
> A Joomla site is made up of content (articles and other content displayed by components), a template, and modules. The template selects and positions the content that appears on the page, and it controls all the presentation and aesthetic aspects of the web page. It does not have any content (except that it can include logos).

Summary

Joomla is a great CMS that is capable of powering sophisticated dynamic websites—for little or no cost. This chapter looked at the general nature of a CMS, Joomla's history, what Joomla can do, and what makes up a Joomla web page.

Here are the key points covered in this chapter:

- A CMS separates the content of web pages from the graphical design. This makes it easy to keep sitewide design coherent and makes it easy to change. It also makes adding content easy for nontechnical people.

- Joomla is an example of open source software. It is created by a worldwide community of developers and is available free of charge.

- Joomla provides rich functionality in its default package. It can be further extended with additional features to meet the needs of almost any niche application through the availability of free (GPL) and low-cost (commercial) extensions that can be downloaded from extensions.joomla.org and other commercial extension sites.

- The main body of a Joomla web page displays content generated by a component. The most important component is the one that manages, selects, and displays articles stored in the database.

- A Joomla site is made up of content (generated by components), a template, and modules. The template determines what content is displayed on a page and its placement within the layout. It also controls all the presentation aspects of the web pages. It does not have any content, but it can include logos.

- Modern websites separate content from presentation by using a technology known as Cascading Style Sheets (CSS). Templates utilize CSS style sheets to control the aesthetic appearance of the content displayed by that template.

Chapter 2

Downloading and Installing Joomla!

In This Chapter

Joomla is one of the most popular open source CMSs on the planet. The first step in becoming part of the "Joomlaverse," the vibrant community that exists around Joomla, is to download Joomla and install it on your web server.

This chapter describes the first two stages in getting a Joomla-powered site up and running: finding and downloading the latest files and installing them on a web server. This chapter describes both local installation (which you'll want to use if you don't have a hosting account or if you have a slow Internet connection) to use as you read this book and a real web server installation. This chapter covers the following topics:

- How do you install Joomla?
- Where can you find the most current Joomla files?
- How do you unpack the Joomla files on your desktop computer or on a hosting account?
- How do you use the Joomla Installation Wizard?
- How can you support the Joomla project?

How to Install Joomla!

The process of installing Joomla involves several steps:

1. Obtain the latest Joomla file package.
2. Create a SQL database.
3. Unpack the package on a server.
4. Use a browser-based wizard to complete the installation.

We look at each of these steps in turn. There are two alternative paths you can take for step 2: You can either unpack Joomla on a remote hosting account or create a web server that actually runs on your desktop/laptop computer. The second technique is useful for trying out Joomla by creating a site and then transferring it to a hosting account.

Obtaining the Latest Joomla! File Package

The home of the Joomla project is www.joomla.org. The Joomla site is actually a collection of separate sections and sites for different aspects of the project. With one exception, all the sections and sites are powered by Joomla. As of this writing, the following sections are available:

- **www.joomla.org**—This is the main Joomla site, where you can find the latest information and news. This site is home to the official news blog for Joomla, which talks primarily about the project's development plans and progress. You can subscribe to news via RSS by clicking the link in the left-hand column.

- **community.joomla.org**—A portal for all the community activities of the Joomla project, this site includes blog posts from both the Leadership Team and community members, as well as information about events, user groups, and the "Joomla Magazine" and JoomlaConnect—an aggregated RSS feed from the third-party developer community.

- **forum.joomla.org**—With more than 394,850 members at the time of this writing, the official Joomla forum is one of the biggest forums on the Web.

You can get help from the active Joomla community, whether for templates, translations, components, using extensions, or just help in general. When you are asking for help, remember that the forum is all-volunteer, so provide as much detail on your problem as you can in a concise note and be respectful.

- **extensions.joomla.org**—The Joomla Extensions Directory is packed with more than 5,000 third-party GPL extensions, including components, modules, and plug-ins. This is the place to look when you're ready to extend the functionality of your Joomla website. It even includes useful reviews and rating tools so you can see what other people think of various extensions.

- **resources.joomla.org**—This is a listing of third-party individuals and companies that provide products and service for Joomla, including education, extensions, and support.

- **docs.joomla.org**—This site provides documentation and help for Joomla. This section is a community-generated Wiki that provides a lot of useful information about using Joomla.

- **developer.joomla.org**—This is where developers can find documentation on the Joomla API.

- **shop.joomla.org**—Get your Joomla T-shirt here!

- **people.joomla.org**—This is a new social portal where you can join and create a user profile, make friends, and join discussions on Joomla. You can find me at http://people.joomla.org/my-page/compass.html.

- **www.joomlacode.org**—This site is the only one that doesn't run on Joomla, but it's the one we are interested in right now. Known as *the forge,* it serves as the code repository both for the main Joomla files and many of the thousands of GPL third-party extensions.

 NOTE
This book is about the newest version of Joomla, Joomla 1.6.

Let's take a look at the forge so you can get an idea of how to find the files you need. On the Joomla home page are some buttons that link to the forge files. The buttons have changed over various redesigns of www.joomla.org. When you click the Download Joomla button, you are sent to a page where you can grab the latest zip files that make up a base Joomla installation.

> **NOTE**
>
> At the time of writing, Joomla 1.6 was in beta, and the page http://www.joomla.org/download.html always shows the current version (1.5). If you ever need to get beta versions, you can get them at http://developer.joomla.org/code.html or http://joomlacode.org/gf/project/joomla/frs/.

Joomla! Package Naming Conventions

Before we move on, let's take a quick look at how the Joomla packages and releases are named.

The naming convention for Joomla versioning is *A.B.C*, which represent the following elements:

- *A*—This is the major release number. Currently all versions of Joomla begin with 1 (that is, 1.*B.C*).
- *B*—This is the minor release number. The current minor release number is 1.6, and this book is based on Joomla 1.6.
- *C*—This is the maintenance release number; for example, 1.5.20 was a recent security release of Joomla 1.5.

> **THE LEAST YOU NEED TO KNOW**
>
> The core Joomla files are available for free at www.joomlacode.org. The Joomla home page, www.joomla.org, provides links to the files. When downloading them, make sure you are getting the correct version, either the full package or an update.

> **IMPORTANT NOTE**
>
> You cannot upgrade from Joomla 1.5 to Joomla 1.6. There are significant enough changes in the code that simply overwriting files would break your site. Migrating a site from 1.5 to 1.6 is a complex process that is beyond the scope of this book. For many sites, it is easier to construct the site over again in 1.6 and copy and paste the content.

After you've located and downloaded a compressed Joomla file package of several megabytes, what do you do with it?

Creating a MySQL Database

Whether set up at home or on a hosted server, Joomla needs a MySQL database to serve as a repository for site content. SQL (pronounced "sequel") stands for Structured Query Language and has become a shorthand reference to any database structure that responds to requests written in the SQL language. One particular brand of SQL database software is the very popular MySQL, which can be set up on almost any hosted web server, including your home computer.

If you are installing Joomla locally (on your home or office computer) with WampServer 2 or XAMPP, as described in the following section, the wizard will have the permissions necessary to automatically create a database.

If you are installing Joomla on a web host, you will need to pre-create a SQL database. When you do, make sure to note the username, password, and database name. The most common way to set up a database is through some sort of button/link in your hosting admin panel; look for something that talks about MySQL databases.

Unpacking the Joomla! Package

You need to choose whether you will be setting up your Joomla site on your home computer, on a hosted server, or both. The following section, "Unpacking Joomla! on a Local Desktop Computer," walks through setting up a home computer to serve as a host and installing Joomla on it. This approach is ideal for designing a new site and testing the extensions you might use with it. The section, "Unpacking Joomla! on a Hosting Account," walks through setting up a Joomla site—which will serve as your production website—on a hosted server.

IMPORTANT NOTE
Before you begin installing Joomla, you need to have a MySQL database ready for Joomla to use.

Unpacking Joomla! on a Local Desktop Computer

If you unzip the Joomla file package and try to run/open the main index.php file, it will not work and will instead open in an editor where you can see all the code.

Joomla is not a self-contained program like Microsoft Word or Mozilla Firefox. With those sorts of programs, you simply install them onto your computer by running an installation file. Joomla is very different. Joomla is client/server software and needs an installation of PHP in order to execute.

Joomla is a complex series of Hypertext Preprocessor (PHP) scripts that run on a web server. When you browse a Joomla site, these scripts are generated on-the-fly and create what you see on the pages of the site. The key term here is web server. This is an example of client/server scripting: The software is actually running on a different computer (the server), and you are interacting with it from a client (your web browser).

NOTE
No, the acronym *PHP* doesn't quite match the words *Hypertext Preprocessor*. It used to stand for Personal Home Page. PHP is principally a programming language for web pages/servers.

Thus, you cannot download Joomla and try to run it on your computer as if it's an EXE file. It has to have a server, which means you need to have a hosting account at a hosted server or a set of programs on your local computer that emulate a hosted server.

Before you shell out your hard-earned money for a hosting account, there is something else you can do first: You can run a web server on your local computer—that is, your desktop or laptop. This is known as having a localhost. It may sound like I just contradicted myself from the previous paragraph, but I really didn't. You can't "run" Joomla itself on your own computer, but you can install a localhost web server for it to "run on." In this scenario, your computer is acting as both the server and the client. One advantage of this setup is that your website will load very fast because it's coming from your own computer. One disadvantage is that you will have to move, or "port," the site to a real web host later on. Setting up a localhost is a great way to learn about Joomla before you start to develop your site.

THE LEAST YOU NEED TO KNOW
Joomla needs a web server to run on. A good way to learn about Joomla is to run a web server on your own computer, known as using a localhost. This makes your "practice" site blazingly fast (if not available to the world).

To set up your localhost, you need some software that runs Apache, PHP, and MySQL on your computer. These are the component scripts of a remote web server on a hosting account. Two popular packages include all these scripts, and both are free:

- **WampServer 2**—This package, available at www.wampserver.com/en, is for Windows.

- **XAMPP**—This package, available at www.apachefriends.org/en/xampp.html, is for Windows, Mac OS X, and Linux.

Let's quickly run through Joomla setup using WampServer 2 for the localhost:

NOTE
WampServer 2 is Windows-specific.

1. Download WampServer from www.wampserver.com/en and then install it. At the end of the installation, you will have a folder called c:\wamp\www, which serves as the root folder of a local website. If you use XAMPPLite, the folder will be called c:\xampplite\htdocs.

2. Extract/unpack the Joomla package you downloaded into a folder inside \www\ or \htdocs\. It doesn't matter what the new folder is called (for example, c:\wamp\www\Joomla would work). Make sure that you don't unpack it in such a way that you end up with two folders, one inside the other (for example, c:\wamp\www\Joomla\Joomla_1.6-Full_Package.zip).

3. Run WampServer. You should get a handy icon in your system tray (the icons at the bottom right of the Windows desktop). Figure 2.1 shows three possible versions of the icon. (For XAMPP, you run start-apache.bat and then start-mysql.bat.)

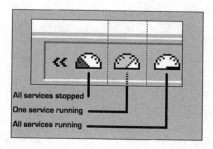

FIGURE 2.1   WampServer icons in the Windows system tray.

4. Make sure that the dial is white.

5. Now open a browser and go to http://localhost (no "www") or left-click the icon and select localhost. You should see a page that looks like Figure 2.2.

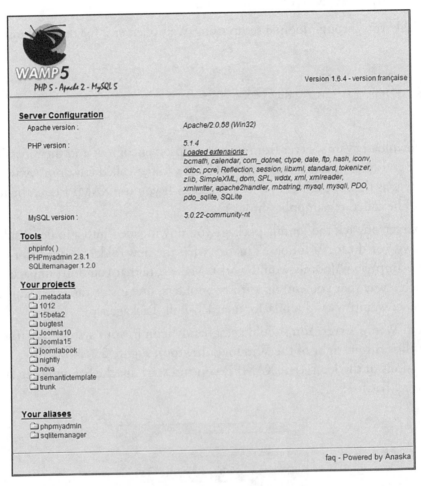

FIGURE 2.2   Browser view of WampServer http://localhost.

NOTE
If you are not seeing the page shown in Figure 2.2, you should stop and figure out why. You have to get this page before you can proceed. The WampServer site has some helpful troubleshooting FAQs and a forum. You should see your folder called "Joomla" (or whatever you called it) in the Your Projects list. Click that folder, and you are taken to that website, running locally on your computer.

NOTE
If you get stuck with this part of the process, you can refer to Appendix D, "Install-ing WampServer," for more information on how to install WampServer.

At this point, all you have done is set up the localhost web server and unpacked the Joomla files so they are ready to install. Before we look at how to install Joomla, let's take a quick look at what the upload process involves if you have a hosting account and want to install Joomla on a hosted web server.

THE LEAST YOU NEED TO KNOW
Several free packages include all the files and scripts needed to run a web server on a desktop computer. WampServer is one for Windows.

Unpacking Joomla! on a Hosting Account

This section assumes that you either have a hosting account or are going to get one. Joomla has some minimum requirements to run, and Joomla 1.6.X has slightly higher requirements than Joomla 1.5.X.

Here are the minimum requirements for Joomla 1.6:

- **PHP 4.2.x or above**
- **MySQL 5.0.4 or above**—See www.mysql.com

You must ensure that you have MySQL, XML, and Zlib support built into your PHP. For assistance in making sure you have the proper support, refer to the Joomla Help Forums (see help.joomla.org).

When you have a host that meets the requirements, you need to upload the main Joomla files. There are two ways to do this:

- You can upload the zip file and then extract the contents on the server by using a shell command or Cpanel file manager.
- You can extract the contents of the zip file onto your desktop and then upload the contents individually via FTP.

If you have Cpanel with your hosting company (almost all hosting companies provide it), the first method is usually the fastest and easiest way to do this. You can use this file manager to upload the zip file to the public_html folder (or whatever folder you have as the root folder on your host; www and htdocs are sometimes used). You can then use it to extract the files.

> **NOTE**
> Many web hosts offer a tool called Fantastico, which enables you to instantly create a Joomla website, along with all the databases needed. I actually don't recommend using Fantastico. Although it makes the process easier, many hosts don't have the most current releases of Joomla in the available Fantastico installation scripts.

> **THE LEAST YOU NEED TO KNOW**
> To install Joomla on a web host, your account needs to meet some minimum requirements. Make sure your host does, or you will have problems later.

Running the Joomla! Installation Wizard

If you are this far along, you have unzipped the Joomla package to either a remote web host or a localhost root folder on your local computer. Now for the fun stuff—actually installing Joomla.

You install Joomla via a browser-based wizard that walks you through several steps.

Getting to the Joomla! Installer

Using your browser of choice (mine is Firefox), navigate to the location of your Joomla files. (In my case on a localhost, it is http://localhost/Joomla.) You will see the first installation screen (see Figure 2.3). If you don't see this screen, be sure the Apache/MySQL/PHP host software is all running, you have the Joomla files unpacked into the root folder, and the path (folder names) to the index.php file within the Joomla folder is typed correctly.

Before you start, make sure you have pre-created a SQL database for the site to use.

Step 1: Language

Figure 2.3 gives you a first look at some of the internationalization features of Joomla 1.6. You can select among many languages for the installation instructions.

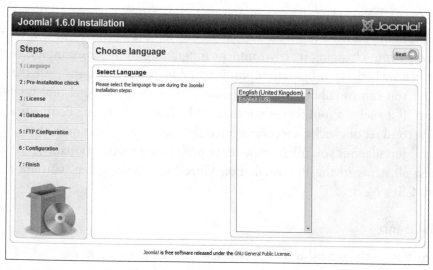

FIGURE 2.3   The Choose Language screen.

Step 2: Pre-Installation Check

After you have selected your language, the next screen you are presented with is the Pre-installation Check screen (see Figure 2.4). A critical part in the installation process, this screen checks to see if all the minimum system requirements are met.

FIGURE 2.4   The Pre-installation Check screen.

The first set of checks is for the required minimums for installation. If they are red (not met), then you need to find a new environment (change hosts) or talk your hosting provider into changing its environment (upgrading PHP, for example). Note that the last item, whether configuration.php is writable, is a permissions issue that is easy to rectify. You can usually change permissions through the Cpanel tool provided by your host. (Cpanel is a tool that is standard with almost all hosting companies.)

The second set of checks is recommended settings. If you don't meet them, you can still install Joomla, but you might experience problems with functionality and security.

When all items in the Pre-installation Check screen are green, you are ready to proceed. Click Next.

Step 3: License

The next step of the wizard is the License screen (see Figure 2.5).

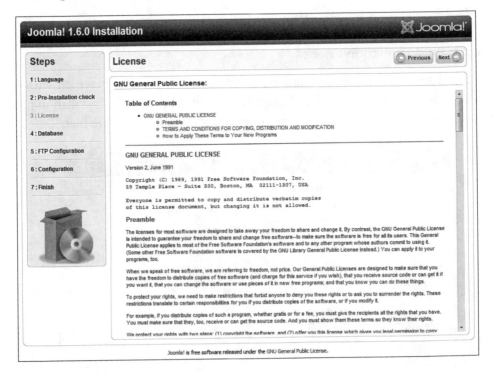

FIGURE 2.5   The License screen.

Joomla is released under a GNU/GPL license. One of the most common questions regarding this license is, "Can I remove the footer link that says Powered by Joomla?"

It's actually perfectly okay to do this; you just have to keep the copyright statement in the source code.

Step 4: Database Configuration

The next screen is Database Configuration (see Figure 2.6).

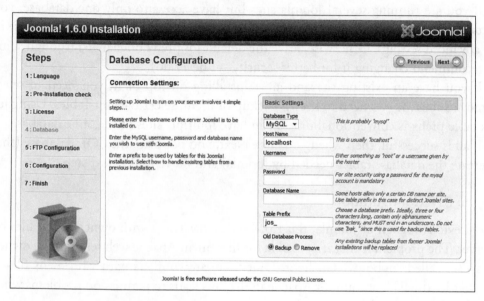

FIGURE 2.6   The Database Configuration screen.

The Database Configuration screen is one of the main pages of the installation process; it's where you enter important information about how Joomla can access the MySQL database that your Joomla site will use. You will see a drop-down for the database type.

The hostname will almost always be localhost, and the username and password are provided by your hosting company, usually in an email you receive when you create the account.

If you are installing on a localhost using WampServer or XAMPP, the username is usually root, and the password is nothing or blank.

At this point, you need to choose a name for the SQL database that Joomla will use.

NOTE
Use some sort of name that is not confusing because other scripts also use SQL databases, and before you know it, you might have several on your server and need to tell them apart. Don't use spaces in the name.

If you are running several Joomla sites but have access to only one database, you need to use different table prefixes to distinguish them, and you need to enter these in the advanced settings. Otherwise, leave the default jos prefix unchanged (though some do recommend changing it for better security—I never do).

If you have an existing site and are reinstalling on top of it, you need to select Remove Tables. If you need to keep a backup of them, select Backup Tables. Using jos as a table prefix is conventional unless you have multiple sites in the same database.

If all is successful, then when you click Next, you populate the SQL database (that is, create the database tables needed by Joomla) and move to the next step.

Step 5: FTP Configuration

The previous version of Joomla, the 1.0.X series, has issues with ownership of files on a server. The problem is that it's possible for files on an Apache web server to be owned by a user called "nobody." Go figure. But there are conflicts with who owns files—whether it's the FTP account or Apache itself. This leads to permission problems when Joomla tries to upload files.

Joomla 1.5+ has a solution to this problem: It actually uses an FTP account for everything, so no conflicts arise.

When installing Joomla 1.6, if you are getting permission/ownership issues, you need to create an FTP account (or use the one provided by your hosting company) for Joomla to use and enter the details in the FTP Configuration screen shown in Figure 2.7.

Step 6: Main Configuration

On the Main Configuration page, you enter some information about your new site; the information you enter determines how you will insert content into your site (see Figure 2.8).

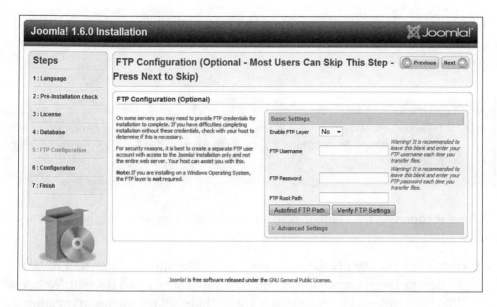

FIGURE 2.7   The FTP Configuration screen.

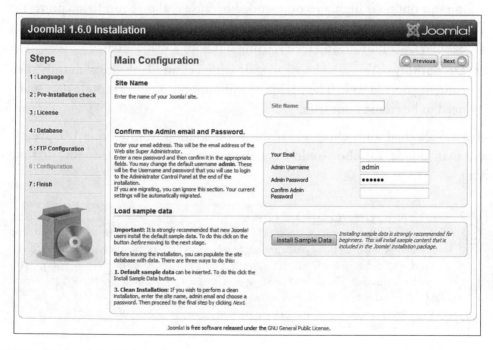

FIGURE 2.8   The Main Configuration screen.

Give your site a name and then enter the "super administrator" information. The first user created in the site will be created using this information and will automatically get super administrator status.

CAUTION

Make sure you write down the password! Feel free to eat the sticky note you wrote it on once you have committed it to memory, but if you forget it immediately (which I have done), you will need to reinstall Joomla.

When it comes to the content of your sparklingly new site, you have a couple of choices:

- **Install default sample data**—If you choose this option, the wizard installs the default Joomla content that you have probably seen all over the Web, with "Welcome to Joomla." Note that it also includes all the menus, navigation links, and sections/categories. If you are learning how to use Joomla, selecting this option is highly recommended because it allows you to adapt, revise, and examine how things can be set up. (Note that if you don't click the Install Sample Data button, you'll be starting out with a blank site!)

- **Do nothing**—You can choose to start with a clean blank site with only the content you add to it. The upside of this option is that no sample data will need to be cleaned out later.

Joomla 1.5 also had some choices available for migration from Joomla 1.0. We might expect that Joomla 1.6 also would have these options, though it doesn't at time of writing.

THE LEAST YOU NEED TO KNOW

If you are new to Joomla, you should install the sample data. But realize that it's only a suggestion of how you can organize content, and it allows you to browse around and get familiar with the inner workings of Joomla. In later chapters, you start with no sample data. On a local computer, it's easy to simply delete the WampServer or XAMPP folder and repeat the steps above to reinstall WampServer or XAMP plus Joomla but without the sample data so you can follow along with the rest of this book.

Step 7: Finish

Cross your fingers, close your eyes, click Next, and hopefully you see the screen shown in Figure 2.9. You now have a website "Powered by Joomla," and you can investigate different language options, view the site, or jump right to the administration of your site.

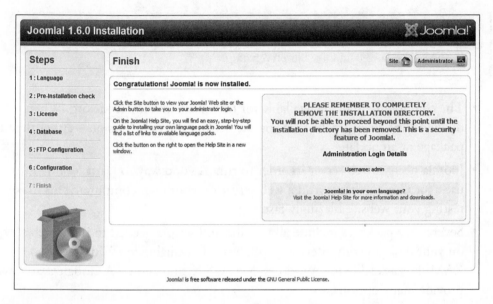

FIGURE 2.9   Finish!

 IMPORTANT NOTE
Make sure you remove the installation directory as directed on the Finish page.

If you don't get this page, then you have some work to do. Issues often arise because of server environments. If the solution is not obvious, a useful step is to copy the error message or the main part of it and then search for it on the Joomla help forums, at forum.joomla.org, and using Google. Chances are that someone else has already run into the same error and has posted the solution online. (To search for the exact phrase, include the message in double quotation marks.)

Summary

Installing Joomla is perhaps the biggest hurdle to getting started on creating your website. You'll need to create a MySQL database for Joomla and upload all the files to a server. After these two steps are complete, it's relatively easy to use the Joomla Installation Wizard, which runs in a browser:

 NOTE
If installing Joomla is a challenge for you, there are some one-click services that host Joomla websites like SimplWeb.com.

- The core Joomla files are available for free at www.joomlacode.org. When downloading them, make sure you are getting the right version—either the full package or an update.

- Joomla needs a web server in order to run. A good way to learn Joomla is to use a localhost—that is, run a web server on your own computer. This makes testing your website blazingly fast.

- Several free packages include all the files and scripts needed to run a web server on your desktop computer. WampServer 2 is available for Windows, and XAMPP is available for Windows, Mac OS X, and Linux. A Google search will provide many options.

- To install Joomla on a web host, your account needs to meet some minimum requirements, or you will have problems later.

- Installing Joomla is an easy four-step process:

  1. Obtain the latest Joomla file package.

  2. Unpack the package on a server.

  3. Pre-create a MySQL database (not needed if installing locally).

  4. Use Joomla's browser-based wizard to complete the installation.

- If you are new to Joomla, you should install the sample data. But realize that it's only a suggestion of how you can organize content.

Chapter 3

Joomla!
Administration Basics

In This Chapter

The term *site administration* usually refers to the day-to-day tasks of adding content, managing users, and making sure installed components and modules are running correctly. With a properly configured Joomla site, the administration burden is relatively low, and most of the effort can be dedicated to generating that all-important content.

This chapter takes you on a whirlwind tour of the core administrative functions you'll need. It doesn't go step-by-step, explaining every last button in the administrative backend; rather, it picks out key functions, tips, and tricks that you'll need to know to keep your site humming. I highly recommend reading the official documentation Wiki at docs.joomla.org, which provides a great deal of detail. This chapter covers the following topics:

- What is the difference between the frontend and the backend of a Joomla-powered website?

- What are the main administrator menu functions?

- What types of users are there, and how do they relate to the frontend and backend?

What Are the Frontend and Backend of a Joomla!-Powered Website?

After you install Joomla, you actually have two sites:

- The public site (commonly called the *frontend*) that people view at www. yoursite.com
- The administration site, also called *admin* for short (commonly called the *backend*), whose URL is www.yoursite.com/administrator

While some administration is possible via the frontend of the site, it's most efficient to manage your site through the backend.

THE LEAST YOU NEED TO KNOW
A Joomla website consists of two sites: the public frontend and a private administrative backend.

When you browse to the backend, you are greeted by a login prompt, as shown in Figure 3.1.

To get any further into the backend, you'll need an administrative password. I hope you remembered it!

NOTE
When you installed Joomla, on the final screen, you were asked for an admin password. That is the first account created, and it is given the access control level (ACL) group Super User. The username is admin, and the password is whatever you entered at that time.

If you log in with a Super User account, you are presented with the administrative backend of your site. How it looks depends on your administrator level. Figure 3.2 shows one possibility.

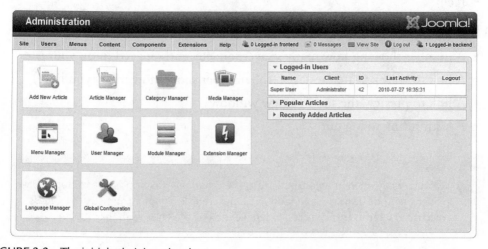

FIGURE 3.1   Backend login screen.

FIGURE 3.2   The initial administrative view.

TIP
If you want to take extra steps for security, you can create a new Super User with a name other than admin when you install Joomla.

At the top of the page is a menu bar, immediately under that is a toolbar (which is not visible in Figure 3.2), and the large area is called the workspace. This page you see when you first log in to the backend is called the Control Panel.

The Menu Bar

The menu bar is the tool for navigating the admin backend. This horizontal menu enables you to access all the functions of administration by providing the following menus:

- Site
- Users
- Menus
- Content
- Components
- Extensions
- Help

On the right of the menu bar are some additional information and functions:

- A number showing how many viewers are currently logged in on your site
- A link to your private messages (the number shows how many you have)
- A link to preview the site in a new window
- A button/link to log out

NOTE
If you are logged in as an administrator or a manager (as opposed to a Super User), fewer menu options are available. The different levels of administrator access are discussed later in this chapter, when we look at the User Manager.

The Toolbar

Immediately under the menu bar is the toolbar. It's collapsed in the initial Control Panel view, but it appears when you navigate to a particular function, such as the Article Manager, as you can see in the rest of the figures in this chapter.

The toolbar displays various context-sensitive icon buttons for different functions. For example, Figure 3.3 shows the Article Manager toolbar.

FIGURE 3.3   The Article Manager toolbar.

While you're in the Article Manager screen, you have the toolbar buttons New, Edit, Publish, Unpublish, Archive, Check In, Trash, Options, and Help.

The buttons you see in the toolbar change depending on what screen you are in. For example, Figure 3.4 shows the Menu Manager toolbar. Here you have only New, Edit, Delete, Rebuild, Options, and Help buttons.

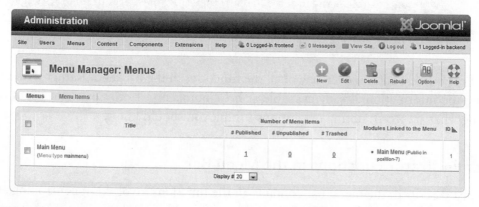

FIGURE 3.4   The Menu Manager toolbar.

NOTE
Although the icon buttons displayed are different for each function, the actual button itself always does the same thing. For example, the publish button does the same thing in each manager screen.

The Workspace

The mainbody of the admin page is the workspace, not to be confused with the Control Panel, which is the first view you see after you log in. The workspace area is structured in a number of different layouts depending on where you are in the backend and what you are editing. One common format is a basic table, usually used for various managers, articles, menus, and so on.

CAUTION
There is no current set of workspace layout standards for third-party extensions. The creator of an extension is free to make the administrative interface look however he or she likes. This can sometimes lead to inconsistency, though, and most developers usually take the lead from the core Joomla functions for their design.

THE LEAST YOU NEED TO KNOW
The admin workspace is the main tool in administering a Joomla site. Different parts of it are visible to different administrators. Third-party extensions often have workspaces that are organized differently than the workspaces used for managing the core Joomla functions.

Let's quickly take an overview of all the functions in the backend. Rather than reiterate the information already available at help.joomla.org, I only pause to point out things that are worth noting or cautions I think you should know.

Administrator Functions in the Menu Bar

As just described, the menu bar contains all the functions involved in controlling and managing a Joomla website. The following sections add to the basic information available in the Joomla documentation, briefly touching on the important roles of several of the menu bar functions.

THE LEAST YOU NEED TO KNOW
To get information about the specific functions of all menus and buttons, click the Help button on any page of your site's backend. It's much more accurate and up-to-date than a book can be as it's linked directly to www.joomla.org.

The Site Submenu

The Site menu contains several functions you can use sitewide, including the very important Global Configuration screen. Figure 3.5 shows the submenus in the Site menu.

FIGURE 3.5   The Site menu.

Control Panel

When you first log in to the Joomla backend, you see the Control Panel. It has on the left icon buttons that you can use to access common functions; on the right it has a series of Ajax-powered lists that slide out items when you click them.

What is visible in your Control Panel (and in your menu bar) depends on what type of admin group you are when you log in.

Joomla 1.6 allows you to create your own groups with their own permission, but when you first install, it gives you three administrator levels to get started. Most sites might never create any more backend user groups and just stick with these default ones. The initial three backend administrator groups are:

- Super User (highest permissions)
- Administrator (medium permissions)
- Manager (lowest permissions)

Each administrator group sees a slightly different view/Control Panel in the backend. For example, a manager, who has the lowest level of permissions, cannot see or access the Global Configuration screen.

Previously, Figure 3.2 showed the Super User view. Figure 3.6 shows the manager view. The administrator view is actually the same as the Super User view. Although this type of user has reduced functions, they are incorporated in the menus so they cannot be seen from a simple screenshot.

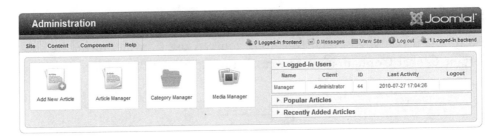

FIGURE 3.6   The administrator and manager views.

The administrator view does not have global sitewide functions, such as the ones you find in the Global Configuration screen. The manager view does not have menus or extensions. In both cases, the number of accessible functions is less than what's available as a Super User.

THE LEAST YOU NEED TO KNOW
Depending on which administrator group you log in to the backend as, you see different options in the functions you can perform.

TIP
The navigation of the backend depends on JavaScript. You must have it enabled to use the site fully.

The Global Configuration Screen

The Global Configuration screen is important for your site. It's available only to Super Users and contains critical settings to keep your site running (see Figure 3.7). The Global Configuration screen has the following four tabs:

- **Site**—This is the initial active tab, which contains some general information about your Joomla website:
  - ◆ **Site Settings**—Here you set your Site Name (used in various places like the backend) and can take the site offline, giving visitors the offline message. You can also customize the offline message with HTML, images, a logo, and so on by placing a file named offline.php in your template folder.

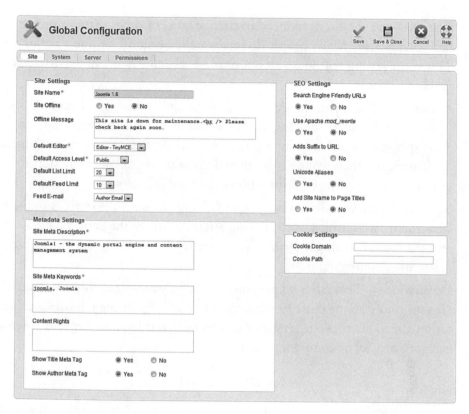

FIGURE 3.7   The Global Configuration screen.

- **Metadata Settings**—Most of these settings are not that useful, as we will override them on a menu basis. But it's still worth filling them in. Much more critical is to set the Show Title Meta Tag option to Yes.

- **SEO Settings**—These are somewhat misnamed as they are about making your URLs be "human friendly" words rather than complex strings of characters. For example, the Amazon link to this book is

http://www.amazon.com/gp/product/0137012314?ie=UTF8&tag=compassdesign-20&link_code=as3&camp=211189&creative=373489&creativeASIN=0137012314.

This is not to say that Amazon uses Joomla—it doesn't—but note that the Search Engine Friendly (SEF) URL Settings are not a silver bullet. As you can see, Amazon doesn't even bother with SEF! You should turn them all on with Adds Suffix to URL and Unicode Aliases based on preference.

- **System**—You should never need to change most of these settings, such as debug and cache. Many people do increase the Session Lifetime a bit longer. This is the setting that logs you out of the backend when you are inactive/grabbing a coffee.
  - **Cache** —These options are for setting the site cache—and hopefully speeding it up. If you are making a lot of revisions to your site, especially on the template, it's worth turning off the cache while you do, so you don't make changes and then wonder why they don't take effect. You really start to notice having cache on with 4,000+ visits a day on a site.
- **Server**—Again, you should not need to change most of the settings in the Server tab. Two settings worth paying attention to are the Server Time Zone and the From E-mail and Name. These are used to send system emails like the registration confirmation.
- **Permissions**—This tab is where you can assign various functions to your User Groups (more about this in a moment). The settings in the Global Configuration screen are sitewide settings that can be overridden on a specific menu, category, article, or component basis.

Site Maintenance

Located in Site > Site Maintenance, this submenu item includes the Global Check-in and Cache functions. The Global Check-in tool checks in all content items that are open, such as those unintentionally left open for editing. Joomla has a built-in function that allows only one person to edit a content article at a time. This is very important for content management. Joomla does this by "checking out" items so no one else can open them. However, if a user clicks the Back button or closes the browser while editing, the item can remain checked out. The Global Check-in function allows the Super User to make all content items available for editing again. Needless to say, before using this option, the Super User needs to make sure no one is actually editing content at the time, because unsaved revisions could be lost.

If the cache on your site is enabled (see the section "The Global Configuration Screen" earlier in the chapter), you can purge all cached pages and files by using the Clean Cache function. This is useful if you make changes to various aspects of a site and want to immediately see the new changes on all the affected pages.

Users Menu

One of the most powerful features of Joomla is its capability to handle complex systems of users and permissions. Access Control Levels, or *ACL*, is the grand-sounding name given to assigning different privileges and functions to different user groups. With Joomla 1.6 you can customize the access to your site and create different groups to do different jobs/roles. In Appendix B, "A Guide to Joomla! 1.6 ACL," we give a more detailed guide to ACL in Joomla 1.6.

When you first install Joomla, it gives you eight user groups, or roles, to get started. You assign these different ACL roles to groups through the User Manager in the Site menu. The initial groups are

- Public
- Registered
- Author
- Editor
- Publisher
- Manager
- Administrator
- Super User

Selecting the User Manager brings up a table with all the users who have an ACL of Registered or higher. Near in mind that "the "Public" group contains the permissions associated with people who are just browsing your site. Figure 3.8 shows an example of a site with just a few users.

Simply put, you use the User Manager to manage users, and only administrators and Super Users can view it.

There is a search function (shown on the left side of Figure 3.8), where you can enter a name, a username, or an email, and it will find all users who have what you typed present in their fields. On the right, you can also select a specific group or see only users who are logged in.

TIP
You can't currently export users from Joomla or import users into Joomla without either a third-party component or accessing the SQL tables directly through a tool such as PHPMyAdmin.

FIGURE 3.8   The User Manager.

Each of the eight user levels in a Joomla-powered website has different permissions and capabilities in the frontend and the backend of the site. Table 3.1 describes them.

TABLE 3.1   Joomla! Access Control Levels

ACL User Level	Frontend Privileges	Backend Privileges—Menus & Functions
Public Frontend or Guest (Any visitor)	Browse only pages published as "public"	None (see Public Backend)
Registered (A logged-in user)	View both "public" and "restricted" content	None (see Public Backend)
Author	Can create new (unpublished) content	None (see Public Backend)
Editor	Can edit content created by others	None (see Public Backend)
Publisher	Can publish content—make it viewable	None (see Public Backend)
Public Backend (A visitor before login)	n/a (see Public Frontend)	None—can only view login screen
Manager	Same as Publisher	Article Manager Category Manager Media Manager Featured Article Manager Component Manager (Banners, Contacts, Newsfeeds, Search, and Weblinks) Help

ACL User Level	Frontend Privileges	Backend Privileges— Menus & Functions
Administrator	Same as Publisher	Same as Manager plus: Site Maintenance User Manager Massmail Menu Manager Component Manager (Messaging, Redirect) Extension Manager Module Manager Plug-In Manager Template Manager Language Manager

NOTE
These permissions are additive, so an editor can do everything an author can—that is, both edit and create content.

Guests, registered users, authors, editors, and publishers are termed *frontend users*. Very often a Joomla site will have many of these users. This makes it possible to establish content publication workflows. It also allows the responsibility of content creation, editing, and publication to be distributed among many users without having to grant access to the backend; this is one of the many advantages of a CMS.

NOTE
If you want a lot of content, you will want to have many authors, editors, and publishers.

Managers, Administrators, and Super Users are termed *backend users*. These users are designed to manage and control the site rather than just focus on content. Usually there is only one Super User.

THE LEAST YOU NEED TO KNOW
There are two main types of users: frontend users and backend users. Frontend users generate and manage content; backend users manage the site.

Users are either created automatically though the registration link on the frontend login form or created manually in the backend.

TIP
You can turn the automatic registration function on or off in the Global Configuration screen. If you want your site to grow quickly, offer something of value for free and ask people to register to view it. Make sure you prominently display your privacy policy and adhere to it!

The Menus Menu

Menus are a critical part of a Joomla site. They not only provide navigation but also determine the layout of a page. Menus are difficult to understand, and we examine them in much more depth in Chapter 5, "Creating Menus and Navigation." For now, we take just a quick overview to provide some context for the more challenging concepts explained later.

Figure 3.9 shows the Menus menu, with only one menu set up. Note, that when you only have one menu, it is always called the main menu. You can add more menus, with different names, as we'll see in Chapter 5.

FIGURE 3.9   Menu drop-down options.

The Menus option contains all the menus that are used in the website. In Figure 3.10, you can see the Menu Manager and a quick link to this example site's sole menu.

NOTE
These menu names are totally arbitrary; they are just names given to menus in a "fake" set of content as an example. Your actual menu names will appear here.

Clicking the Menu Manager takes you to a summary table of all the menus used in the site, as shown in Figure 3.10.

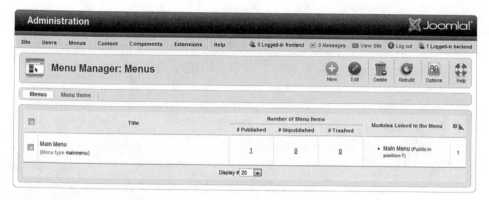

FIGURE 3.10   The Menu Manager.

NOTE

Clicking a Menu Items icon in the Menu Manager is the same as just clicking that menu in the drop-down main menu: It opens a menu for editing. Using the drop-down menu just skips a step.

Clicking the menu name takes you to the Menu Items tab with the items filtered—that is, you only see the items in that menu. Figure 3.11 shows the Menu Items tab when you click on this example Main Menu with only a single Menu Item, the home page link.

We revisit menus in much more detail in Chapter 5.

The Content Menu

The Content menu (see Figure 3.12) contains the all-important Article and Category Managers. Articles are the individual content items that form the core of a site. This menu also contains the Featured Articles and Media Manager.

The links in the Content menu—Article Manager, Category Manager, and Featured Articles—link to the corresponding three tabs on an aggregated Content Manager page. Once there, you can also navigate quickly between them with the matching tabs.

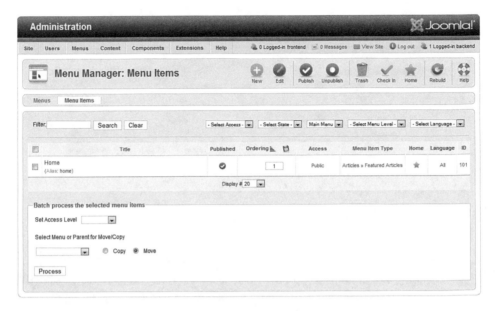

FIGURE 3.11   A menu within the Menu Manager.

FIGURE 3.12   The Content menu.

Article Manager

The Article Manager displays all your articles (see Figure 3.13). You can sort the list of articles based on any column (ascending or descending) by clicking that column heading.

NOTE
Categories allow multiple related articles to be displayed together as a dynamic page. Notice that the article in Figure 3.13 has no category. This is because it is "uncategorized," which allows it to be treated as a single-article static page.

FIGURE 3.13   The Article Manager.

Category Manager

The Category Manager allows you to add, edit, and delete Categories, the main organizational structure for articles. We look more at Categories in Chapter 4, "Content Is King: Organizing Your Content."

Featured Article Manager

Called the Frontpage Manager in Joomla 1.5, the Featured Article Manager in Joomla 1.6 allows you to create a page on your site that can show any article from any other category. For example, if you had a website that featured the work of artists, you could use the Featured Articles function to show a selection of art (which would be articles) from different artists and easily be able to change them each week.

NOTE
Joomla 1.6 has a built-in trash function. To see articles/categories that are in the trash, you view them through the respective managers. There is a drop-down, Select State, where you can select to view all trashed items.

The Media Manager

The Media Manager is a one-stop shop for managing all the media that might be used on a site; it includes all types of media, not just images (see Figure 3.14).

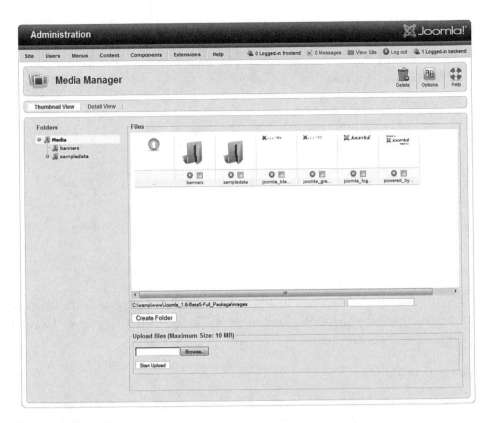

FIGURE 3.14 The Media Manager.

The Media Manager shows a basic File Manager–type view of all files that are in the /images folder. The Media Manager automatically points to this folder; you can't browse to any other folders in the Joomla installation.

You use the Media Manager to change, add, and edit folders and upload or delete media in them. It's a handy tool for putting some organization in your media storage so all your images (for example) aren't dumped into one big folder, which would make them difficult to locate.

> **TIP**
> Make sure you have a logical structure for your media. Your actual structure doesn't matter, but creating folders for certain sections or categories or types of images makes it easier to handle numerous files. It's worth documenting your structure if multiple administrators are managing your site.

The Components Submenu

Components are the most important extensions for a Joomla site. The other extension types are modules, plug-ins, templates, and languages. We go into more detail on each of these in dedicated chapters. You use the Components menu to administer the functionality of components that are part of the Joomla core as well as any components you have installed (see Figure 3.15).

FIGURE 3.15   The Components submenu.

Components

A component adds a significant amount of functionality to a Joomla site—for example, a forum or shopping cart. The most important component is one that is part of the Joomla core and manages and displays all the content articles!

Modules

A module adds a smaller amount of functionality than a component. Most often they are small widgets around the sides of the main component view—for example, a login module or a latest news module.

Plug-ins

A plug-in is a function that runs in the background across your site, For example, it might cloak email addresses from spam bots or load a gallery in an article.

Templates

Templates control the look and feel of a Joomla site, including CSS and images. They also define all the positions where modules can be loaded on a page.

Language

Joomla has the capability to use many different languages. A Language Pack modifies the text that is controlled by the CMS—for example, the word *submit* on a button. You'll still need to translate the content yourself!

So a component is a specialized mini-application that runs in Joomla to generate the mainbody of a page. Thousands of extensions are available both for free and commercially from third-party providers. You can find out more about them at extensions.joomla.org.

> **NOTE**
> Some component-level extensions also include and make use of modules and plug-ins in addition to the component itself to achieve full functionality.

The following core components are included by default in a base Joomla installation:

- Banners
- Contacts
- Messaging
- Newsfeeds
- Search
- Weblinks
- Redirect

The Extensions Menu

As just mentioned, extensions come in several types: components, modules, plug-ins, templates, and languages. Components are fundamental to the functionality of a Joomla site and have their own menu. The rest of the extensions are found in the Extensions menu, shown in Figure 3.16.

FIGURE 3.16   The Extensions submenu.

The Extensions menu provides access to all the extensions you might have installed in Joomla to extend its functionality. Each type of extension has its own manager.

> **NOTE**
>
> In the Extensions menu, there are managers for modules, plug-ins, templates, and languages. The manager for components, however, is in a separate menu item. This is because components are more complex than these other extensions, and it would make navigation difficult if they were all together; therefore, components have a menu item of their own.

Extensions

The Extensions > Extension Manager menu link takes you to the Extensions Manager. Here you can install new extensions, uninstall any that you no longer want, or search for updates. The Extensions Manager is shown in Figure 3.17.

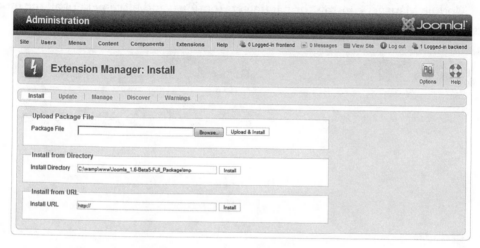

FIGURE 3.17   The Extensions Manager.

Joomla allows the installation of extensions from their packaged installable zip files. Joomla automatically detects what type of extension is being installed. The Extension Manager also details individual extensions on pages for each extension type so they can be uninstalled.

> **TIP**
>
> If you are not using a particular component, it's a good idea to disable it in the Extension Manager under the Manage tab. Just click on a check mark icon in the Enabled column to disable (or re-enable) a component without uninstalling it.

To be installed automatically into your Joomla site, a package must be zipped, and the zip file must contain an XML file with instructions to Joomla detailing how the installer is to unpack and install it.

> **TIP**
> Sometimes third-party developers have a zip file that contains the real installable zip file as well as supplemental files such as documentation. It's a zip file within a zip file. If you get an error during installation, try unzipping the file on your computer to see if another zip file is within it. Usually a filename such as UNZIPME is a giveaway.

Module Manager

The Module Manager controls the parameters (options) and placement of all the modules in a Joomla site (see Figure 3.18).

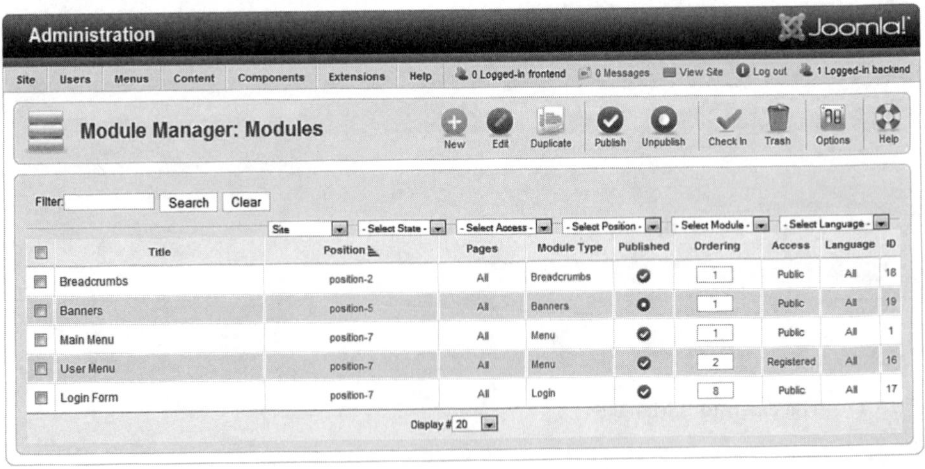

FIGURE 3.18   The Module Manager.

Modules can be thought of as mini-components. Whereas a component always displays its content in the mainbody of the page, a module displays its content in designated peripheral places on the page. For example, the Log In module might have its position set as "left." (In most templates, this would mean in the left column.)

Often, a component has a number of modules bundled with it. For example, Virtuemart, a popular shopping cart component, has a module that shows the latest items for sale.

> **TIP**
>
> The module positions are totally arbitrary in that they are names selected by a template designer to designate positions (locations to place content) in a design, based on the template designer's whims. If I wanted to, I could have all my "left" modules be displayed in a column located on the right. This is not something to be concerned about, though. Most designers generally follow reasonable position naming conventions. It's worth noting, however, when using templates created by others.

Plug-in Manager

With the Plug-in Manager, you can control the options of all the plug-ins you have installed. Plug-ins act as event handlers that enhance sitewide functionality without having a visual presence on the page. The Plug-in Manager is shown in Figure 3.19.

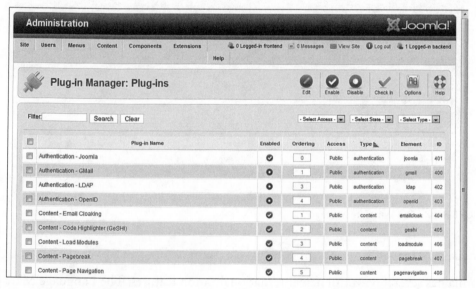

FIGURE 3.19   The Plug-in Manager.

Many plug-ins don't have options; they simply provide some function. The following are two examples:

- **Content-Mail Cloaking**—This plug-in automatically checks all pages for email addresses and replaces them in the code using JavaScript so email spam bots can't harvest them.

- **Content-Load Module**—This plug-in allows you to load modules in the middle of a content article.

Template Manager

The Template Manager, which shows all the templates that are currently installed, controls how a template is implemented on your site (see Figure 3.20). You can edit the HTML or CSS files, assign a template to specific pages, and preview it with the module positions shown.

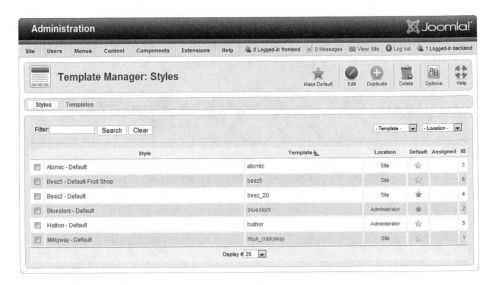

FIGURE 3.20   The Template Manager.

Language Manager

Joomla has several powerful new internationalization features. The Language Manager shows all the language packs that are currently installed (see Figure 3.21).

There are more than 40 accredited translations available for the core, ranging from German to Swedish to Bulgarian to Arabic.

The Help Menu

The Help menu contains helpful links to the official Joomla site (see Figure 3.22).

FIGURE 3.21   The Language Manager.

FIGURE 3.22   The Help submenu.

Joomla also provides a contextual Help button on each page. The Joomla Help function is a searchable knowledge base of most of the basic functions; it is a mirror of the Help documentation at help.joomla.org.

Another great place to get answers to troubleshooting questions is the official Joomla forums, forum.joomla.org. It's a large community with many users who are immensely helpful.

View Site

When you use the View Site function, Joomla opens a new browser window, with the frontend of the site shown. The preview link is to the right of the menu bar.

Joomla provides a useful feature that enables you to take the site offline. You can access it by selecting the Preview link at the right of the menu bar. When you make the site offline, visitors are greeted with the simple message shown in Figure 3.23.

FIGURE 3.23   An offline site.

When you take a site offline, if you log in as an administrator, you get to see the site as outside visitors would see it. This is tremendously useful because it enables you to work on a site before going live; you can see your edits, but the public can't see the site.

You can adjust the offline message to your taste. Maybe you want to include a brief message about your site and a note that it is coming soon. If you need to customize the offline message more, you can edit the offline.php file in the template directory, or create a new version of that file in your template folder.

Summary

This chapter described both the frontend and backend of a Joomla-powered website and quickly showed how to navigate the administrative backend. The menus covered thus far are referred to often throughout the rest of this book.

This chapter explored the following:

- A Joomla website consists of two sites: the public frontend and an administrative backend.

- There are two main types of users: frontend users and backend users. A frontend user manipulates content, whereas a backend user is responsible for site management.

- The way to get information about the specific functions of all menus and buttons is to click the Help button that appears on most admin pages and accesses the latest context-sensitive help posted at help.joomla.org. It's much more accurate and up-to-date than any book can be!

- The Control Panel is the main tool for administering a Joomla site. Different parts of it are visible to different levels of administrators. Third-party extensions often have workspaces that are organized differently than those of the core Joomla functions.

Chapter 4

Content Is King: Organizing Your Content

In This Chapter

As a CMS, Joomla's primary function is to organize and present all the content in a site. It does this through content articles. These discrete pieces of content exist in the database as independent entries. A Joomla website can quickly grow to be hundreds or thousands of articles. To keep these all organized, it's best to have them structured into categories.

THE LEAST YOU NEED TO KNOW
The previous version of Joomla—1.5—had only two levels to organize with, called Sections and Categories. Joomla 1.6 allows an infinite number of levels, simply called *categories*.

This chapter provides an in-depth explanation of how Joomla displays its content articles and how you can organize their hierarchical structure. It details how to plan and organize the content and user experience for a site. It also explains the hierarchical structure currently used in Joomla and how to best shape content into this hierarchy for small and large sites. This chapter covers the following topics:

- How does Joomla generate web pages?
- In what different ways can you present content items?
- How can you organize your content?
- How do components and modules present information?

How Does Joomla! Generate Web Pages?

For those new to Joomla, one of the most difficult things to figure out is how content is organized. The relationship between categories, blogs, and lists can be confusing.

The key to understanding how to organize content is in how Joomla generates pages. We began talking about this topic in Chapter 1, "Content Management Systems and an Introduction to Joomla!" If you have a firm grasp of PHP-served dynamic pages, you can skip ahead to the next section of this chapter, but if part of your brain still harkens back to static HTML pages, this topics is worth a quick revisit.

To get a better idea of how a Joomla site can be organized, let's make a sitemap for an imaginary site. Say that this company is called Widget Inc., and it sells widgets in both blue and green. (This example could easily be generalized into any sort of brochure site for a small company.)

A sitemap is a standard planning tool that web designers use and that is critical for a Joomla website. It's often implemented as a tree diagram that shows all the pages in the site. Figure 4.1 shows an example.

THE LEAST YOU NEED TO KNOW
Having a sitemap is critical to creating a well-organized site. You must make an effort to draft one before you start working in the administrator backend.

In this sitemap, each web page is represented by a box, and the lines are links within the site. A sitemap represents the architecture (links) of a site rather than its content organization. It is a useful planning tool for organizing the site, however. Figure 4.1 shows seven pages; from an organizational point of view, it seems as if there are four main paths in the site:

- About Us
- Services
- Contact Us
- Widget Blog

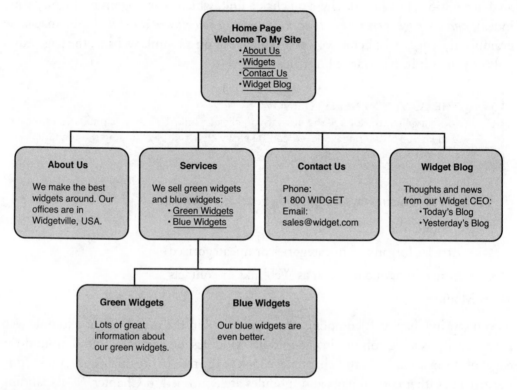

FIGURE 4.1   A website sitemap.

The first step in trying to understand how Joomla structures its content is to realize that *there are no pages!* What does this mean?

In Chapter 1, we talked about the idea of a CMS using "placeholders" for the content. Remember, the content is stored in the database and needs to be placed onto the pages by Joomla. The CMS has spaces on its pages to place content, and it needs to know what content it should put there. Joomla only knows what content should be used after the viewer clicks a link. When it detects a click, Joomla then knows what page to generate, gets the content, and puts it into place.

Consider a different example—a magazine. You turn to the index, look something up, get the page number, and turn to that page. For that page to be filled with content, the magazine author, editor, and designer needed to have chosen the content and arranged it as they wanted on that page. When you turn to that page, you see the content. This seems like an overly simple example, but it illustrates how pages are generated in a CMS. On a Joomla site, you click a link, which is analogous to the magazine index), *and the page is created at that exact moment you clicked the link*. In the magazine example, the pages exist before you go to them, but on a Joomla website, the page exists only as you visit it. It's strange but true.

> **THE LEAST YOU NEED TO KNOW**
> Joomla generates a page the instant you click its link. This means that the content and layout of the pages viewed can be easily changed by changing the menu links rather than the content itself.

There are two main ways that Joomla generates content:

- Components:
  - ◆ Articles (organized in categories or uncategorized)
  - ◆ Other components, such as Weblinks or contacts
- Modules

As you saw in Chapter 1, components are presented in the mainbody of a Joomla web page, usually as a big column in the middle. Modules are generally found around the edges of the mainbody. In this chapter, we look at the task of organizing and presenting the articles. Other components and modules are examined in Chapter 7, "Expanding Your Content: Articles and Editors."

How Joomla! Organizes Content Articles

Joomla gives you two options for how to organize all your content articles. Remember that each article is a discrete piece of content; for example, it might be a two-paragraph news announcement about your company. While a small site might have only five to ten articles, a big site could have thousands. The size and complexity of your site are huge considerations as you organize your articles.

Let's take a conceptual look at these two organizational options, and then we will see how they apply to our imaginary Joomla website for Widget Inc.

Uncategorized Articles

Using uncategorized articles is by far the simplest way to organize a Joomla website. As the name implies, there is basically no hierarchical structure.

Let's consider an analogy. Imagine that you are trying to organize a stack of papers on a desk. Each piece of paper represents a single content article, and the website is represented by a filing cabinet next to the desk.

If you were to organize your articles as uncategorized, you would simply place them in a drawer of the filing cabinet. If there weren't many articles, this would be a fast and easy way to organize them. You can easily find what you want by just picking up the small stack of papers and flipping through the sheets (that is, following links to the different articles). If you have many more articles than a dozen, however, using uncategorized articles isn't going to work. If you pick up the stack, you might have to flip through 1,000 pieces of paper.

Categories

Like almost all other CMSs, Joomla provides a hierarchy for organizing large numbers of content articles called *categories*. You can have an infinite number of nested categories. For example, you might have the kind of structure shown here:

- **Category 1**
  - Category A:
    - Article i
    - Article ii
  - Category B:
    - Article iii
    - Article iv
- **Category 2**
  - Category C:
    - Article v
    - Article vi
  - Category D:
    - Article vii
    - Article viii

Let's return to our filing cabinet analogy. In the cabinet, you have drop-down folders, and inside them you have manila folders, and inside those are sheets of paper (see Figure 4.2).

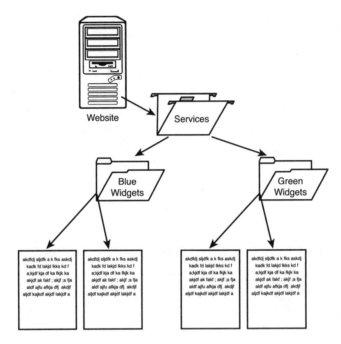

FIGURE 4.2 How Joomla stores its content.

The filing cabinet is the website, the drop-down folders and the manila folders are the nested categories, and the papers are the articles.

Categories

Categories make up the main tier of the hierarchy. Categories are "folders" that can be nested as needed. Categories are also the parents of articles. A category can have one or more children (articles). A category can also be an empty set with no children (articles), but it will not be visible to site visitors.

Articles

Articles are the lowest tier of the hierarchy and also the most important. They are what most people think of as "pages" of a website: You create content articles to add content that you want to display to site visitors. An article must be assigned to a category; it cannot exist without one. (Note that Joomla considers "uncategorized" as a category in its database.)

A Sample Hierarchy

Let's say you want to create a website that discusses classic American automobiles. The following shows how you'd create a sitemap for this site.

Planning the Categories

Assume that you have decided that one type of automobile you want to discuss on the website is the muscle car group—those big beefy performance autos that were so popular in the United States in the 1960s and 1970s. You make this type of automobile your highest tier—a category. So first you create a new category and name it Muscle Cars.

A logical subset of Muscle Cars (parent item) would be a list of the manufacturers that made muscle cars. So next you create a category for each manufacturer: Chevrolet, Chrysler, Pontiac, and Ford. You assign each of these subcategories to the category Muscle Cars.

Planning the Articles

Now you get to the meat of the matter: building the pages for the various car models. The models of cars are, in other words, the lowest level of your hierarchy. To create pages for the models, you create a content item that represents each. You then assign each model (content item) to the proper manufacturer (category). Let's look at one specific category: Ford. For this manufacturer, you want to create pages for each of the following models: Mustang, Fairlane, Falcon, and Galaxy. In this case, you create content items for each model and assign each to the category named Ford.

Visually, you have created a content hierarchy that looks like the following:

- Muscle Cars [category]
  - Chevrolet [subcategory]
  - Chrysler [subcategory]
  - Pontiac [subcategory]
  - Ford [subcategory]
    - Mustang [article]
    - Fairlane [article]
    - Falcon [article]
    - Galaxy [article]

THE LEAST YOU NEED TO KNOW
Joomla offers two methods for organizing articles. The first is to use uncategorized articles, which are suited for very small sites. For larger sites, you need to use the second method: creating categories.

Creating the Widget Inc. Website with Uncategorized Content

Let's return to our imaginary widget company and go through two examples of organizing the content using the two methods that were just explained: uncategorized and categories. The simplest way to create a site with Joomla is with uncategorized content. So you can better understand how to set up content on a site, let's not organize our content into sections and categories here, but just make all the content items uncategorized. With this method, it is much easier to understand how a Joomla site is driven, so it is a good place to start. A single uncategorized content item in the database will correspond to a single page of content on the website.

Remember that the uncategorized method is not much use if you have more than a dozen pages because the content gets too difficult to manage.

THE LEAST YOU NEED TO KNOW
Making your pages with uncategorized content items is the simplest way to build a Joomla site, but it is difficult to manage with more than a dozen pages.

If you want to follow along with the creation of this site, you need to install Joomla (see Chapter 2, "Downloading and Installing Joomla!") somewhere. I would advise installing it as a localhost.

NOTE
For this example, I installed Joomla but used no default content. This means I started with a blank content database.

Without any content, the site looks as shown in Figure 4.3.

To make this example more appropriate, you need a slightly simpler sitemap for the Widget Inc. site. Let's say you have a simple website that consists of three pages: a Home page, an About Us page, and a Services page (see Figure 4.4).

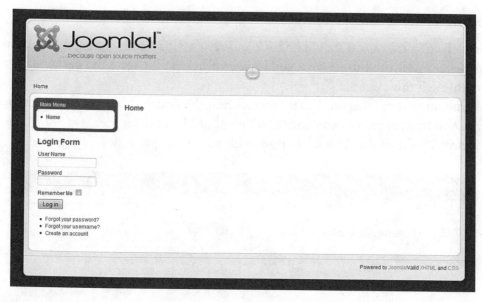

FIGURE 4.3   A fresh installation of Joomla with no content.

FIGURE 4.4   Simple sitemap of the Widget Inc. site.

First, you need to create some articles for this example.

Creating Content Articles

If you haven't already, you should go back and review Chapter 3, "Joomla! Administration Basics." You need to havve a good sense of how to navigate the backend as you work through this example.

Remember from Chapter 3 that you can find the Article Manager in the Content menu. You need to create two content items: About Us and Services.

Figure 4.5 shows the Article Manager with no articles yet added.

FIGURE 4.5   The Article Manager.

When you click the New button in the Article Manager, an editor appears, and you can fill in the desired content. In Figure 4.6, you can see where I added a sentence in the editor.

We will look at adding content and the editor in much more detail in Chapter 7. For now, we are focusing on site organization. So enter About Us as the title (leave the Alias field blank) and set the category as uncategorized (see Figure 4.6).

You might have noticed if you are following along with an empty content Joomla installation that there was only one choice for category in the drop-down box—uncategorized. This makes sense because you have not created any categories yet; you create categories as they become available as options in this drop-down.

Click the Save icon, at which point you should be told, "Article successfully saved."

We then add another article, with the title Services, in the same way. You now have two articles in your Article Manager, as shown in Figure 4.7. Notice that the category column says uncategorized.

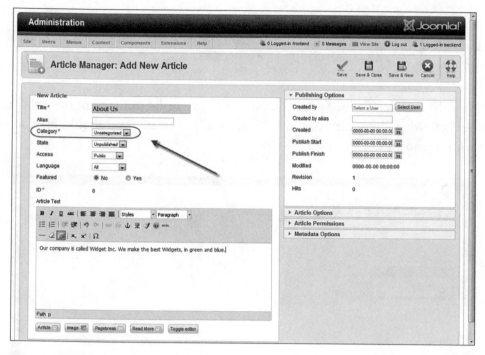

FIGURE 4.6   Adding an uncategorized article.

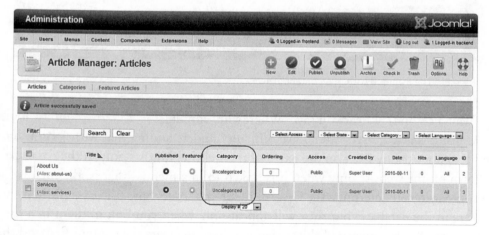

FIGURE 4.7   The Article Manager with About Us and Services content articles.

NOTE
Make sure you publish the two articles by clicking on the red circles in the published column so that they become green ticks.

Now that you have added your content, let's look at the frontend of the website. If you are following along carefully (there will be a quiz later!), you should see a screen like the one shown in Figure 4.8.

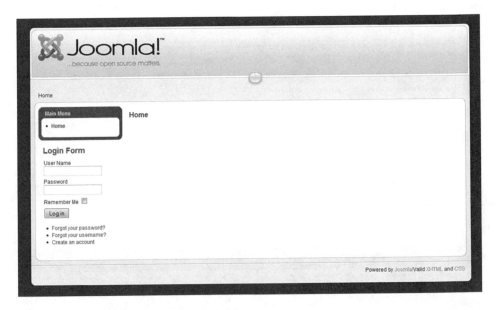

FIGURE 4.8   The frontend with two content articles.

"Wait a second," I hear you say. "Where's my content?!"

As just discussed, users often have difficulty understanding that with Joomla, content does not exist by itself on the pages of the website; it exists only in the database. It is shown on the website only when it is linked to in a menu—that is, the menus (not the content items) determine the content of a Joomla site. Sure, the content items will be there in the database, but they will appear only when you link to them in a menu somewhere. A consequence of this is that you have to create the content first and then create the links to it.

For all content that is in the mainbody of your pages, you must create the content first and then create the links to it. Each of these content items must have a link to it to cause it to appear on the site. Just to increase the confusion, each must also be "published" in the Content Item Manager. Your two items for this example are published, so you can now add links to them in the menu.

NOTE
Content items that are in a module *do* appear on pages without having to be linked to. They have to be told what pages to appear on, however, and by pages, we of course mean links! More on modules later in this chapter.

THE LEAST YOU NEED TO KNOW
Menu links determine both what will a page will contain and how it will be laid out.

TIP
You can use an advanced menu technique I like to call a landing page or hidden menu, in which case the menu that causes the content item to be shown on a page does not need to be published or visible itself. You can create a menu that is not itself published but links to various other pages. You can then use it in various situations without having to link to it off your site. Maybe you want a special page that offers one of your products at a discount and gives the URL in an offline newspaper ad or a landing page for your Google AdWords campaign. To find these URLs, you just look at the URL line in the menu item.

Creating Menu Items

Now that you've created your content items, let's head over to the menu that is in this site; it's called Main Menu. If you look back at Figure 4.8, you will see this menu in the left column. It has only one link in it at this point—one that links to the home page of the website.

Go to Menus>Main Menu. In the Menu Manager, you see a screen like the one shown in Figure 4.9. Currently it's showing only the single link to the home page.

You create a new menu by clicking the New button. You then see a screen from which you can add a new menu item, shown in Figure 4.10.

The first step in creating the menu is to select the type. Circled in Figure 4.10 is the Menu Item Type button. Click it and a pop-up appears. For this exercise you want to select Single Article.

FIGURE 4.9 Initial main menu.

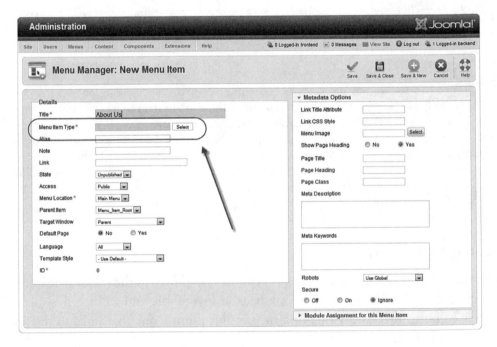

FIGURE 4.10 The admin screen for adding a menu item.

Note that you could have a link to a whole category. Because you don't have any of those, you should go for the article and click Single Article, as shown in Figure 4.11.

On the next screen, New Menu Item (see Figure 4.12), you need to fill out the various parameters for a new link. It's not immediately obvious how to select the article you want to link to it. Under the basic parameters on the right side is a button to select the article (shown in Figure 4.12).

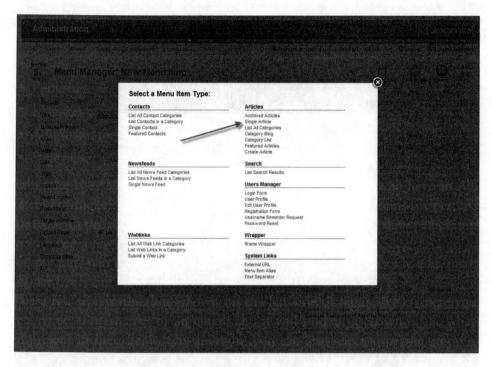

FIGURE 4.11 Creating a link to a single content article.

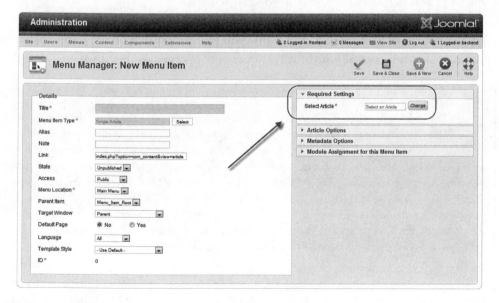

FIGURE 4.12 Adding new menu item parameters.

Clicking Select opens a pop-up box where you can select the article you want to link to (see Figure 4.13).

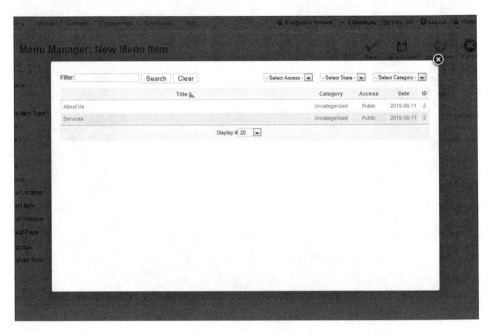

FIGURE 4.13   Selecting the article to which a menu item is linked.

Finally, give your link a name. The name you give it here will be the name displayed as the link. This is a critical point for search engine optimization (SEO).

NOTE
The link name does not have to be the same as the title of the content item. Now, SEO wisdom says that the anchor text of a link, the actual wording that is underlined, is very important to achieving a good search engine rank position (SERP) with that key phrase. This makes our example good for showing what not to do. It would be pointless to try to achieve SERP for the phrase "About Us." If my website sold widgets, then it would make more sense to have a link that said "About Our Widgets." Then at least you'd get Google points for having "widgets" in the link. For the most benefit, the title of the page you are linking to should also have the keyword phrase/anchor text in some version, perhaps "About Widget Inc., Your Quality Supplier for Widgets."

While we are discussing link text and SEO, I should mention something else: When you're making a site, it's important to make it as "usable" as possible. Usability experts tell us that the words in a link should match very closely with the page we end up on. Steve Krug talks about this in his book *Don't Make Me Think*, saying, "If there's a major discrepancy between the link name and the page name, my trust in the site will diminish."

Taking both these factors into account, trying to place important keywords in the link text along with making the link usable is a balancing act. Often, doing better at one means that the other is worse. Don't think you can dismiss usability. What's the point of having substantial traffic if visitors leave your site out of frustration? Needless to say, it takes work and some careful thought to decide on link text. Fortunately, however, it's easy to change later; you just go in and edit the menu item!

THE LEAST YOU NEED TO KNOW

You can create links to a content item, but the content needs to exist first. The name of a link (anchor text) needs to be chosen very carefully.

After you create another link to Services in the same way, your main menu will look as shown in Figure 4.14.

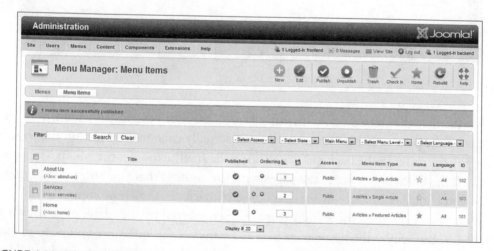

FIGURE 4.14   The main menu, with Home, About Us, and Services menu items.

NOTE

Make sure you publish the two menu items by clicking on the red circles in the published column so that they become green ticks.

When you go to the frontend now, you see three menu items—Home, About Us, and Services—in your main menu in the left column (see Figure 4.15). You can click any of those three links to navigate around the simple, three-page Joomla website.

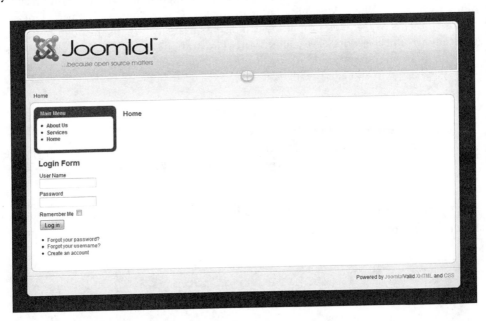

FIGURE 4.15   The frontend of a three-page Joomla website.

Notice that the names of the menu items in the main menu (in Menu Manager) appear on the page in the same order. You can actually change the order on the page by changing the order in the backend (by clicking the small arrows in the Menu Manager).

Click the links, and you get the pages with the content that you entered. For example, if you click About Us, you see that content article, as shown in Figure 4.16.

When you click the Home link, you are again greeted by the blank page shown in Figure 4.8. But why is the home page blank? To answer this question, you need to look at the Featured Article component, the one used by the Home link/menu item when you first install Joomla.

The Featured Article Component

You now have two content articles, About Us and Services. You also have two menu items in the main menu that link to those articles. Now you need to set up the last page of the Widget Inc. website, the home page. Now we're getting to some of the aspects of Joomla that are rather difficult to understand. When Joomla is freshly installed, the home page is not a simple link to content articles; it's actually a special component called the *Featured Article component*.

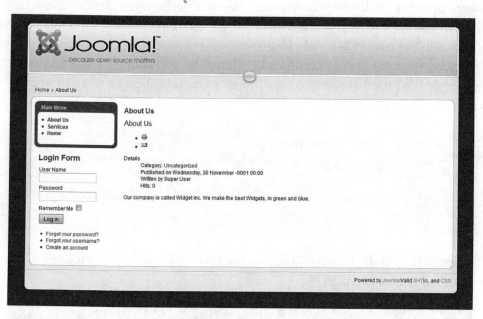

FIGURE 4.16   The About Us article, viewed from the frontend.

As discussed in Chapter 1, content in the mainbody is generated by any number of components. Until now in this chapter, we have been discussing the component that deals with articles and presents them in various ways. Several components in the Joomla core generate mainbody content in this way:

- Contacts
- Newsfeeds
- Polls
- Weblinks
- The Featured Article

The first four of these do not use articles but pull their content from various places, either within the Joomla site database (contacts) or even other sites (RSS newsfeeds). The Featured Article component uses articles and presents them in a specialized way. Basically a *component* is a mini-application that presents data in the mainbody of a

Joomla site in some fashion. A good example of a component is a forum. The content presented is highly specialized and different from the rest of the site.

In almost every case (except the case of the Featured Article component), all components installed are in the Components menu. The Featured Article component is unique in Joomla in that it is not managed from anything in the Components menu, but rather in the Article Manager and from within content articles themselves. Quite simply, the Featured Article component allows the publishing of *any* content item in a Joomla site's database on the front/home page, regardless of where it appears on the site.

THE LEAST YOU NEED TO KNOW

Components are mini-applications that present content in the mainbody in a special way.

The home page of a Joomla site is a component. It allows you to pull content from anywhere in your site for its use.

While in the Article Manager, click on the Featured Articles tab. Figure 4.17 shows the Featured Article Manager.

FIGURE 4.17   The Featured Article Manager with no articles.

You don't have anything in the Featured Article Manager yet. Maybe that's why your home page is blank!

NOTE
You cannot use the Featured Article Manager to add content articles to your home page; it only arranges them. You have to add articles from the Article Manager or from the article parameters.

Click on the Articles tab and you'll go to the Article Manager. If you look closely at the Article Manager, you can see a column about the Featured Article component (see Figure 4.18).

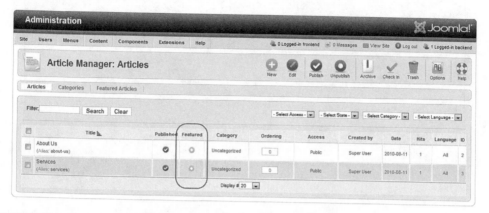

FIGURE 4.18   Featured Article publishing icons in the Article Manager.

These publishing icons in the Featured column control whether an item appears on the home page of the site. You can simply click these circles and check marks to have the items included on the Featured Article. Note that the two articles have gray circles. If you click them, you get a blue star. You can also change this setting in the Publishing tab in the actual content. In Figure 4.19, you can see the About Us article with the Featured Article publication parameters shown.

If you publish your two articles to the Featured Article (either by clicking the icons in the Article Manager or setting the parameter within the two articles), your home page will look like the one shown in Figure 4.20.

The order of the articles on the home page is controlled by menu link parameters. It can be ordered by date, alphabetical, or several other options. (We look at menu link parameters in much more detail in Chapter 5, "Creating Menus and Navigation.")

> **NOTE**
> You add articles to the Featured Article from the Article Manger. You arrange their order in the menu parameters of the default link in the main menu. You can see what articles are on the Featured Article and have further fine-tuned control over them in the Featured Article Manager.

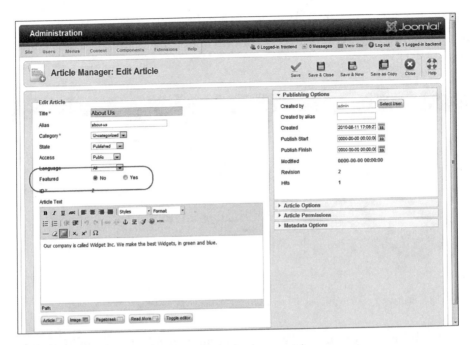

FIGURE 4.19   A Featured Article publishing parameter in an article.

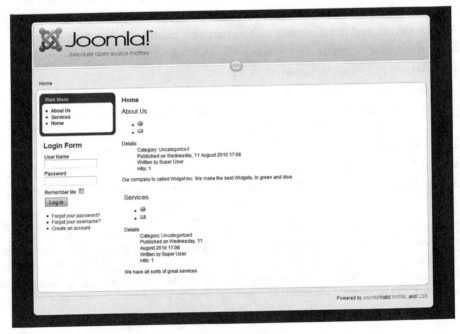

FIGURE 4.20   A home page with two Featured Article published articles.

The home page of a site doesn't have to be controlled by the Featured Article Manager. Sometimes you need more control over its layout, among other things. *The default item in the main menu —the one with the star next to it—will be the home page of the site.* In the default Joomla installation, this is set to be the Featured Article Manager (the Home link), but it could just as easily be a single content item, a whole category, or another component.

Figure 4.20 shows a very simple three-page Joomla website based on the sitemap in Figure 4.4. At the beginning of this chapter, you considered a slightly more complex site of a whole seven pages!

To build this bigger site, you need to use the second article organization method Joomla can use: categories. Read on!

Creating the Widget Inc. Website with Categories

Let's go back to the example we started with in this chapter—the seven-page site shown in Figure 4.1. Now that you have a better idea of how to create articles in Joomla and how to link to them with menu items, let's examine how to create this site by using categories.

Two of the pages will be components: the Featured Article component for the home page and the contacts component for the Contact Us page. That leaves five other pages. You can see that there are actually seven web pages here:

- About Us
- Services
- Green Widgets
- Blue Widgets
- Widget Blog
- Today's Blog
- Yesterday's Blog

Remember that Joomla gives you unlimited organizational levels, so you can just create categories and nest them as needed.

For this example, let's have About Us as uncategorized and then two categories:

- Services:
  - Blue Widgets

- ◆ Green Widgets
- Blog:
  - ◆ Widget Blog
- About Us (uncategorized)

Now it seems as though the Widget Blog will have a redundant level, as there is only one article in it right now. If you are the site designer, you might as well organize it this way, however. If the site grows, as hopefully it will, you will have the ability to add more categories for the blog, for different areas of discussion. It's easier to add categories if you already have the structure built in, even if it does not seem to make sense at first.

To start setting up the content, it's easiest to follow this order:

1. Create the categories.
2. Create the articles.

Creating Categories

If you go to the Category Manager (by selecting Content>Category Manager), you see that it has one entry—Uncategorized. This is because you installed your site with no content in the installation process. Click New, and you see the editor screen for a new category, as shown in Figure 4.21.

In Figure 4.21, you can see the title and category name. Set up the Services category, and the Widget Blog category. After you have set up the category for the Widget Blog, the Category Manager should look as shown in Figure 4.22. Don't forget to publish them both!

Note that there are no active articles yet. Now that you have your category structure created, you can add some articles.

Creating Content Articles

If you have been following along with this chapter's example with your own fresh installation of Joomla, you will already have two articles in your site. The About Us article can remain as it is—uncategorized. Rather than just delete the Services article, you can move it into the correct category.

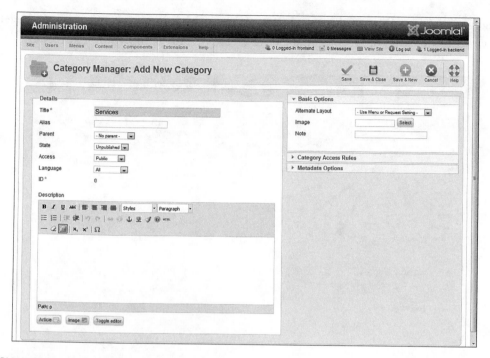

FIGURE 4.21   Adding the Services category.

FIGURE 4.22   Category Manager with two categories created.

Go to the Article Manager (by selecting Content>Article Manager) and open the Services content article. You can turn this article into one about blue widgets. First, change the title to Blue Widgets and then make sure that its category is Services. Delete any text in the Alias field so Joomla can re-create it. This is shown in Figure 4.23.

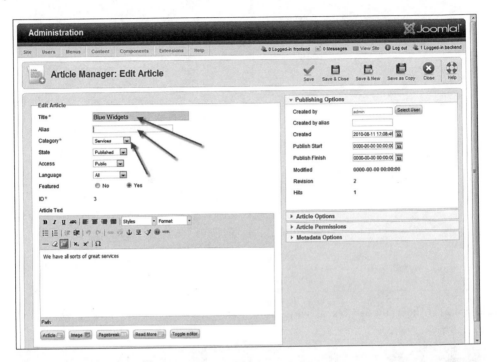

FIGURE 4.23   Editing the Blue Widgets content article.

You can now create two more articles, one for green widgets and one that will be your first post in the blog. Make sure as you are doing this that you are getting the articles in the correct categories.

After you create all your articles, the Article Manager should look like the screen shown in Figure 4.24. Notice that the two articles from before, About Us and Blue Widgets (formally Services), are shown on the Featured Article. Before moving on, make sure that About Us is the only Featured Article article by clicking on the blue star in the Featured Article column for the Blue Widgets article.

If you take a look at the frontend of the website after making that Featured Article adjustment, you should see a screen similar to the one shown in Figure 4.25.

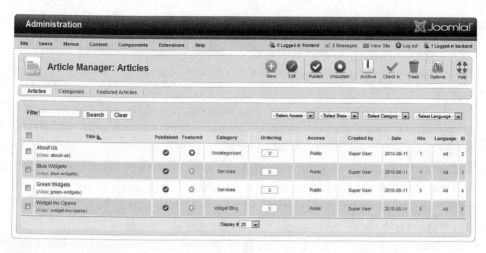

FIGURE 4.24   The Article Manager with four content articles.

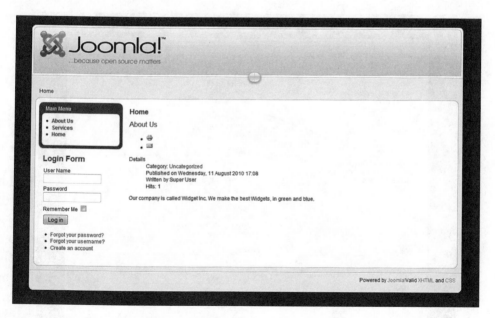

FIGURE 4.25   The home page after you add content.

If you navigate around a little, you quickly see that the links you created are still pointing to the individual content articles. We want them to point to more general pages—categories—that will show more than one article. Although you have set up your content, you haven't set up your menu items. You can do that now.

Creating Menu Items

Chapter 5 goes into much more detail about the relationship between menus, menu items, modules, and the content presented on a page. Right now, we're going through a complete process of creating a simple site. We revisit the same process in the next chapter because the repetition will help you understand a difficult concept in two different contexts. Go to the main menu (Menu Manager>Main Menu) and delete the link to Services; leave the link to About Us.

Next, create two links to your blog and services. When you click the New button in the Menu Manager, as before, you go to the New Menu Item screen. Last time we created a menu item, we pointed the link to an article by clicking the Select Menu Type button. Here we do the same but select a category as the target.

When we click Select Menu Type, we get our pop-up box and we choose Category Blog as our layout, shown in Figure 4.26.

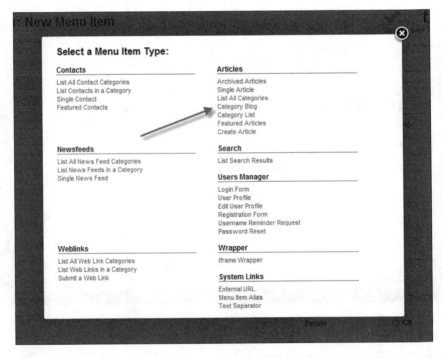

FIGURE 4.26   Adding a link to a category. Chapter 5 explains in more detail the various other options here. For now, just click away!

As you did when you were creating menu items that linked to single content articles, you have to choose where the link points from the drop-down box. This time, however, you are selecting a category rather than a single content item (see Figure 4.27).

When you select the menu item type, give this Menu Item a name (I chose Services) and your Menu Item screen should look like Figure 4.27.

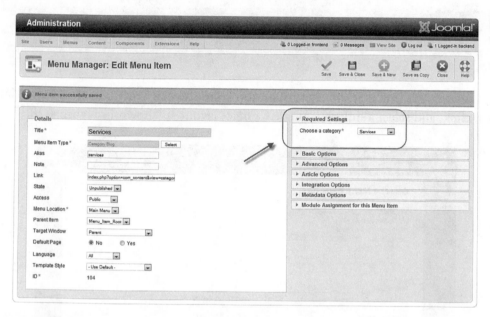

FIGURE 4.27   Selecting the category for a new menu item.

You can then create another menu item (in exactly the same way) that links to the Widget Blog category.

Don't forget to publish both your menu items!

> **NOTE**
> When you go to save the Menu Item you might get an error saying one with that name already exists. This is because your old Services Menu Item might still be lurking in the trash. In the Main Menu Manager, just select Trash in the State drop-down, select the old Services Menu Item, and click the Empty Trash button.
>
> Of course, instead of deleting the old Services Menu Item and creating a new one, you could have just changed where the first one links to by clicking the Menu Item Type button and changing it. In a database-driven content management system, everything can be quickly and easily changed.

Linking to Components

You now need a link to the Contact Us page. As explained previously, this link will be to the Contacts component, which will show a form in the mainbody that visitors can use to contact the administrator of the website.

 THE LEAST YOU NEED TO KNOW
Menu items can link to any kind of component, not just the one that controls articles.

Creating this link is relatively simple: You go to the main menu in the Menu Manager, click, and select a link to a Single Contact layout, as shown in Figure 4.28.

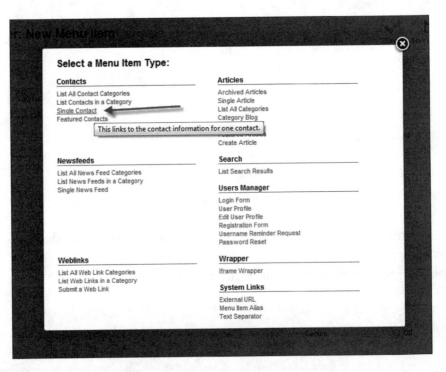

FIGURE 4.28   Creating a link to the contacts component.

Selecting this option takes you to the New Menu Item dialog. Here, as shown in Figure 4.29, you enter Contact Us as the title.

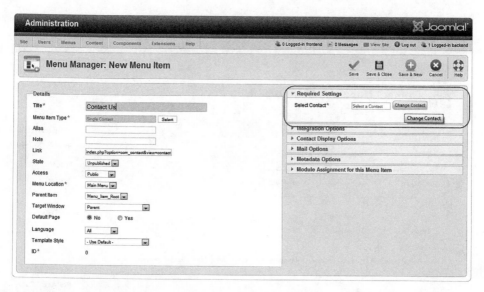

FIGURE 4.29   The New Menu Item dialog for a component link.

In the same way as all our Menu Items so far, you have to tell Joomla what to point the link to. Here, instead of an article or category, we need to point it to a contact. Again, this is the button on the right shown in Figure 4.29.

But when you click the button to select a contact, the list is empty! This is because your initial Joomla installation currently has *Users* but no *Contacts*. If you were following closely, we set up this site we are working on with no sample content. Joomla considers Contacts a type of content in your database, and doesn't set up any. Let's cancel making this Menu Item and go make a contact.

Go to Components>Contacts>Contacts to get to the Contacts Manager, which should be empty. To create a new contact, click New, and you get the Contact screen shown in Figure 4.30. The most important step here is to make sure you link this contact to a user. The Linked User field is shown on the left. The only user you currently have in this site is your original Super User, so choose that one in the pop-up box.

You also want to make sure this contact shows a form. In my example, I want people to be able to contact me by filling this out on my website. In the contact, on the right-hand side, click on the Contact Form tab and set the form to show.

Again, make sure this contact is published.

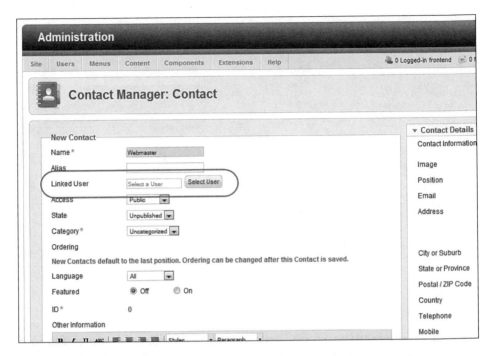

FIGURE 4.30   Creating a new contact.

Now you can go back into the Menu Manager and create that Menu Item to Contact Us. When you click Change Contact you should now see the contact you just created as a single option. (I called mine Webmaster.) Select this one and click Save. Don't forget to publish the Menu Item. The frontend of the site should now look as shown in Figure 4.31 when you follow the Contact Us menu item link.

NOTE
Notice that each time you created a menu item, you had to select what the menu item links to in a parameter on the right-side drop-down box. This is common with all menu items, whether articles or components.

If you look back at your sitemap, you see that you had one link for each article, green widgets and blue widgets, each on its own page. Currently, you have a link called Services that shows content from both of those articles.

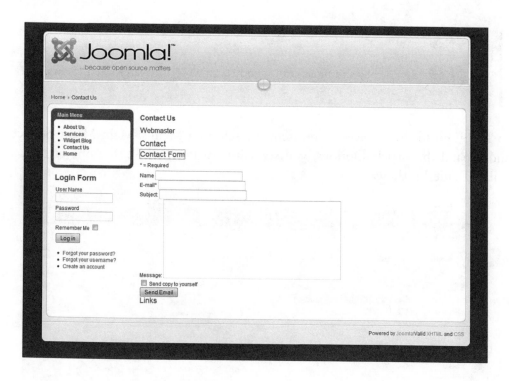

FIGURE 4.31   The Contact Us page from the frontend.

How do you get two more pages for each of those articles? Doing this is easy and gives you a glimpse into how powerful a dynamic CMS can be. All you need to do is change a parameter on that menu item, and you instantly create two new web pages. The following describes the process.

"Read More" Links and Individual Pages

A CMS has all the articles stored away as database entries. As this chapter explains, a single content article can appear on several pages merely through manipulation of the menu items. (Chapter 5 goes into much more detail on this topic.)

You can use this to your advantage when you create a blog layout page. (This is a menu item to a category that shows articles from that category with a snippet of introductory text shown and then a link to read more.) You only need to create the menu item to this page, and it will suck in all the articles, as appropriate, and display them according to the menu item parameters.

NOTE
You also need to make sure that the articles have a "read more" break in them. You create a breaks by editing an article and clicking on the Read More button at the bottom of the editor window.

If you go to the Services menu item (by selecting Menus>Main Menu>Services) and expand the Article Options, you see a list. In Figure 4.32, the one of concern (Linked Titles) is shown.

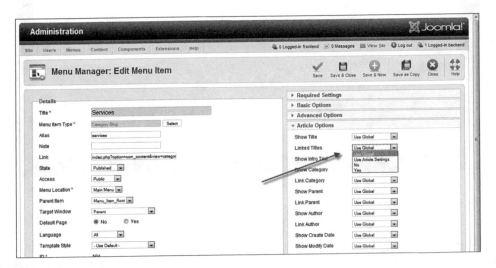

FIGURE 4.32   Article Options for a menu item.

When you change Linked Titles to Yes and save the menu item, it has the effect of turning all the titles in the Services Category blog into links that go to the individual content articles, represented as a single page.

As shown in Figure 4.33, the title now has a hover effect, and if you inserted a Read More break in the article, there is also a Read More... link.

NOTE
If you are linking to a single uncategorized article, you'll never see the "read more" link/intro text. The feature is observed only when you are linking to blog layouts.

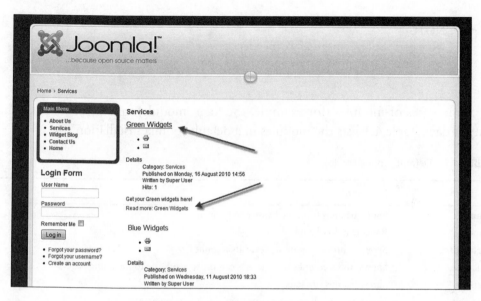

FIGURE 4.33   Frontend linked titles.

Following these links now takes you to individual pages for the articles. You could have had a large number of articles showing in that category blog layout and could have created instant links to new pages by changing that simple parameter.

THE LEAST YOU NEED TO KNOW
You create individual web pages for a content article by adjusting the menu parameters, not by creating new content.

Module Content

Until now in this chapter, we have looked at how content can be organized and presented in the mainbody of a web page. It's also possible to use modules to have snippets of content appear around the edges of the mainbody.

The content presented in a module is very different from that of articles or other components. Modules can be anywhere on a page. Most commonly, you find them around the top, sides, and bottom of a page. (Refer to Figure 1.6 in Chapter 1.)

NOTE
Note that the layout is totally dependent on the designer of the template—one, two, or three columns; footer; no footer; and so on.

Some types of modules (for example, the login module) take in data rather than output data. Table 4.1 lists the modules in a default Joomla installation.

TABLE 4.1   Default Joomla Modules

Module	Description
Banner	Shows banners from the banner component
Menu	Presents links of a menu
Login Form	Shows a form to log in or create an account
Syndicate	Shows RSS feed links that viewers can use to syndicate to the home page
Statistics	Shows various site stats
Category	Shows a list of all categories configured in your database
Related Items	Shows links of content items that have similar keywords
Wrapper	Presents another URL inside an iframe (a page within a page)
Who's Online	Shows the number of viewers currently on the site
Random Image	Shows a random image
Newsflash	Shows a random content item from a chosen category
Latest News	Shows a link list of the most recently published content items
Popular	Shows a link list of the most popular content items (by page view)
Search	Shows a search box
Custom HTML	Contains any sort of HTML

The Custom HTML module is very flexible. You can think of it as a tiny module article that can go on a particular page. We don't go into too much detail here about how modules work because we look at them in detail in Chapter 6, "Extending Joomla!"

For now, you can add to the home page a custom module with some text in it. You go to the Module Manager (Extensions>Module Manager) and click New.

Select the Custom HTML module. The Module Manager: Module Custom HTML screen appears (see Figure 4.34). Here you enter a title and some content in the editor, and you make sure that it's in the correct module position (here you can use right) and has the correct menu assignment (all of them). A small snippet of content appears in the right-hand column.

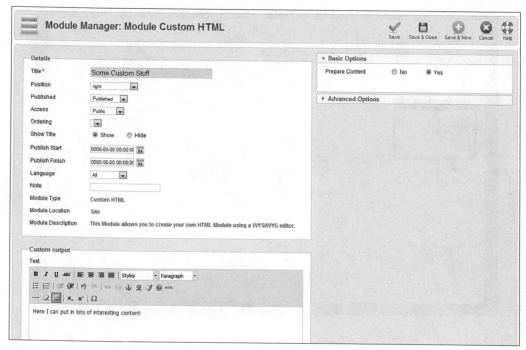

FIGURE 4.34   Editing a custom module.

Your small example is now finished; it should look something like the screenshot shown in Figure 4.35.

You have organized content and used some uncategorized content and a link to a component. The result is a dynamic site that has a logical navigation scheme and some interactivity, including a Contact Us form. In later chapters, you see how to set up much more complex sites, such as a school website.

THE LEAST YOU NEED TO KNOW

Creating a Joomla website from a sitemap always requires a combination of content articles, other components, and modules. From the backend, they are administered in different ways (that is, articles versus other components), but in the frontend, they appear seamless.

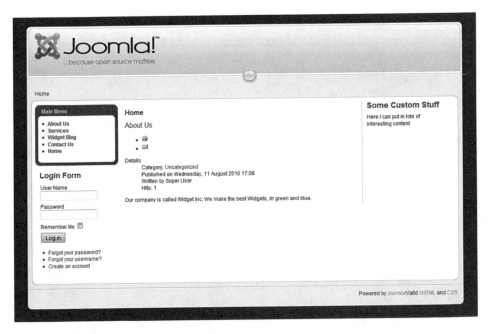

FIGURE 4.35 The completed seven-page Joomla site.

JOOMLABOOK.COM CHAPTER 4 DEMO SITE
www.joomlabook.com provides a SQL dump of the site created in this chapter. It is an exact copy of what you should have if you followed all the steps in this chapter. You can log in to the administrative backend to see the site framework and the categories and menus. The username/password is admin/joomla.

Summary

This chapter tackled one of the trickiest parts of creating a Joomla site—organizing content into Joomla's content hierarchy:

- Having a sitemap is critical to maintaining a well-organized site. You must make an effort to draft one before you start working in the administrator backend.
- Joomla generates a page the instant you visit it. This means you can easily change the pages viewed by changing the menu links rather than the content itself.

- Joomla offers two methods for organizing articles. The first method, suited to very small sites, is to use uncategorized articles. For larger sites, you need to use the second method: creating categories.
- Making your pages with uncategorized content items is the simplest way to build a Joomla site, but it is difficult to manage with more than ten pages.
- Menu links determine both what will be on a page and how it will be laid out.
- You can create links to a content item, but the content needs to exist first. The name of a link (anchor text) needs to be chosen carefully.
- Components are mini-applications that present content in the main body in a special way. The home page of a Joomla site is a component. It allows you to pull content from anywhere in your site.
- There are many ways to organize the same content in a Joomla site.
- Menu items can link to any kind of component, not just the one that controls articles.
- You create an individual web page for a content article by adjusting the menu parameters, not by creating new content.
- Creating a Joomla website from a sitemap always requires a combination of content articles, other components, and modules. From the backend, they are administered in different ways (that is, articles versus other components), but in the frontend, they appear seamless.

Chapter 5

Creating Menus and Navigation

In This Chapter

Menus and Menu Items are important to a Joomla site. In a static HTML site, they merely serve as navigation. In a Joomla site, on the other hand, they serve that purpose and also determine what a dynamic page looks like and what content appears on that page when you navigate to it.

The relationship among menus, Menu Items, pages, and modules is perhaps one of the most confusing concepts in Joomla. This chapter explains this relationship so that you can create a navigation scheme that works for your site.

This chapter examines how to build navigation (menus and their Menu Items) for a Joomla website and how the different aspects interact to produce both a coherent navigation structure and effective page layouts. This chapter covers each of the following questions:

- How do menus and modules work together?
- What do Menu Items do?
- What is a blog layout?
- What is a list layout?

- How can you change a menu's appearance through the Module Manager?

- How do you get submenus or drop-down menus?

How Menu Modules Work

Each Joomla menu has a module that controls where and how the menu appears on a page. If you install Joomla with no sample content, it installs a single menu that it calls the *Main Menu*.

The sample content for Joomla 1.5 contained six example menus. At the time of writing, the sample content is still being worked on, but we can imagine it will also include some combination of example menus.

> **THE LEAST YOU NEED TO KNOW**
> This sample data menu structure is only Joomla's suggestion or example. I personally created the sample pages and key concepts menus and content as part of a team working on Joomla sample content. It's very likely that the sample content will change and evolve over time with new releases and their features.
>
> These six menus are installed when you choose to install sample data during the installation. In most cases, you need to create your own menus or revise these. You could even just delete them and start over again.
>
> If you do not install the sample data, you will only see one menu called Main Menu with only one Menu Item that generates a default home page using the Front Page component.

Each menu has at least one module associated with it. This module controls where and how the menu appears. For example, you could have a module that appears only on the home page, in the left column.

Remember from Chapter 1, "Content Management Systems and an Introduction to Joomla!" that a CMS is dynamic: The content is pulled from the database and put into placeholders on the pages. You can think of the menu as the content in the database and the module as a placeholder for it. If you want to position the menu, you move around its *placeholder* (the module) from the left to the right column, for example. If you want to manage the *content* of the menu (the links), you use the Menu Manager.

You manage the appearance of a menu—for example, whether a link gets underlined when you hover, what color the link is, and whether it looks like a button—through the Module Manager. All these characteristics are defined in the template's CSS file (more on that in Chapter 9, "Creating Pure CSS Templates") and are controlled in the Module Manager by using a module suffix (explained further in Chapter 11, "Creating a Restaurant Site with Joomla!").

The basic building blocks of menus are the Menu Items. Each Menu Item corresponds to a single link in the frontend. Next we'll look at the importance of these Menu Items and what they do.

THE LEAST YOU NEED TO KNOW
The backend part of a menu, what links appear in a menu and the content of the page they generate, is controlled by the Menu Manager. The frontend part of a menu, where it is placed and what it looks like, is controlled by a menu module's settings in the Module Manager.

What Menu Items Do

In a Joomla site, Menu Items do a lot! In a Joomla site, all pages are generated dynamically. Joomla uses information from whatever link a site visitor just clicked to decide what the web page will contain and look like when the user gets there.

You can think of a menu link as doing four different things:

- Designating the content that the link will display
- Organizing articles in the page layout
- Selecting the template to control the page's style and appearance
- Controlling the menu link's appearance

The links on a menu are controlled by the Menu Items in that menu (here the Main Menu) in the Menu Manager. This determines what pages they go to and the appearance of those pages. This is the *where* and the *what*.

In this example, the menu's appearance (left column, brown background, and so on) is controlled by settings in the Main Menu module. This is the *how*.

TIP
You can actually have more than one module for a specific menu. For example, you could have the same menu appear in the left column on the home page and in the right column on other pages in the site.

You saw in Chapter 4, "Content Is King: Organizing Your Content," that menus and links have some important characteristics:

- Menus control the site. Pages are dynamic and do not exist until generated by clicking a Menu Item link.
- Menus/links and content are completely independent of each other in the database; content must be created and then linked by a Menu Item to be displayed on a page.
- Menu Items can be created as you are creating the content, after it is saved.
- Menu Items can link to Content (articles) or other components.
- Menu Items determine both the content and appearance of the pages they generate.

Let's look in more detail at the three parts of a Menu Item: the *what*, *where*, and *how*. To do this, let's create a Menu Item.

Creating a Menu Item

The Menu Manager contains all the menus on a site. Each menu controls where links go to and what the page looks like when the user gets there within a specific module.

When you create a Menu Item, as you saw in Chapter 4, you get a screen that presents what type of Menu Items you can have. Figure 5.1 shows the choices.

NOTE
Chapter 5 starts off exactly where we left off in Chapter 4. If you are following along with an example site, you'll need to have completed that chapter or import the SQL dump of Chapter 4 available from www.joomlabook.com.

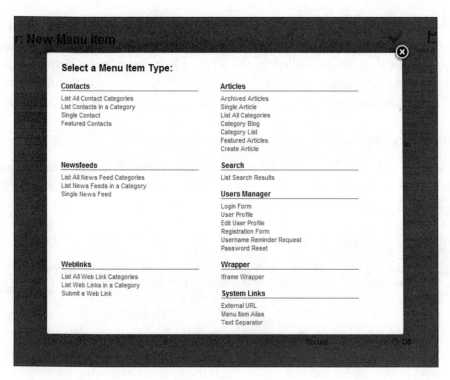

FIGURE 5.1   Menu link options.

Now, this list is intimidating, but don't panic. In Chapter 4, we saw two of them, a Single Article and a Category Blog. Now we are going to look in more detail at two of these options:

- Articles→Category→Category Blog Layout
- Articles→Category→Category List Layout

Where Does a Menu Item Link?

For most websites, a Menu Item for content can go to two basic pages: a single article or an entire category. It could also go to the equivalents in a component (for example, a single component item, a component category). Which one you choose depends on the site structure you want.

The difficulty here is that the content structure/hierarchy is arbitrary, and there are several ways of setting up a site, as you saw in Chapter 4. This makes for a flexible system but one that can be challenging to set up. Once you have set it up, you have to decide how you will construct the menus to link to it. So you need to plan the site content structure in categories and then plan the menus and how you will link to them.

What Does a Page Look Like After a Link Is Followed?

Now that we've briefly looked at the *where* of pages for your Joomla site, let's look at the *what*—what the pages look like. You can have two basic layouts when you follow a Menu Item:

> **NOTE**
> It is possible to create your own customized layouts of articles by creating overrides in the template. We look at this in more detail in Chapter 9.

- **Blog**—A blog layout is so named because it is similar to the layout seen on many blogs—a series of paragraphs with the opportunity to read more. The blog layout shows content articles with the option of showing some introductory, or teaser, text. There are also more presentation options: You can have one column or ten, and the first few items can have summary text while the rest are just links. The blog format is much more flexible than the list layout.
- **List**—The list layout is a table, with all the articles listed as titles only. The titles are links to the items themselves.

> **NOTE**
> We have been talking about two types of blogs (sorry). The Widget Blog for our widget site is like the blogs you see all over the Web (at www.blogspot.com, for example). Joomla, however, uses the word *blog* to describe a specific article *layout*. Be aware that this term has a specific meaning in Joomla.

Continuing the Widget Inc. Site Example

Let's develop the Widget Inc. site a little bit more so you can see what the two layouts look like.

At the end of Chapter 4, your site had four articles in two categories (refer to Figure 4.24).

Now you have a few articles, and you are going to create some menu links to them in blog and list formats. You will actually have them pointing to exactly the same content; the layouts will simply be different. From this example, you'll be able to more clearly see that there is not a one-to-one relationship between menu links and content.

THE LEAST YOU NEED TO KNOW

There are two main layouts for a Joomla page: blog and list. The blog layout shows intro text with a "read more" link. The list layout shows a table of linked titles. Which layout is used is determined by the menu link parameters.

Blog Layout

Go to the Menu Manager and open the Main Menu. If you were following along in Chapter 4, you will have a few Menu Items already

In Chapter 4, you created links to blog layouts. Let's open one of these Menu Items and find out more details about what a Menu Item is.

Open up the Services Menu Item, as shown in Figure 5.2.

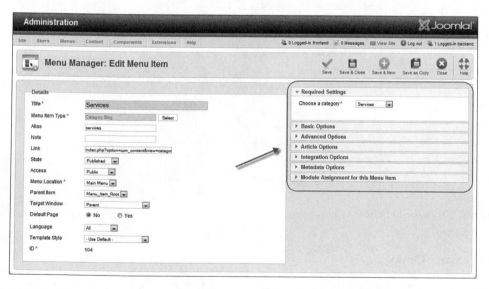

FIGURE 5.2   Blog layout menu item.

A host of *options* (Required Settings, Basic, Advanced, Article, Integration, and Metadata.) control what a page will look like when a menu link is followed. This is the *what* that we talked about earlier in this chapter.

The choice of blog or table and the option settings in the Menu Item are the biggest factors in controlling the look and flow of a Joomla site.

Blog Layout Parameters

Rather than reiterate the information from the Joomla Help site (accessible by clicking the Help button), let's look at some of the most common and important parameters shown on the right side in Figure 5.2. The most important settings are those that determine how many items will be shown and in what format.

Basic Options

The basic options are shown expanded in Figure 5.3. These are mainly about displaying information about the category. The most critical of these is whether to show the category description.

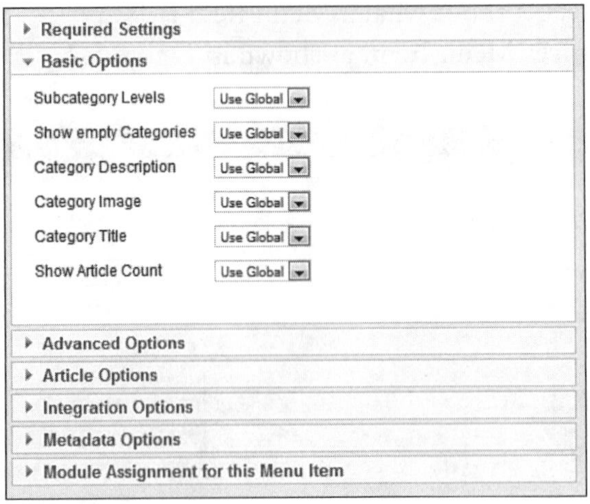

FIGURE 5.3   Basic options for a blog layout.

Blog Layout Options

Figure 5.4 shows some of the options that are more significant in controlling what the page will look like, i.e., how the articles will be arranged.

The basic choices are full width or multiple columns. It's also possible to have some full-width items and then break them into columns. It's not currently possible to do this the other way around—to have, say, a couple columns and then some full-width items.

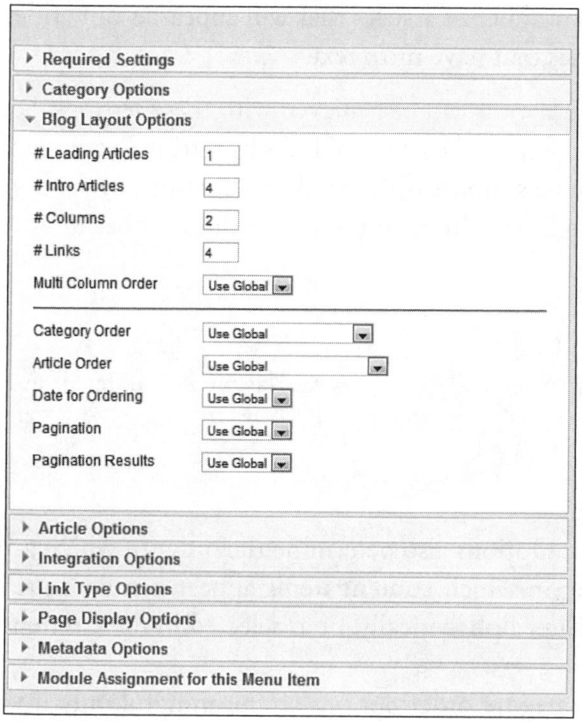

FIGURE 5.4   Blog layout options.

Blog layouts divide the main body of the page into three regions. The topmost region is called *Leading* referring to the place to display the most prominent leading articles. It is always full width. The middle region is called *Intro*, and articles in this region can be displayed in more than one column to make the page more visually interesting. The bottom region is called *Links* and is a full-width table-style listing of article titles as links.

The options that control a blog layout are

- **Leading Articles**—The number of articles that will show their "intro" text across the full width of the main body. (Usually set to 1 or 2.)

- **Intro Articles**—The number of articles that will show their "intro" text arranged in columns

- **Columns**—The number of columns to use in the Intro region. (Usually set to 2. More than three will probably not look very good.)

- **Links**—The number of articles that will appear as only titles with links. They follow the ones that have intro text.

Many different page layouts can be achieved with these settings. Several articles can be displayed full width, followed by a list of links by setting Leading to 3 or 4 and Intro to zero. All articles can be simply displayed in two columns by setting Leading and Links to zero, Columns to 2, and Intro to the maximum number of articles to be displayed on a page.

> **TIP**
> Another way to achieve a Category List layout with different aesthetics is to use a blog layout with Leading and Intro both set to zero so all articles are displayed in List style.

The Blog Layout Options also determine the order in which articles appear

The actual order in which content items appear can be quite complicated. They could be listed by date, alphabetically, or as selected in the Content Manager, to name a few.

Obviously, the category order options are meaningful only if you have items from more than one category in the link.

Article Options

Article Options control many aspects of how an article is displayed. The options can be set at two levels within Joomla. The highest level is the Article Options found by clicking the Options icon in the Article Manager. These settings act as the sitewide defaults that are inherited for articles that do not have these settings overridden at the Menu Item or article level. The next level is the Article Options that appear in the Menu Items that display articles, such as a Category Blog. The final level is the Article Options set specifically within each individual article in the Article Manager. The Article level settings for any Article Options override any settings in the two higher levels.

The component parameters, shown in Figure 5.5, are duplicates of ones in the Article Manager Preferences (Global Configuration parameters), such as whether to Show Author. Having these options allows you to set the global settings to best accommodate the majority of site pages and then override the global settings on a Menu Item (page-by-page) or individual article basis as needed.

▶ Required Settings	
▶ Basic Options	
▶ Advanced Options	
▼ Article Options	

Show Title	Use Global ▼
Linked Titles	Yes ▼
Show Intro Text	Use Global ▼
Show Category	Use Global ▼
Link Category	Use Global ▼
Show Parent	Use Global ▼
Link Parent	Use Global ▼
Show Author	Use Global ▼
Link Author	Use Global ▼
Show Create Date	Use Global ▼
Show Modify Date	Use Global ▼
Show Publish Date	Use Global ▼
Show Navigation	Use Global ▼
Show "Read More"	Use Global ▼
Show Icons	Use Global ▼
Show Print Icon	Use Global ▼
Show Email Icon	Use Global ▼
Show Hits	Use Global ▼

▶ Integration Options	
▶ Metadata Options	
▶ Module Assignment for this Menu Item	

FIGURE 5.5   Article Options in a Menu Item.

If you keep all the default options, your live site will look as shown in Figure 5.6. The only change I made was to rename the Menu Item Services-blog layout.

Figure 5.6 shows the blog with your two content articles.

THE LEAST YOU NEED TO KNOW
A blog layout presents content items in any number of columns, with the option to show intro text along with a "read more" link.

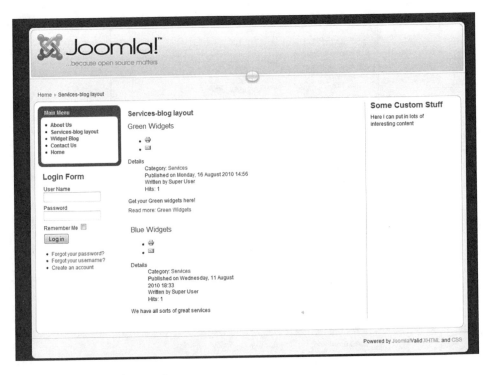

FIGURE 5.6 A basic blog layout of a category.

List Layout for a Blog

Go to the Main Menu in the Menu Manager, click New, and select Category List Layout from the choices.

The New Menu Item screen is more or less the same as for the section list layout, but the options are now different in the List Layout Options (see Figure 5.7).

Again, you give the menu link a title and make sure to select the correct category. Figure 5.8 shows the result in the frontend.

Category List Advanced Options

The main difference in parameters between the category list layout and the blog layout is in the basic settings. As you can see in Figure 5.8, you can set various options for how the articles are listed.

▶ Required Settings

▶ Category Options

▼ List Layout Options

Display Select	Use Global ▾
Filter Field	Use Global ▾
Table Headings	Use Global ▾
Show Date	Use Global ▾
Date Format	
Show Hits in List	Use Global ▾
Show Author in List	Use Global ▾
Pagination	Use Global ▾
Pagination Results	Use Global ▾

▶ Article Options

▶ Integration Options

▶ Link Type Options

▶ Page Display Options

▶ Metadata Options

▶ Module Assignment for this Menu Item

FIGURE 5.7   List Layout Options for a category list layout.

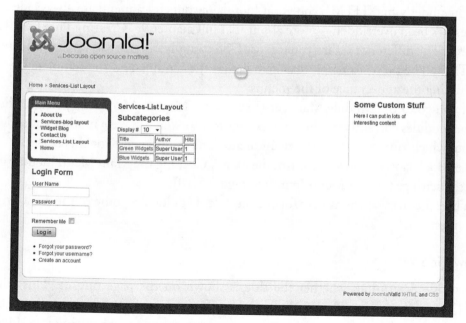

FIGURE 5.8   Frontend view of a category list layout.

THE LEAST YOU NEED TO KNOW
A list layout shows articles as linked article titles in a table. The presentation for a section is slightly different than for a category.

Managing Menu Modules in the Module Manager

You use the Module Manager to control the placement and appearance of a menu (for example, whether you want the menu to be in the left or right column, whether the links have a hover effect).

As mentioned previously, when you create a menu, a corresponding module is created for it, and the module is called by the same as the menu.

NOTE
Any visual look and feel, like a hover effect, you want for a menu must be defined in the CSS files of a template. Most commercially available templates have a number of alternative appearance options pre-created, and you select between them using the module suffix parameter.

The underlying XHTML code that Joomla outputs for a menu are always identical (unless it's been overridden—more about that in Chapter 9, "Creating Pure CSS Templates"). The difference is that you can use CSS to apply different styles to this identical XHTML. The point to emphasize here is that the module and the template CSS are controlling the appearance of the menus.

If you go to the Module Manager (Extensions>Module Manager), you see a list of all the modules currently on the site (see Figure 5.9). You can see a module called Main Menu, which corresponds to the main menu. The module type for this is menu.

Let's look closer at how to control the menu. Clicking the Main Menu module gives you the settings for that Menu Item (see Figure 5.10).

There are many options here for the module. Let's look at some of the most important ones.

Show Title

Show Title determines whether the title is shown on the page output. This will be an H3 tag unless overridden in the template. Typically, titles are not shown for main menus and are shown for special purpose menus or submenus appearing in a sidebar.

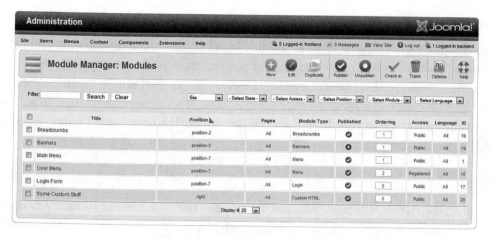

FIGURE 5.9   Module Manager showing the Main Menu.

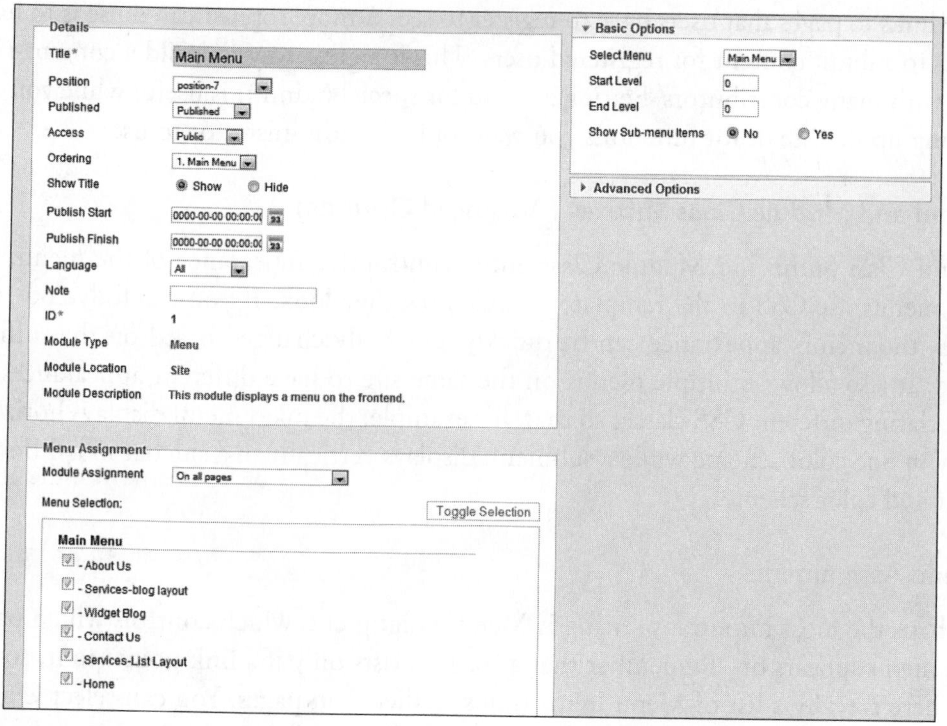

FIGURE 5.10   Main Menu settings.

Position

The Position option controls what module location the menu appears in. The list of possible positions is set by the designer of the template you are using. The options in the drop-down are determined by the currently active (default) template. Note the descriptive location of a module; for example, "left" doesn't necessarily have to actually be on the left. It depends where the designer put it. If using a third-party template, refer to the documentation provided.

Access

By using the Access function, you can make your site much more interactive. Public is, well, public. Anyone can see it. Registered means only registered users can see it. Special means it is visible only to administrators.

You can use this parameter in several ways. The most obvious use is to have a menu that links to pages that users have to register to see. A more sophisticated use is to have links to submit content for registered users. This is a great way to build a content-rich site with many contributors. Setting a menu for special (admin) is useful while you are setting up the site or for functions you want only the administrator to use.

Menu and Module Class Suffixes (Advanced Options)

Menu Class Suffix and Module Class Suffix control the appearance of the menu. All the menus use CSS in the template to style how they look. If you carefully code the CSS, the menu's appearance can be quickly and easily changed based on the suffixes used. It also allows multiple menus on the same site to have different appearances by associating different CSS classes so that, for example, the main menu displays horizontally in one color scheme while a submenu displays vertically in a sidebar in a different font and color scheme.

Menu Assignment

Perhaps the most important setting is Menu Assignment, which controls which pages the menu appears on. Remember that a "page" exists only if a link points to it, so the list here is really a list of Menu Items (links) rather than pages. You can select On All Pages, or be more selective. You can also Ctrl+click to select multiple pages...I mean links!

NOTE

You can have more than one module corresponding to the same menu; just copy the module. For example, you could have a side menu (or any other module) that is in the left column on the home page but in the right column through the rest of the site.

THE LEAST YOU NEED TO KNOW

The module for a menu controls its placement on a page and its appearance. It also controls what pages the menu appears on and what access level can see them (that is, guest or registered user). The menu appearance is determined by code in the template's CSS.

Summary

This chapter looked at menus and navigation for a Joomla website. It's important to realize that with Joomla, the menu links actually control the appearance of the page to which the menu links. You can change a menu link's settings by editing its Menu Item in the Menu Manager.

- You control the backend part of a menu—where the links go and what they do—with the Menu Manager. You control the frontend part of a menu— where it is and what it looks like— with a menu's module.

- A menu link can point to content categories, or individual content articles. It can also point to a component.

- There are two main layouts of a Joomla page: blog and list. The blog layout displays intro text and a "read more" link. The list layout shows a table of linked titles. The layout that is used is determined by the menu link options.

- A blog layout presents content items in any number of columns, with the option to show intro text and a "read more" link.

- A list layout shows articles as linked titles in a table.

- The module for a menu controls its placement on a page and its appearance. It also controls which pages the menu appears on and what users (guests or registered users) can see them. The menu's appearance is determined by code in the template's CSS.

- Various submenus (for example, expandable menus, drop-downs) are possible using advanced CSS techniques.

Chapter 6

Extending Joomla!

In This Chapter

It's difficult to find a Joomla-powered website that has not added functionality beyond the basics with some sort of extension. The word *extension* collectively describes components, modules, plug-ins, templates, and languages.

Thousands of extensions are available both free and commercially from third-party providers. You can find out more about them at extensions.joomla.org (for GPL) and other commercial directories (for non-GPL).

2010 saw the release of Joomla 1.6, which signified a major rewrite of the software. It was a significant enough change that extensions had to be rewritten to operate efficiently in the new version. Always make sure that any extensions you plan to install are Joomla 1.6 compatible.

This chapter looks at some examples of core and third-party Joomla extensions. It also examines how they are installed and managed in Joomla. This chapter covers the following topics:

- What are extensions?
- How do you install Joomla extensions?

- Where can you get third-party extensions?
- What are components?
- What are modules?

Extensions

Extensions are installable packages that extend the core functionality of Joomla in some way. There are five main types of extensions:

- **Component**—A component is the most complex type of extension. It is a sort of mini-application that usually renders the primary content that makes up a page and appears in the mainbody (the large middle column) of the page. The core Content component (`com_content`), for example, is the mini-application that manages and displays all your articles in some way. Another example is a forum component that shows boards, threads, and so on. Not all components are about content; some handle complex functions. For example, the Registration component (`com_registration`) handles user registration.

- **Module**—Modules are usually much smaller (that is, take up less screen area) and less complex than components. They also usually appear around the edges of the mainbody—in the header, side columns, or footer—and do specialized tasks that may or may not be related to the content displayed in the mainbody. For example, the latest news module shows links to the articles that have most recently been added to the site. Often, a module works with a particular component. A related article module shows titles of articles that are somehow related to the articles being displayed by the content component in the mainbody of the page. As another example, the login form module allows site visitors who registered using the contacts (registration) component to log in to the site.

- **Plug-in**—A plug-in is a special piece of code that can be used across a site and runs when a page is loaded. An example is the email cloaking plug-in, which hides email addresses with JavaScript so spam robots cannot see them. Plug-ins are typically event handlers that work in the background to add functionality.

- **Template**—A template controls the graphical look and feel of a site. Templates usually control the layout of a page, along with colors, graphics, and typography.

- **Language**—By installing a language pack, it is possible to internationalize Joomla to a different language. All the words that are part of Joomla for example, "read more") can be displayed in a foreign language.

Installing Extensions

All Joomla extensions come in the form of compressed files and are installed via the Extension Manager. Select Extensions>Extension Manager to open the Extension Manager (see Figure 6.1).

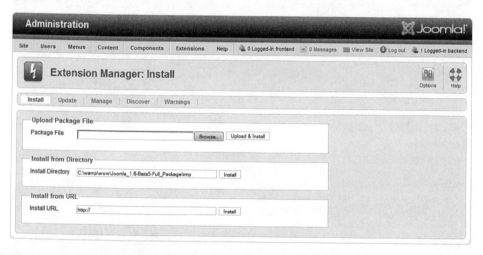

FIGURE 6.1   The Extension Manager.

On the first tab, labeled Install, is a tool to upload the installation package (the zip file of the extension). When you browse to the file and upload it, Joomla automatically detects what type of extension it is and installs it. You then see a screen that tells you whether the installation has been successful. Often, depending on the third-party extension being installed, you also see some more details about the extension, such as setup instructions or where to seek support.

NOTE
If you have an error in the installation, the two most common problems are (1) the zip file contains another zip file, and it is the zip within the zip that is to be uploaded, or (2) problems with permissions and ownership of folders (Joomla can't write or create a folder needed for the installation of the extension). The easiest way to solve permission problems is to use the FTP layer, which you set up in the Global Configuration.

You also use the Extension Manager to uninstall components. If you go to the Manage tab in the Extension Manager, shown in Figure 6.2, you see a list of extensions that can be uninstalled. You can select to view different types of extensions: component, module, and so on, by selecting them in the drop-down Select Type field.

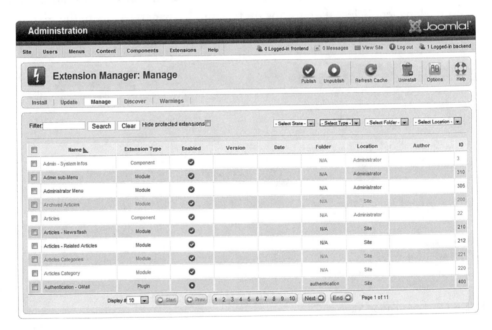

FIGURE 6.2 The Manage tab of the Extension Manager.

NOTE
Notice in Figure 6.2 that many of the components are grayed out. These are core components of Joomla that cannot be uninstalled.

After a component is uninstalled, if you want to use it again, you need to reinstall it. There is no "undo," and any data associated with a component that you delete will likely be purged from the database. If you are unsure whether any data is associated with a component you want to delete, try temporarily disabling a component and verify that important functionality will not be lost before uninstalling it.

Managing Extensions

Each type of extension *except component* has its own manager in the Extensions menu. Figure 6.3 shows the Extensions drop-down menu.

FIGURE 6.3   The Extensions menu.

NOTE
Components have their own menu because of the complexity of components compared to, say, modules.

The Module and Plug-in Managers have a similar table-style layout (which is also similar to the Article Manager's layout). Figure 6.4 shows the Module Manager.

The Template and Language Managers are slightly different from the other managers, mainly because you can have only one template and language active at any one time. For example, Figure 6.5 shows the Template Manager.

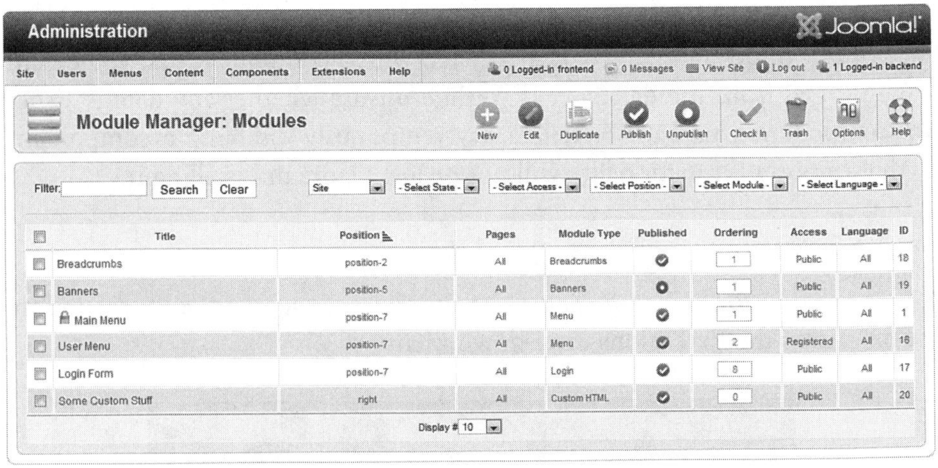

FIGURE 6.4   The Module Manager.

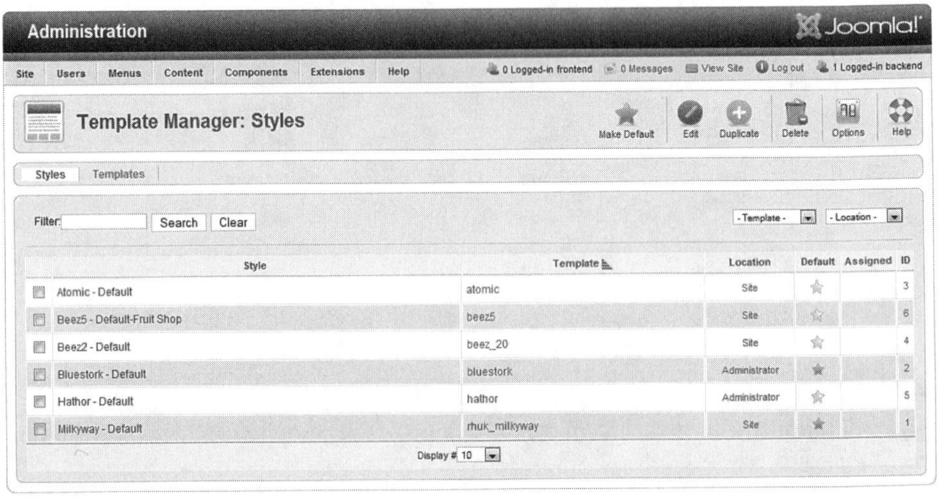

FIGURE 6.5   The Template Manager.

Components

A *component* is a specialized mini-application that runs in Joomla. As you learned in Chapter 1, "Content Management Systems and an Introduction to Joomla!" anything that is shown in the mainbody of a Joomla site (usually the main center column) is generated from a component. It could be a forum, directory, gallery, and so on. You could argue that content is the component at the center of Joomla, the component that is able to present content articles in the form of a single-article page, a blog of several articles, or a table of article titles. But really, several components are part of the core of Joomla. Some extensions are considered components, even though they do not fill the main body of a page on the frontend. This is because their functionality needs to be managed using a backend manager.

NOTE
Some components make use of modules as well as the component itself to achieve full functionality.

Core Components

The following are the core Joomla components:

- **Banners**—You can use this tool to rotate advertising banners on your site. The complete banner extension is made up of a Banner Manager backend component and a banner display module.

- **Contacts**—By using this component, you can present a list of contacts on the site. A manager using the backend contacts component also has the ability to add, delete, and set categories for contacts. When linking to the component with a menu item, you can link to individual contacts or list a whole category of contacts as a roster or directory.

- **Newsfeeds**—Using the newsfeed component is a great way to effortlessly build relevant content for your site. It makes use of RSS technology, and if another website has an RSS feed, you can use the newsfeed component to present that feed on a page of your site.

- **Search**—Joomla has a powerful built-in search function. Along with its corresponding module, it allows visitors to search all the articles of a site with keywords.

- **Weblinks**—Any web page can have links to other sites. The Weblinks component takes this a step further by storing the links and showing a count of how many times they have been clicked. A useful feature of this component is that it allows site users to submit a link by creating a corresponding menu item. This type of tool generates what is commonly called a web directory, or a links page.

- **Messaging**—This tool allows emails to be sent to all registered users. It is a simple tool and does not approach the functionality of third-party email components. It is difficult to ensure that emails sent using the mass mail component conform to the CAN-SPAM Act, but it is useful for sending out a quick email blast to a user group, such as administrators.

- **Redirect**—The redirect tool is a useful feature to help you manage old pages and URLs. Whenever a visitor tries to go to a page that does not exist, a 404 error will be recorded in the server logs. The Redirect component, checks these logs and allows you to enter in a new URL/page for the visitor to be redirected to.

Third-Party Components

One of the exciting things about Joomla is the huge range of extensions available for it. Joomla is unique in the open source world, where open source GPL advocates and commercial vendors work side by side to grow the project. The main repository for third-party extensions is extensions.joomla.org, though a number of commercial alternatives exist.

More than 5,000 GPL extensions are available for Joomla, and it's impossible to provide any generalities on how they work. Each one tends to have a slightly different structure in the backend, based on the decisions of the creator.

Modules

Modules can be thought of as the little brother of components. They are much smaller and simpler to manage, and they supplement the content functionality or interactivity of a page. As just discussed, a component might actually have several modules bundled with it.

Module Display

You can select Extensions>Module Manager to open the Module Manager. Notice that in this table view, listed modules display some common options for how they are presented. If you select a module and choose to edit it, you see its options and settings (see Figure 6.6).

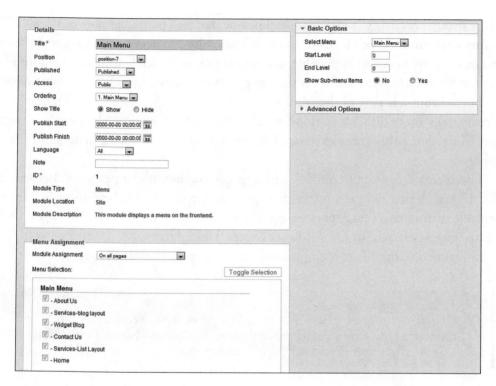

FIGURE 6.6   Module details and menu assignment options.

At the top-left part of the Module Manager are the module's details:

- Title
- Published (whether it is published)
- Access
- Position (the location where it should appear within the layout, as defined in the template)
- Ordering (placement among modules also located in that position)
- Show Title
- Publish Start
- Publish Finish
- Language
- Note

These details are fairly self-explanatory. The one that is of particular note is Access. This setting determines which levels of users will have the privilege of seeing content from this module on a page. It is possible to create almost completely different versions of a website for different levels of users such as guests, registered users, and administrators.

The bottom-left part of the Module Manager shows the menu assignment, which is potentially more difficult to understand. Chapter 5, "Creating Menus and Navigation," introduces this complex idea of assigning modules to menu items rather than to pages.

The menu assignment controls which pages the module appears on. Remember that a "page" exists only if a menu item generates it. So the list here is really a list of available menu items that generate pages. You can select On All Pages, No Pages, Only On the Pages Selected, or On All Pages Except Those Selected.

In Figure 6.6, the Main Menu module is set to appear on all the pages of the site.

> **TIP**
> Figuring out which modules should appear on various pages can quickly become confusing. I recommend using pen and paper to map out what your main pages will look like and what modules will be located on those pages.

Usually modules are placed and controlled by a site administrator according to the aesthetics of the template, considering that they are usually set to appear sitewide.

Core Modules

A number of modules exist in the core default installation of Joomla. They can be split into several types: core content modules, core component–related modules, and core miscellaneous modules.

Core Content Modules

Joomla includes a number of modules as part of the default installation, the more commonly used ones are

- **Archived Articles**—This module shows a list of months that link to all archive content on the site. As mentioned previously, archiving content on a site has advantages and drawbacks. The main drawback is that the URL is changed.

- **Latest News**—This useful module displays a linked list of the most recent content items (articles) created on the site. Despite its name, it can be set to take content from only specific sections or categories. This is a great way to dynamically show recently added content on your home page.

- **Articles-Newsflash**—Next in the series of modules that show content dynamically (along with Latest News and Most Read Content), the newsflash module shows random content items that match a selection criteria. Slightly different from the other two dynamic-content modules, newsflash can show an introductory text excerpt of an article as well as just the title. It can show content from any section or category, not just the newsflash category (which is one of the default categories of a base Joomla installation.)

- **Random Image**—Another content presentation module, this is the equivalent of the newsflash module for displaying images.

TIP

With some careful planning in the design of a template, it's easy to have the random image module generate the header of your site. This has the effect of showing randomly alternating images as your header.

- **Most Read Content**—This is a useful module for easily showing dynamic content; it shows a linked list of the most popular articles currently on your site. As with the latest news module, it can show articles from specific sections and/or categories.

- **Articles-Related Articles**—This module shows a list with links for all articles related to the one currently being displayed. Joomla decides whether an article is related based on what keywords have been entered in the Article Manager's Metadata Options>Meta Keywords field for that content item. Note that it's not possible to limit the number of items displayed with this module as it is with other modules.

We talk more about metatags at length in Chapter 8, "Getting Traffic to Your Site."

Core Component–Related Modules

The default Joomla installation includes a number of modules that work with core components:

- **Syndication Feeds**—This is the module counterpart of the newsfeed component. It is an RSS feed of the articles from the page on which the module is currently displayed. It is therefore best used on pages that display categories or sections.

Core Miscellaneous Modules

A number of modules provide special functionality to a site:

- **Login**—This is a critical module for most Joomla sites. It displays a simple form for users to log in or to create a username or retrieve a password. A login form can also be linked to from a menu, for display on the mainbody. In this case, the module is not used.
- **Menu**—This is another vital module. The main menu module shows menus of the site.
- **Who's Online**—This simple module shows the number of registered users and guests currently at the site.
- **Statistics**—This module shows simple visitor statistics, with the option of showing more technical server statistics.
- **Feed display**—This module's ability to show an RSS feed makes it the module equivalent of the newsfeed component, which can show a feed in the mainbody.
- **Wrapper**—This module loads an external page in an inline frame into the module's position, much as the wrapper component does for the mainbody. Its usefulness is limited in a module; it can load only small amounts of content, as modules are usually placed in columns and other smaller parts of the page.
- **Custom HTML**—The Swiss Army Knife of modules, this accepts any kind of custom HTML, including JavaScript code snippets.

Third-Party Modules

As with components, a diverse collection of third-party modules has been created for Joomla.

Plug-ins

A plug-in offers some form of sitewide functionality. Most Joomla users find that they do not need to manage plug-ins as often as they need components or modules.

Core Plug-ins

Joomla offers the following core plug-ins:

- **Authentication**—Joomla has several plug-ins (Gmail, OpenID, and LDAP) that can be used to allow authentication (login) integration with different systems.

- **Content - Code Highlighter (GeSHi)**—This plug-in highlights code included in content (when you use the `<cpre>` tag), according to GeSHi standards.

- **Content - Email Cloaking**—This plug-in converts any email address written in an article to JavaScript. This makes it undetectable by spam email harvesters.

- **Content - Load Modules**—This plug-in allows you to load a module into a content article by putting `{loadposition user1}` at the point where you want modules assigned to the *user1* position to load. You can actually replace the position with any word; it doesn't need to be defined in the template. For example, for the position blobber, when you edit the corresponding module, you just type "blobber" directly into the position in the module rather than use the drop-down and type `{loadposition blobber}` into the article.

- **Editor button—Button – Article, Button - Image, Button - Pagebreak, and Button - Readmore**—This plug-in controls the Image, Page Break, and Read More" buttons in the article editor.

- **Editors**—There are three editor choices in the Joomla core: None, TinyMCE, and CodeMirror. Other more advanced or commercial editors can also be installed.

- **Search**—This plug-in controls the indexing and thus searching of content.

- **System–cache**—This plug-in controls the caching features of Joomla 1.6.

Third-Party Plug-ins

As with components and modules, many third-party plug-ins exist.

Templates

Chapter 1 examined how a template controls the look and feel of a Joomla site. Chapter 9, "Creating Pure CSS Templates," looks in much more at detail how to create templates.

Core Templates

Joomla 1.6 ships with seven core templates:

1. **Bluestork - Default**—This is the administrator template in the backend. (Yes, you can make new administrator templates to customize the look and feel of the administrative interface!)
2. **Hathor - Default**—An alternative—accessible—backend administrator template.
3. **Milkyway - Default**—This is the default frontend template for a new Joomla installation.
4. **Atomic**—Another frontend template.
5, 6, 7. **Beez2 – Default, Beez2 – Parks Site, and Beez5 - Default**—Two special proof-of-concept templates that focus on accessibility through the use of template overrides.

Third-Party Templates

Thousands of third-party templates are available for Joomla. Perhaps the easiest way to find a template for your site is to search Google for "Joomla 1.6 templates" or "free Joomla 1.6 templates." I offer many free templates for download on my blog at www.compassdesigns.net.

Third-party template providers are of two types: clubs and individual template providers. Clubs charge an annual fee and are good if you like to frequently update your site design. Generally, new club templates are added monthly. Individual template providers offer templates individually, and using them is usually slightly less expensive for sites that do not anticipate changing the template once it's implemented.

NOTE

Joomlashack.com provides great professional templates at an affordable price. (I'm a cofounder of this company.) We focus on easy to use and customize templates that load fast while still looking professional.

Summary

Joomla has an extension for nearly every possible website need. Extensions are available from a variety of places, for a variety of prices. Many are licensed under the GPL and are available for free. Here are some recap points for this chapter:

- Thousands of extensions are available both for free and commercially from third-party providers. The free repository is at extensions.joomla.org.

- Joomla is supported by a diverse community of developers who create the critical extensions needed to increase the basic functionality of Joomla.

- Many Joomla extensions are available for free under a GPL license; others are commercial. Non-GPL commercial ones can be found at various third-party websites on the Web.

Chapter 7

Expanding Your Content: Articles and Editors

In This Chapter

There are two main ways to add to and manage content in a Joomla site—through the frontend and through the backend. Part of the biggest attraction of Joomla is that it enables you to easily add and edit content through the backend via a "what you see is what you get" (WYSIWYG) editor.

This chapter begins by looking at WYSIWYG and how it functions in the backend for managers, administrators, and Super Users. It then examines how authors, editors, and publishers manage content through the frontend. This chapter covers the following topics:

- What is WYSIWYG editing?
- How do you manage articles in the backend?
- How should you use metadata?
- How do you add images and other media to articles?
- How do you manage content from the frontend?
- What is the difference between authors, editors, and publishers?
- What is global checkin?

WYSIWYG Editors

You've probably used a WYSIWYG editor, but you might not even be aware that you have. If you've ever used some sort of editor where you can highlight words, change their formatting, and have those changes be instantly visible to you, then you've used a WYSIWYG editor. For example, Microsoft Word is a WYSIWYG editor (albeit a complicated one)!

WYSIWYG editing is different from directly editing using a markup language, such as HTML or XHTML. When you use a markup language, you must type in tags that assign styles instead of just clicking a button. Joomla and web-based email, such as Yahoo! and Gmail, use simple WYSIWYG editors that let you format content by highlighting text and clicking a button. Figure 7.1 shows an example of an editor taken from a Yahoo! email account.

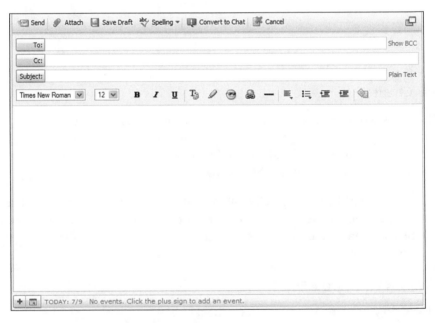

FIGURE 7.1   A Yahoo! web-based email WYSIWYG editor.

The default Joomla editor is similar to other editors, with various formatting buttons that will be familiar to you from Microsoft Word. Figure 7.2 shows the default Joomla editor, TinyMCE.

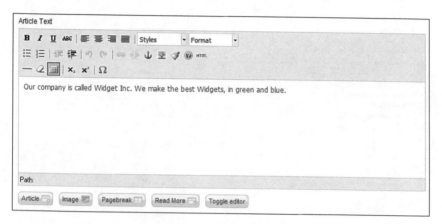

FIGURE 7.2   Default Joomla editor: TinyMCE.

Joomla ships with the TinyMCE editor. This is a platform-independent web-based JavaScript HTML WYSIWYG editor (see tinymce.moxiecode.com).

Many other Joomla editors are also available.

Managing WYSIWYG Editors

It's possible to have a number of editors installed as plug-ins to Joomla. There are three main aspects to managing the editors you have installed.

First, you need to set your sitewide global editor. You do this in the backend in the Global Configuration dialog box, which you open by selecting Site>Global Configuration. You see a drop-down box for your default WYSIWYG editor (see Figure 7.3).

After deciding what your sitewide default editor will be, you also have the option to set a different editor (that is, designate another tool) for individual users. You do this in the User Manager. Select Users>User Manager. Click the user to open up the User Manager—Edit User screen. Circled in Figure 7.4, you see the setting to select a different editor. If the User Editor drop-down box is simply left as Use Default, the global editor will be assigned to that user.

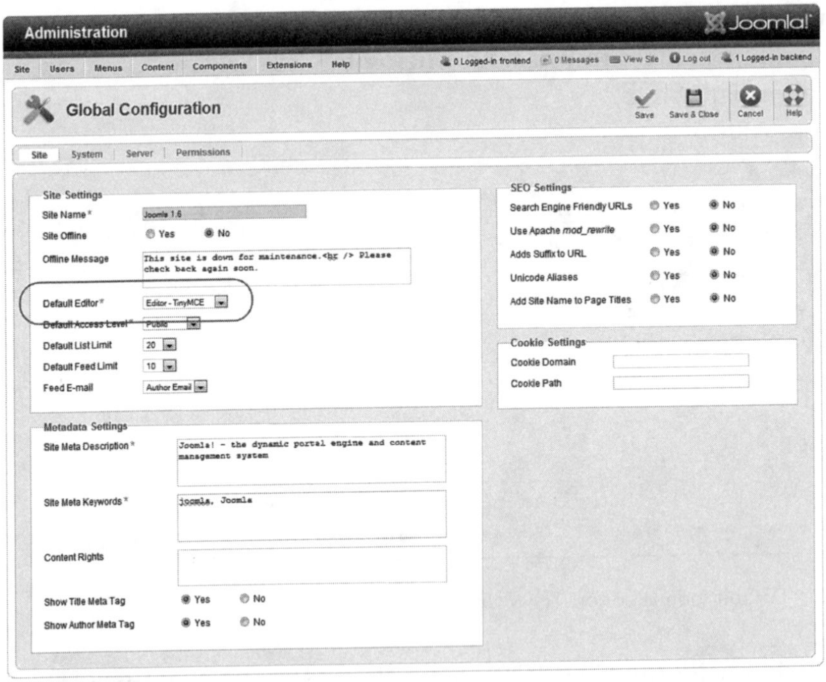

FIGURE 7.3 Default WYSIWYG editor setting.

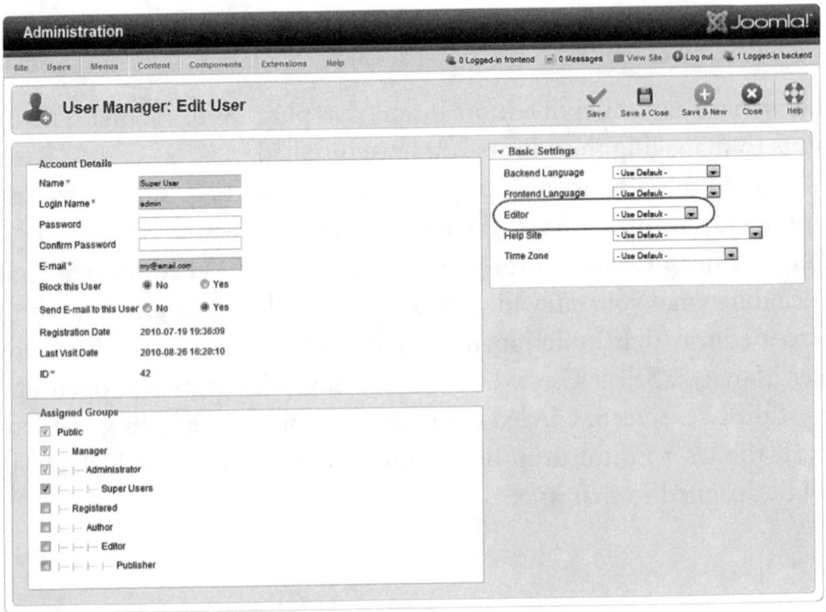

FIGURE 7.4 Individual user WYSIWYG editor setting.

The last aspect of managing WYSIWYG editors is within the editors themselves. In the Plug-in Manager, some editors have special parameters that you can set to achieve varying functionality. Figure 7.5 shows the parameters available for the TinyMCE editor.

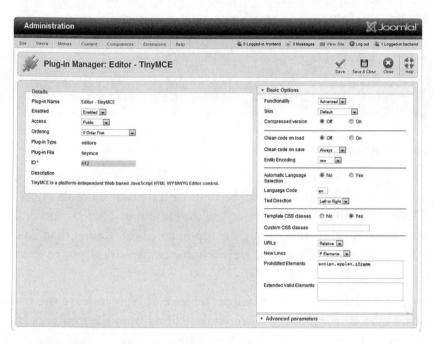

FIGURE 7.5   WYSIWYG editor parameters.

Most of these parameters do not need to be adjusted. There are two important parameters that you must adjust, however:

- **Clean Code on Save**—Code Cleanup makes TinyMCE clean the code/ HTML elements. Usually you want this parameter turned on, but occasionally, if you are trying to paste code, you might need to turn it off to do that. Otherwise, the editor strips out elements that you actually want to be there.

- **URLs**—You can select either relative or absolute URLs. You will almost always want to use relative URLs. Then, when you create a link to a page, it will not include the root. It will be /apage.html instead of www.*yoursite*.com/apage. html. If you use absolute URLs, if you ever change your domain name, your links will not work because they will point to the old domain.

NOTE
Another way to write or paste HTML and be sure that it is being entered properly is to turn off the WYSIWYG editor, either at a sitewide level or on a user-by-user basis. You can, for example, create a special admin user called noWYSIWYG, which has its editor turned off (set to Editor—No Editor). This allows you to log in and work in pure HTML if you need to.

NOTE
You can find out more about using the features of TinyMCE by opening an article for editing in the Article Manager and then clicking the Help icon.

Other Third-Party Editors

TinyMCE is the editor that comes with the core Joomla 1.6 installation, but many additional editors are available and can be found at extensions.joomla.org.

All WYSIWYG editors work more-or-less the same way. There are generally several small icons for various functions along the top of an editor. Rather than go over these types of details in too much depth, let's examine some critical points and common problems:

- **You must click Save, Save & Close, or Save & New to leave the editor—** This is especially important when you're editing from the frontend. If you click Back or click away, you will lose your work.

- **You shouldn't apply font style, such as making a font smaller, to big sections of content in the editor**—Instead, you should do this in the CSS file of the template. That was the whole point of separating content from presentation! (See Chapter 1, "Content Management Systems and an Introduction to Joomla!")

- **Always make sure you have the correct section and category**—I have lost count of the times I forgot to set the category and then couldn't find my content.

- **If something happens to your connection while you are editing, *you'll lose everything***—I recommend that you write longer pieces offline and copy and paste them into the editor.

- **Be careful when copying and pasting from Microsoft Word**—Word uses a lot of CSS that's peculiar to Microsoft. Unfortunately, it gets pasted in along with your text. An easy way to strip it all out is to paste into Notepad (or another simple text editor), copy again, and then paste into Joomla or save your document as text. Note that if you do this, paragraph returns (`<p>`) will be turned into hard returns (`<br>`).

- **If you have a lot of writing to do, an efficient way to do it is to actually write in an HTML editor**—Sure, you usually use editors for creating web pages, but in this situation, they make pretty good word processors. A great open source choice is available at www.nvu.com.

- **Make sure you are using the right editor**—If the site administrator installs a new editor, after configuring it he or she should set it to be the default editor in the global configuration.

We look in more detail at the editor and the various extra Joomla options it uses later in this chapter. For now, let's move on to looking at how to add content articles.

THE LEAST YOU NEED TO KNOW
WYSIWYG stands for *what you see is what you get*. a WYSIWYG editor allows editing of content without knowledge of HTML or XHTML. Several editors are available for Joomla and can be installed as plug-ins.

Creating and Managing Articles

Adding content to a Joomla-managed website is relatively easy. You have already done most of the hard work: understanding categories, lists and blogs, and menus. When the setup is finished, Joomla starts to show its CMS power, enabling you to add content quickly and simply.

This chapter continues with the sample site for Widget Inc. that you began setting up in Chapter 4, "Content Is King: Organizing Your Content," and then continued in Chapter 5, "Creating Menus and Navigation." If you followed along and built the site, you will be able to pick up exactly where you left off, as you learn how to create and manage content articles. If you did not create that site, you might want to go back and do so now; otherwise, you can follow along with a default Joomla installation that includes sample data.

NOTE
The description of managing content that follows is based on access controls (permissions) for users being used in the default setup as provided by a Joomla installation.

With Joomla 1.6 it's possible to completely customize user permissions and set up different scenarios for who can edit content and how.

There are two main ways to create and manage content articles in Joomla:

- **Backend editing**—Managers, administrators, and Super Users can manage articles through the Article Manager. In addition, they can manage images (and other media) through the Media Manager. Generally, backend content management is much more efficient than frontend management.

- **Frontend editing**—Frontend editing allows authors, editors, and publishers (which includes all managers, administrators, and Super Users) to manage content articles on the actual page where a content article exists. When you are logged in, a special icon appears, allowing you to edit that article while you are looking at it in the frontend. Managing media is more difficult through the frontend than through the backend.

THE LEAST YOU NEED TO KNOW
Backend editing is more efficient than frontend editing, but generally, not as many users are given backend access.

Frontend editing allows more users to be involved in managing the content. It also allows for the quick and easy editing of single articles.

Managing Content Through the Backend

Let's go to the backend of our Widget Inc. website.

To manage content through the backend, first log in (as Super User) and then go to the User Manager and create a couple administrative users:

1. Create a user called MrManager with an access level of manager.
2. Create a user called MrAdministrator with an access level of administrator.

> **NOTE**
> There may be some confusion here because there are both "admin" and MrAdmin-istrator usernames. The admin name is the default one created by Joomla on instal-lation for the Super User. If that confuses you, open up the Administrator user (the original one) and change its name to MrSuperAdministrator to match the scheme here.

When you now relog into the backend as the MrManager user, you have the fewest menu choices that any backend user will see. The manager access level is useful if you have many people managing your content in the backend. It gives access to everything these users need to create and manage content but not to any other administrative functions that might cause drastic changes to the site.

To take a look at the Article Manager (see Figure 7.6), select Content>Article Manager.

FIGURE 7.6   The Article Manager.

Here, you see the four content articles that you created in Chapter 4. All are pub-lished, and one is on the front page.

Let's quickly look at some important features that the Article Manager offers:

- **Multiple-select check boxes**—The column on the far left with all the check boxes allows multiple selections of content items. You can select the one you want and then use the icons in the toolbar to publish, copy, delete, and so on en masse.

- **Column sorting**—You can click any of the column headings and sort the table in ascending or descending order.
- **Icons and links in the manager**—The small icons in the Published, Featured, and Access columns are clickable toggles. For example, clicking on something that is unpublished publishes it.
- **Filters**—A big site can easily have thousands of content articles. Using the Article Manager becomes difficult if you don't use filters. You can filter by section, category, author, or status, and you can filter the article titles with the search term of your choice.
- **Archiving**—You can archive any content item. Once an item is archived, it cannot be changed in any way until it is unarchived. This can make for a highly managed workflow for writing content: write, review, publish, and archive. In reality, however, there is no real reason an older article couldn't stay a regular content item, just moved to a different menu location in the site (for example, a landing page menu).
- **Ordering**—As with the menu parameters for a blog, you could have an order of Ordering when you present the content items. If you select that option, *this* is where the menu parameter gets that sequencing information. If you look carefully, you will see that the up and down reordering arrows used to reorder articles work only *within a category*. Right now, in Figure 7.6, you can't see any of the up/down arrows because you have only one article in each category. As you add more, the up and down arrows will appear.

In the next section, you'll use a WYSIWYG editor to add a content item and take a look at the content editing interface.

Adding Content from the Backend

To add content to a site from the backend, click New in the Article Manager to go to the Add New Article screen, as shown in Figure 7.7.

Let's create another article for our blog. Put in some text. Next, make sure the category is set to the blog, make sure it's published, click Save & Close, and then look at the result in the frontend.

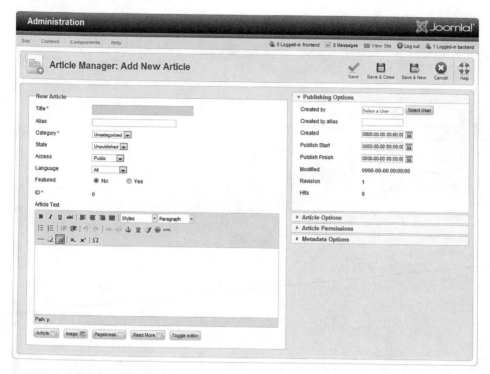

FIGURE 7.7   The Add New Article screen.

Clicking the blog menu item shows all the articles that are in the Widget blog. Figure 7.8 shows the generated blog page.

If you have a longer article, you need to use a "read more" link. When you use this link, only introductory text is shown in the blog layout, and the full article is displayed only when you click the "read more" link.

Longer Articles and the Read More Button

Now you can try opening the second blog entry in the Article Manager and adding another paragraph. After you add a paragraph, place the cursor at the end of the first paragraph (or the beginning of the third) and click the Read More button at the bottom of the editor. When you do this, a line appears between the two paragraphs (see Figure 7.9).

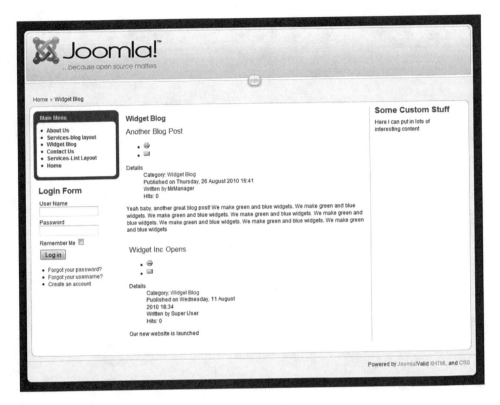

FIGURE 7.8 A blog layout.

FIGURE 7.9 Creating a "read more" link.

This line represents the break that separates the introductory text excerpt on the blog page from the rest of the longer article. Figure 7.10 shows the effect of the "read more" break in the blog layout in the frontend.

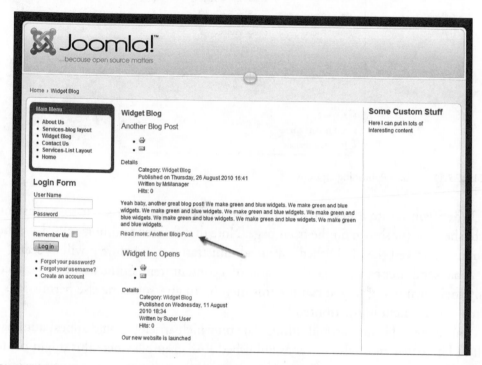

FIGURE 7.10   An article with introductory text, as seen from the frontend.

> **NOTE**
> The "read more" link works only when you are displaying a page using the blog layout. If you link to a single article or to a list layout, the "read more" link doesn't appear, and the break doesn't have any effect.

Publishing Options

When you edit an article, the expandable tabs on the right side of the screen open to the article's Publishing Options, as shown in Figure 7.11.

FIGURE 7.11 Article Publishing Options.

When you create a new article from the backend, you can set it to be instantly published and/or shown on the front page. Note that frontend authors must have their content approved (i.e., Published) by an administrative user before it will be seen.

A backend user can change the creator of a content item. Some user levels can edit only their own work, so you can use this method to give someone else permissions to edit a content item in the frontend.

You can set a future start publishing date on which articles should appear automatically. (The article must also be set as Published.) An example where this might be useful is when you're writing a series of blog posts in advance, before you go on vacation.

You can also use the Finish Publishing date to automatically unpublish articles that are time sensitive, such as special offers that are available for only a set time.

> **NOTE**
> Note that these two publishing dates do not actually toggle the Published setting. An article that is otherwise marked Published must also fall within the date range in order to appear. If it doesn't, you will see a different icon in the Published column in the Article Manager—an icon of a page with a small cross over it, indicating that it's otherwise marked published but not within the required date range to appear on the site.

Article Options

Clicking the Article Options tab expands those settings, as shown in Figure 7.12.

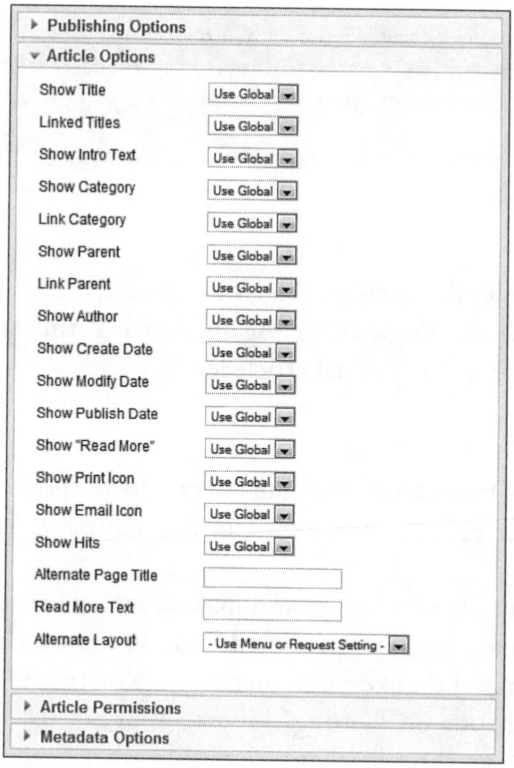

FIGURE 7.12   Article Options.

The Show Intro Text parameter allows better control over the presentation of intro text that has an image when it appears with others in a blog layout. Setting the parameter to Hide causes content above the "read more" link to not appear on the full article display. This allows two versions of intro content within one article. For example, you could use a thumbnail of an image in the intro text but then have a larger image (which would look bad in the blog layout) when the full article is viewed.

The rest of the parameters are explained in detail on the Joomla Help site.

> **NOTE**
> Most of these parameters are contained in the Article Manager Global Options. You should always try to set the global options to have the settings you need for the majority of site pages; then you can customize individual menu links and content item options as exceptions from there.

> If you have several articles that need the same exception settings, make a blank content item first, with filler content, and set the parameters as you need them. Then you can copy and paste that page as a starting point for the other pages, and all the options settings are carried over with it.

Article Permissions

The Article Permissions tab allows you to create specific permission rules for different access levels/groups for that single article. Again, Article Permissions can be set globally and then customized at the individual article level.

Metadata Options

With the Metadata Options tab you can enter article-specific metadata (the `meta` tags that appear in the HTML source code of the web page) for the description and keywords.

I'm going to go out on a limb here and make a somewhat radical suggestion: The best use of the metadata field might actually not be for search engine optimization (SEO); it's well recognized that keyword metatags are pretty much ignored by modern search engines (see Chapter 8, "Getting Traffic to Your Site").

However, Joomla uses these keywords to enable other features besides just appearing in the metadata of the generated HTML source code.

For example, Joomla has a module called *related items* that displays other content items related to the item currently displayed. The determination of what's related is based on the keywords metadata. If you take care and devote attention to choosing a small number of article-relevant keywords, this module will function very well. If you decide, however, that there is a keyword you are going to put in every single article, then every single article is going to be related in this module, and it will be useless to you.

One thing to be aware of is that article-related metadata is appended to the metadata set in the site's Global Configuration. For pages that have several content items, such as a blog presentation, the data from each article gets added together. Again, smaller is, of course, better—a one-sentence description and two to three keywords is adequate.

THE LEAST YOU NEED TO KNOW

The Article Manager lists all articles in a Joomla site. When you create or add articles, you need to take care about the content, what section/category it goes in, whether it's published, and various article parameters (such as metadata).

Inserting Images into Content

Managing images presents some of the biggest problems you might face in creating a website. The most common problem is an image having a resolution that doesn't work well for web pages. If you take a photo with your digital camera and then upload it to the Web, you'll find that the file could easily be a megabyte in size and display several times the size of your computer screen. First and foremost, images need to be optimized with some sort of graphics program for presentation on the Web—this means 72 or 96 dpi. You can find some excellent online tools, such as the following, to do this:

- www.snipshot.com
- www.webresizer.com
- www.picresize.com

Joomla can help you get your images into your content articles quickly and easily, as long as they are properly sized. To try it out, let's create a new blog post and insert an image into it.

Go to the Article Manager and click New to create a new article. At the bottom of the editor screen is an Image button, circled in Figure 7.13. You might notice among the buttons of the editor (TinyMCE, in this case) another button you can click to insert an image. You don't use that one, however. You use the one at the bottom of the editor box actually labeled Image.

NOTE

Remember that TinyMCE is a third-party editor. Because it's used in many applications, it has its own Insert Image button. Using the Joomla Image button is preferred because it allows you to set some attributes for the image, such as a title (`alt` tag content) and the ability to upload an image to the server at the same time as it's inserted.

```
New Article
  Title *              An Article With Image
  Alias
  Category *           Widget Blog   ▾
  State                Published   ▾
  Access               Public   ▾
  Language             All   ▾
  Featured             ⦿ No      ○ Yes
  ID *                 0
  Article Text

  B  I  U  ABC  | ≡ ≡ ≡ ≡ | Styles      ▾  Paragraph   ▾
  ⋮≡ ≡⋮ | ⋮≡ ⋮≡ | ↺ ↻ | ∞ ✂ ⬇ ⬆ ✓ ◎  HTML
  —  ⊘ ▦ | x₂  x²  | Ω

  This post has an image in it.

  |


  Path: p

  Article 🖼   ( Image 🖼 )  Pagebreak 🖼   Read More 🖼   Toggle editor
```

FIGURE 7.13   The Joomla Image button.

If you put your cursor where you want your image and then click the Image button, a pop-up box appears, and you can select the image you want to insert from the Joomla images folder. This pop-up box, as shown in Figure 7.14, is virtually identical to the Media Manager available in the backend.

Navigate to the folder that holds the image and then click it. Next, click the Insert button in the upper right. The image then appears in the content article.

THE LEAST YOU NEED TO KNOW
You insert images in content articles by using Joomla's own insert image function and not a function provided by a WYSIWYG editor. To facilitate accessibility and SEO, you should always give an image appearing within an article a title, which will appear as the value of the `alt` attribute of the generated image tag.

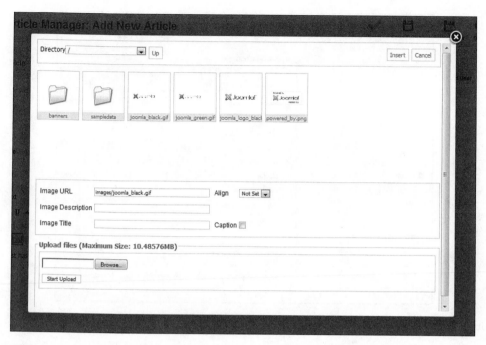

FIGURE 7.14   The Insert Image dialog box.

If your image isn't uploaded yet, you can also use the Insert Image dialog to upload your image before using it. Make sure, however, that you have optimized the image for the Web so that its resolution is appropriate.

NOTE

If you are inserting several images, you will find it easier to pre-upload them, using the main Media Manager (or even FTP) rather than the Article Edit screen.

Editing Image Properties

If you want to edit the properties of the image you just inserted—for example, to align it to the left or right—you can adjust its properties. The method will be based on what editor you have installed. With the default TinyMCE, you click/select the image and then click the Insert Image/Edit Image button in the TinyMCE editor. This brings up the property dialog box shown in Figure 7.15.

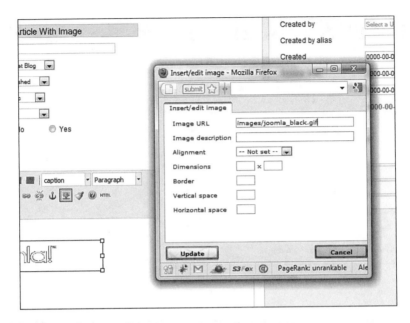

FIGURE 7.15 The Image Property dialog box.

NOTE
You should always make sure that you have a healthy amount of white space around your images. You should aim for at least a 10-pixel margin around the four edges. It's great to have clean, standards-based HTML, but not if your web page looks terrible because the images are all squashed together. I call this real-world web design!

Category Descriptions

So far we have looked at two main vehicles for adding content in Joomla: articles that appear in the main body via the content component and custom HTML modules.

There is a third place where you can add limited content: the descriptions of sections and categories. To do this you must be logged in to the backend of the site. You cannot do this from the frontend.

Each section and category can have some descriptive content associated with it. Based on the parameter settings for the menu item that links to it, you can determine whether this description shows. If the description is set to be shown, it appears at the top of the page for that section/category—but only once on that top-level page. If links connect to individual articles, the descriptions are not shown.

This sounds confusing, but let's look at an example that involves adding a description to the Widget Inc. blog category. Select Content>Category Manager>Widget Blog to open the Category Editor (see Figure 7.16).

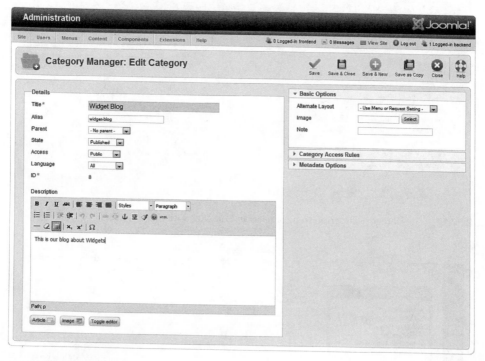

FIGURE 7.16   Editing the category description.

In the Description, you can add content, images, and/or text that will appear as the description for that section.

Save this screen. You now need to go to the menu item and set the parameter to show the description. Go to Menus>Menu Manager>Main Menu>Widget Blog.

In this Edit Menu Item screen (see Figure 7.17), on the right side in the Basic Options, you see the settings to show and hide the description (circled). Set it to Show.

Viewed from the frontend, the blog now looks as shown in Figure 7.18. The clever part is when you drill down to an article, the category description will no longer show. So, it's a way to add content to the "entry" page of the whole category.

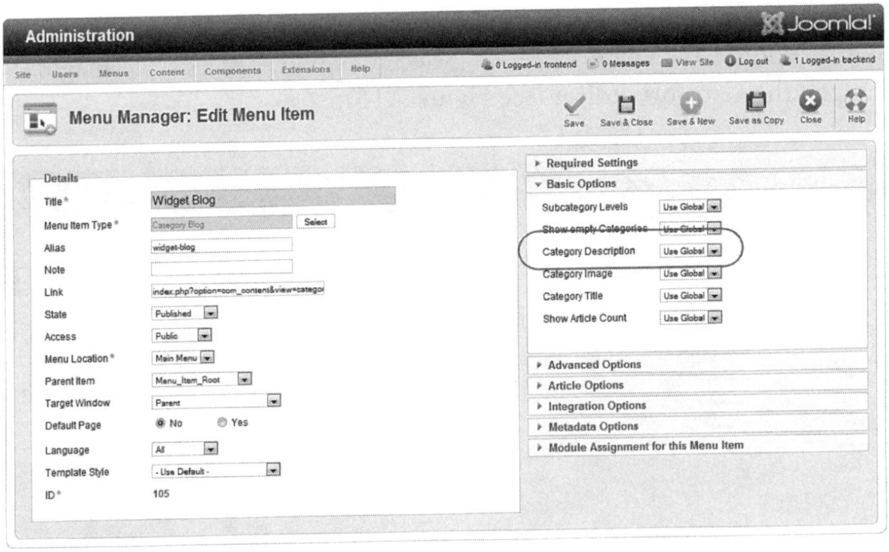

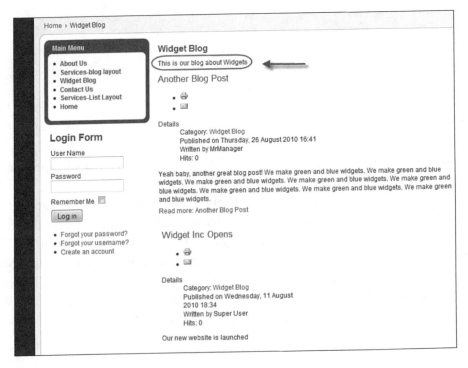

FIGURE 7.17 The Category Description parameter in Edit Menu Item.

FIGURE 7.18 The frontend view of a category description.

THE LEAST YOU NEED TO KNOW
Using category descriptions is a useful way to add a snippet of content/text to the top of a section/category page without having to use an article.

As initially discussed, it's more efficient for a single person to manage content from the backend. If you have several content contributors, however, you might not want to give them all backend access. The answer in this scenario is to let them manage the content from the frontend.

Managing Content Through the Frontend

As you have already seen, the backend of a Joomla site is available only to managers, administrators, and Super Users. Joomla has a system for adding content to the frontend with the frontend user groups: author, editor, and publisher.

In general, a content management workflow includes the following three operations:

1. Submission of new content to the system

2. Editing of that content, if necessary

3. Publication of the content

THE LEAST YOU NEED TO KNOW
Authors are generally responsible for submitting new content; editors for editing content; and publishers for publishing content. However, the permissions are additive, so an editor can edit the submitted content of an author as well as submit and edit his or her own new content.

Before you can properly understand the functions and permissions of the three frontend Content Manager roles, you need to create a menu to link to pages they will need.

Creating a Frontend User Menu

The Joomla sample data you may have installed includes a user menu that can be adapted for use. To create a frontend user menu from scratch for your empty Widget Inc. site, you must first create a new menu (as you did in Chapter 5). Select

Menus>Menu Manager>Menus Tab>New to open the Menu Details screen, as shown in Figure 7.19. Set the title as Frontend User Menu and click Save & Close.

FIGURE 7.19   Creating a new user menu.

When you click Save & Close, you return to the Menu Manager. Open the Frontend User Menu you just created by clicking the menu name, and you should see a menu that has no items.

You now need to add menu items as you have before, but this time you are not linking to articles, sections, categories, or components but to the Users Manager item type. Clicking on Select Menu Item Type gives you a pop-up box that shows the Users Manager menu item types, as shown in Figure 7.20.

You should now create menu links for the following:

- Login Form
- User Profile
- Edit User Profile
- Registration Form
- Username Reminder Request
- Password Reset

You also need to create a link where content can be submitted from the frontend by selecting Articles>Create Article layout.

After you add these menu items, the menu in the backend should look like the one shown in Figure 7.21. Make sure they are all published and set to be in the right menu. Move them there if you accidentally created them in the Main Menu.

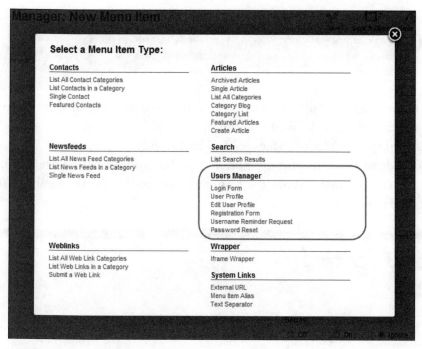

FIGURE 7.20   Users Manager menu item types.

FIGURE 7.21   The new Frontend User Menu.

NOTE
You would normally not have all these links in one menu. You are creating them here only so you can see exactly what each one does.

When a menu is initially created, there is no corresponding module created. Let's create a module to show the menu on the frontend.

Go to Extensions>Module Manager and click New.

Choose Menu from the pop-up module type box and make sure the module is set to show the correct menu. From the frontend, the module for the new menu is presented as in Figure 7.22.

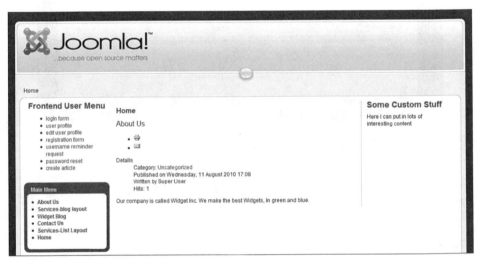

FIGURE 7.22 The frontend view of the complete User Menu.

NOTE
Remember that the *presentation* of a menu (that is, the position on the screen and styling) is controlled by its corresponding *module*. Its *functionality* and where the menu items link to is controlled by its *menu items* in the Menu Manager.

To give the menu the same style as the main menu, you need to find its module. Select Extensions>Module Manager>Frontend User Menu, and in the advanced options, enter the Module Class Suffix as _menu. This allows Joomla to apply the predetermined CSS styles for menus as defined by this template—Milkyway.

Now, the Frontend User Menu you have set up here shows all the possible links you can have. You would not likely use all these links for a real site. Notice that there are already links to register and to recover the password built into the login form, and therefore putting those items on the menu is redundant. Which menu items you choose to display depends on the functionality you want to offer users.

The last step in setting up this menu is to make use of the access control features of Joomla so that some of the menu items are seen only by logged-in users—in particular, the ability to edit a user's profile (Edit Your Details) and submit an article.

Limiting Access to Menus by User Level

If users visit your site, you probably don't want them to see the menu items Edit Your Details and Submit an Article; because they are not authorized to make these changes, seeing these options would just confuse them. Even more, the Submit an Article form will work only if a visitor is logged in and is an author or above.

Fortunately, Joomla allows the easy control of what is visible and what is not. For any Joomla item, whether it is an article, a module, or a menu item, you can set the access level (whether you can see it) to one of three levels:

- **Public**—Anyone can see it.
- **Registered**—Registered users and above can see it.
- **Special**—Any administrator (author and above) can see it.

You do this by changing the access option when you are editing that specific item.

With this in mind, you want to make the Login and Register menu items public and all the rest of the links limited to registered users. Open the various menu items and set the access as described. The menu should look like the one shown in Figure 7.23.

Now when someone visits the site, he or she sees only the Login and Registration links in the area for this menu. If the person logs in, more links appear.

Now you have a means to add articles through the frontend. When a frontend administrator logs in, he or she can go to the Create Article page and see a form. To better understand how this works, let's look at each user role—author, editor, and publisher—in turn. Go to Site>User Manager and create three users for the three access levels: MrAuthor, MrEditor, and MrPublisher.

Your User Manager should look as shown in Figure 7.24 when you're done.

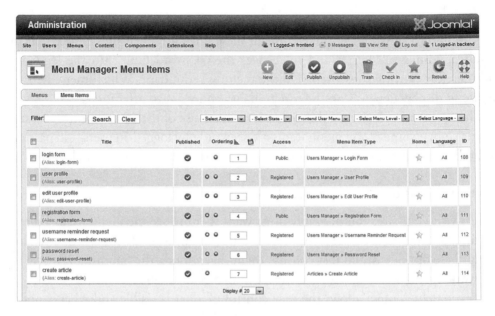

FIGURE 7.23 Changing menu permissions.

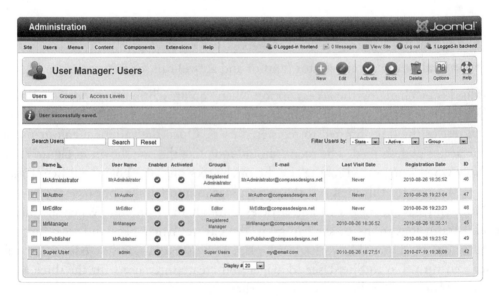

FIGURE 7.24 Creating users in the User Manager.

Now let's take a look at how an author can manage content.

Authors

Authors are the lowest level of frontend content administrators in Joomla. The concept of authors is that they can submit content but cannot publish it or edit the content of others.

If you go to the frontend of the Widget Inc. site and log in as MrAuthor, you see the home page shown in Figure 7.25.

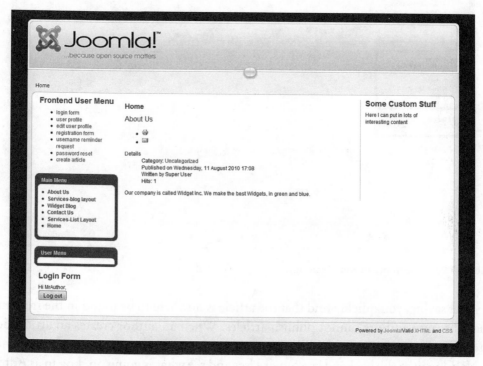

FIGURE 7.25   Logging in to the frontend as MrAuthor.

You can now see the registered-only menu items, and there is no functionality to edit existing articles (more on that in a moment).

If you click the Create Article link, you get the frontend article submission form shown in Figure 7.26.

You need to fill in some information and make sure that you put the article in the Widget Blog category. (This is the fourth blog post!) Save the article, and you get the message "Article Successfully Saved."

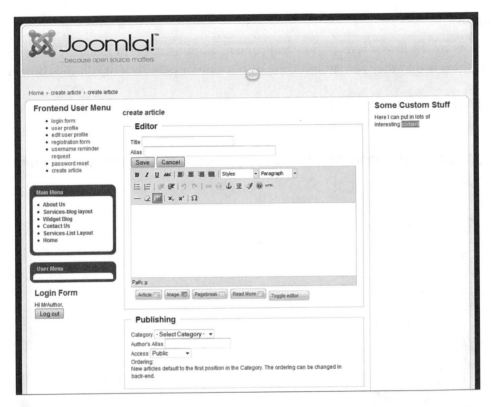

FIGURE 7.26   The frontend editor screen.

After saving, you quickly find that the article is nowhere to be found in the frontend. That's because authors cannot publish articles. When an author creates an article, it is automatically flagged as unpublished.

Now log in to the backend as a Super User and see what is going on. Log in as Admin (or MrSuperAdministrator, if you changed the name). Go to Content>Article Manager. You see the fourth blog post as unpublished. This status is arrowed in Figure 7.27.

You can publish the new article by toggling the Published icon in the Article Manager.

Now let's take a look at what editors can do.

TIP

In the Joomla 1.5 publishing workflow, an author retained the ability to edit his or her articles even after they are published. At time of writing, Joomla 1.6 did not allow this, but it is still under development and likely to change again.

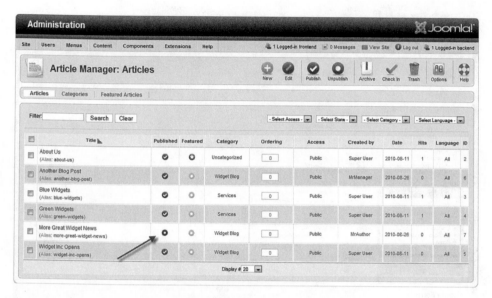

FIGURE 7.27   Approving content articles.

THE LEAST YOU NEED TO KNOW

Authors can create but not publish articles. The author status is useful when you want to have several users able to add content to a site in a controlled way, as their submissions are reviewed by another administrator.

Editors

Editors can submit content exactly the same way as authors. They can submit it, but they cannot publish it, and they can also edit any content on the site—their own or anyone else's—whether published or not.

If you log in to the frontend as MrEditor, you see that the blog has an important difference, as shown in Figure 7.28.

If you are watching carefully, you'll see that a tiny edit icon now appears next to the article title for every article in the site. Clicking it brings up an Article Edit screen almost identical to the submission form.

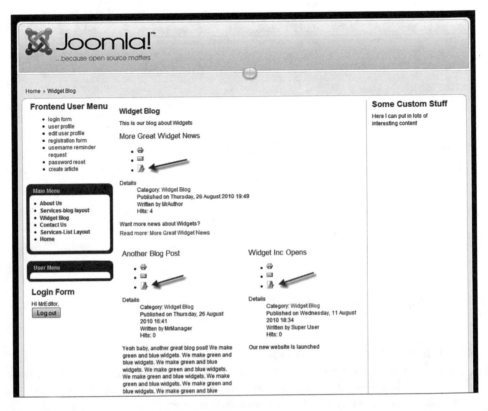

FIGURE 7.28 Logging in to edit articles.

NOTE
Editors can access all the articles on a site. If you want to, say, allow Fred access only to Fred's articles you must use some of Joomla 1.6's advanced access control and group permission features.

So, editors can edit articles but not publish them. How could you take advantage of this in a real site?

From my experience in helping many clients build Joomla sites, only the very big ones have both authors and editors. Most sites have a dozen or so *content producers* who are set at the editor level and are trusted to maintain all content. Clients have found it more useful for these content producers to be able to create and edit all of the articles. Then new articles are passed for final review to a publisher or above for publication, primarily to make sure they are properly inserted into the site's navigation scheme and comply with only using essential styling within the article and leaving the overall selection of fonts and such to the CSS rules set up by the designer.

THE LEAST YOU NEED TO KNOW

Editors can create and edit articles. They cannot publish their own or anyone else's content, but they can edit any article, as long as it has been previously published.

You can also narrow the selection of what can be edited by using Joomla 1.6's advanced ACL features as explained in Appendix B, "A Guide to Joomla! 1.6 ACL."

For the last step in building content articles from the frontend, let's look at publishers.

Publishers

Publishers have all the same abilities as editors, as well as the ability to actually publish articles on the website. All the same controls that you just saw for submitting and editing content are also available to publishers. Publishers can author their own content, edit the content of other authors or editors, and cause articles to be published on the website. A publisher's view of pages includes all unpublished articles in addition to published ones. Note that in the working beta of Joomla 1.6 being used for this book, Publishers can't see unpublished articles. This is a bug that should be fixed in the future.

Try logging in as MrPublisher to see the difference this makes. When you log in, almost everything is identical as for MrEditor. The same Edit button is next to the titles, and the same form is shown to create or edit an article. The minor difference is that there are a couple extra parameters in the create/edit form, circled in Figure 7.29.

Publishers effectively have exactly the same content rights regarding content as backend administrators. They cannot, however, log in to the backend.

THE LEAST YOU NEED TO KNOW

Publishers can create, edit, and publish any article. They cannot, however, change the author (ownership).

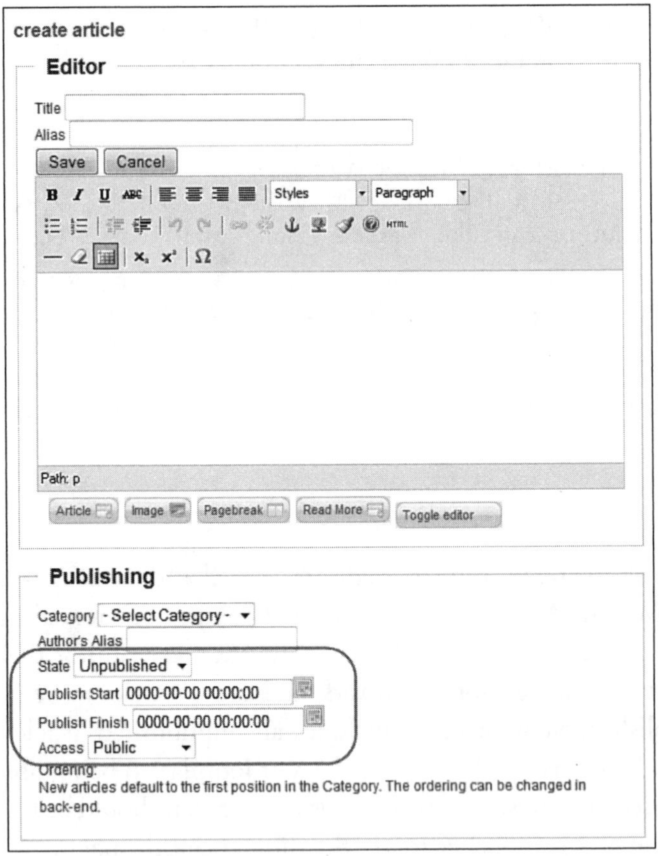

FIGURE 7.29   Frontend publisher functions.

Article Checkin

When working in one of the edit windows, such as when you're working as an author creating new content, you should click the Cancel icon or Save icon to exit the page. The reason for this is that Joomla locks the content while you are editing it, preventing other users such as editors and publishers from accessing it at the same time. This function is referred to as global checkin, and it's managed with the Global Checkin tool found on the Site menu in the backend.

There are times when exiting edit windows improperly could result in content being locked to others. The following are just a few cases in which this could occur:

- The user accidentally closes his or her browser window before canceling or saving a transaction.
- The user uses the browser navigation functions (such as the Back button or a bookmark) to move away from the site before canceling or saving the transaction.
- A power failure knocks out the user's PC at the wrong time or there is an interruption in the user's Internet service.

Whatever the reason, not saving or canceling a transaction properly can lock users from accessing the article later. The checkin function is available in the backend in the Site menu when you're logged in as an administrator or higher.

> **CAUTION**
> If you use the global checkin when users are actively editing articles, their articles will be checked in, making them available to editing by others. Therefore, be careful to use this tool only when you are certain no users are actively editing articles.

> **THE LEAST YOU NEED TO KNOW**
> Joomla has a system for only allowing one user at a time to edit articles. Articles that are accidentally left locked can be released through the Global Checkin tool in the backend.

> **USER'S GUIDE CHAPTER 7 DEMO SITE**
> An SQL dump of the site built in this chapter is available at www.joomlabook.com. It is an exact copy of what you should have if you followed all the steps in this chapter. You can log in to the administrative backend to see the site framework and the sections, categories, and menus.

Summary

This chapter looked at how to manage content articles from the backend and from the frontend. Defining some plan or process for this in your organization is critical to leveraging the power of Joomla as a CMS. Leaving the generation of content in the hands of just one person may result in your site being infrequently updated and stale.

- WYSIWYG allows editing of content without knowledge of HTML or XHTML. Several editors are available for Joomla and can be installed as plug-ins.
- Backend editing is efficient but often not as efficient as it could be when many users are given backend access. Frontend editing allows more users to be involved in managing content while protecting the remainder of the site. It also allows for the quick and easy editing of single articles.
- The Article Manager lists all the articles in a Joomla site. When creating and adding articles, care must be taken regarding the content, what category it goes in, whether it is published, and various article parameters, such as metadata.
- Images are inserted in content articles using Joomla's own function for inserting images and not using functions provided by WYSIWYG editors. Once inserted, content articles can be edited using a WYSIWYG editor's edit feature to set important attributes such as height, width, and title (that is, `alt` tag content).
- Using category descriptions is a useful way to add a snippet of content or text to the top of a category page without using an article that might be sorted away from the top.
- You can use the options of the Article Manager to access and set global options for articles. You should set these options so that they apply to most pages of a site. It is possible to override these global defaults on an individual menu item or article level.
- Authors are generally responsible for submitting content; editors for editing content; and publishers for publishing content. However, the permissions are additive, so an editor can edit the submitted content of an author as well as submit and edit his or her own content.
- Authors can create but not publish articles, and they cannot edit articles. Designating authors is useful when you have many users adding content to a site in a controlled way because their submissions must be reviewed by an administrator.
- Editors can create and edit articles. They cannot publish anyone's content. They can edit any article on the site.
- Publishers can create, edit, and publish any article. They cannot change ownership.

- Joomla has a system called global checkin for allowing only one user at a time to edit articles and for fixing problems when articles checked out for editing are accidentally not saved or canceled. Global Checkin is found on the Tools menu in the backend.

Chapter 8

Getting Traffic to Your Site

In This Chapter

Search engine optimization (SEO) might be one of the most maligned subjects on the Web. From talk of black hat SEO, people who use unethical methods to gain rank in search engines, to their counterparts of white hat SEO, the good guys, how best to get traffic to your site is loaded with opinion and myth.

Trying to learn about SEO is difficult, to say the least. There are a few problems:

- No one knows for sure what works; the search engines won't reveal their algorithms.

- Many people pushing SEO information are in business only to make easy money from providing minimal or poor services.

- The whole topic is complex (see point 1).

In this chapter, I emphasize something slightly different, now known as *search engine marketing* (SEM). I point out some obvious SEO tips and how they apply to Joomla, but I also discuss a more holistic marketing plan including such strategies as Pay Per Click (PPC) and blogging.

This chapter covers the following topics:

- Why do I want traffic to my site?
- How can I get traffic to my site?
- How can I get organic traffic with SEO?
- How can I get referral traffic?
- How can I get PPC traffic?
- How can I use email marketing to get traffic?
- What is an SEF URL?

Start at the Beginning: Site Goals

Why do you want traffic?

Before you actually do any optimization, you need to answer this fundamental and strategic question. You can break it down into the following points:

- What is your website about?
- Who will visit it?
- What will they gain?
- What will you gain?

Write the answers on a piece of paper...no, really!

Unless you have a clear idea of what you are building your site for, you'll struggle to make decisions later in the process of designing and publishing it. It's especially important to think about what your viewers will gain from visiting your site. The answer to this question will form the underpinnings of your search engine marketing efforts.

Now that you have thought somewhat about who is going to visit your site, we can talk about the "how."

Publishing your site is only a small step in the path to getting traffic. Unless you do something else, your site will just sit there and no one will know it exists.

Unfortunately, unlike in the Kevin Costner film *Field of Dreams*, "Build it and they will come" is not true on the Web.

When we consider the bigger concept of SEM, we can split the different tactics to increase traffic into several main categories:

- **Organic**—What was traditionally known as SEO, organic marketing is the idea of having your website visible in various search engines when people search for keywords.
- **Referral**—Quite simply, the idea of having links from other sites to yours. A robust SEM plan will have a comprehensive link building strategy. These can be natural through attracting links to your high-quality content or paid links or other techniques.
- **Pay Per Click (PPC)**—This strategy involves bidding for placement on search results. Submitting such an ad to a search engine such as Google also means that it appears on its distributed ad network, for example, Google's AdWords. So your ads will appear both in search results and on content sites.
- **Email**—Building an email subscription list is a key part of a modern SEM plan. It's important to know who your website viewers are and, if appropriate, to capture emails so that you can present them with information that might draw them back to your site.

If you want your website to be successful, it is absolutely critical that you have a balanced plan that addresses these four components. Just focusing on one will put you at a disadvantage to competitors that have a more balanced approach. It's exactly the same principle that your financial consultant might tell you: Have a diversified portfolio.

NOTE
Disclaimer! I am not an "SEO guy," and I don't play one on TV. What I describe here are things I have read, observed, and, in most cases, implemented that have been found to be successful.

Organic Traffic (SEO)

Let's search Google for the keyword "Joomla." Shown in Figure 8.1 are the results obtained in March 2009. This search greatly illustrates the difference between organic and PPC marketing. The results that appear on the left are ones produced by the

Google algorithm (more on that later in our section about how Google calculates page rank). These are ranked by an insanely complicated formula used by the search engine. The search engine is trying to find the most useful sites connected to the keywords that you used in your search. Here we can see the www.joomla.org site is number one.

FIGURE 8.1   Google results for the keyword "Joomla."

The results on the left are what would be called organic (or natural) results, and the results on the right (and sometimes along the top) are the PPC results. These people pay to appear in this listing.

As we see later on, there are some huge implications in where your website appears on the results page for search terms related to your business.

So let us start learning about how to increase our organic search engine ranking position (SERP). A massive amount of information about SEO, SEM, and SERP is available. You have to be careful though about the quality of the information you're getting. A huge number of people would be happy to take your money for some e-book and run. Here is an example:

"How to earn $1,000's a day with Search Engine Optimization and Joomla.

"How you can profit from the EXACT SAME search engine optimization strategies that I used to charge clients $3,590 a day to implement!

"In this web-based, no-hype guide, I'll reveal my simple step-by-step search engine optimization strategy that I have been using for 2 years on over 350 clients and that anyone can use to get a front page ranking on Google."

See what I mean? That is an actual example from one of the thousands of people selling these services on the Web. The real truth about search engine optimization is that there is no "silver bullet" any more. It used to be true that you could stuff a few keywords into some metatags, list your site to have the search engines spider it, and suddenly get a lot of traffic. Now, search engines are much smarter. Google released information about its patent #20050071741 on its "Information Retrieval Based on Historical Data" (that's that little search page to you and me). In the document were more than 118 factors[1] that affect a website's position in the search engine's rankings!

This is the real truth about SEO: There is no such thing as a "right way" to perform search engine optimization any more. The only reality now, beyond doing the generally accepted steps to properly tag and link your content, is having a long-term web marketing strategy and a commitment to building and growing a site full of quality information.

Having said that, assuming that your site is one of the ones with quality content, SEO still has its place. Look at the statistics shown in Table 8.1.

---

1. You can find out more at www.vaughns-1-pagers.com/internet/google-ranking-factors.htm.

TABLE 8.1   Use of the Internet Among Adults

	% U.S. Adults Online
Total Adults	73%
18–49 Year Olds	86%

	% Commonly Using
Email	91%
Search	91%

Source: Pew Internet 04/06

Trying to get high organic ranking through SEO is important as we can see in the Pew Internet statistics. The search engine is the first step for the vast majority of people trying to find information on the Web.

SEO used to be about trying to play the game to beat the system. This worked until about five years ago, but now search engines are much more sophisticated. Attempts to stuff metatags or put a lot of hidden text on a page are more than likely to get you penalized. This next point is very important to understanding SEO: *A search engine tries to find high-quality content based on a keyword search.*

To be most successful at organic SEO you need to meet this need. Create a site with a lot of high-quality content and make it easy for both search engine spiders and human web visitors to find and read.

> **TIP**
> If you are serious about SEO, you should probably think about allocating some budget to an experienced professional. One tip is if a potential SEO vendor gives any sort of guarantee with regards to results, run to the hills. It's impossible to predict results in this industry and claims like this are recognized as being associated with cowboys (or cowgirls).

Let's look at the steps in a roughly chronological order that you might take as you launch a new site. First, a word about some software called "Information Retrieval Based on Historical Data" (Google).

Introduction to Google

Google is *the* Internet search engine. Even if your business or product is currently listed on Google, do you think that a boost in ranking to the first or second page would increase the number of potential customers coming to your website? It sure would.

How Does Google Calculate Page Relevance?

Although I don't know how the Google algorithm works exactly, (no one does; it's a closely guarded secret), I do know that Google relies on more than 118 different calculations to work out the relevancy of any particular page for a search; the big one is link popularity.

Link Popularity

If you have downloaded the Google toolbar (toolbar.google.com), then you will have seen the green bar that Google uses to rank every site you visit. This ranking is Google's PageRank and is indicated on a scale of 1 to 10. Generally, sites with a PageRank of 7–10 are considered excellent in terms of quality and popularity.

Google's main criterion for the calculation of relevancy for a page is based on the number of websites that link back to that particular site. Each site that links back to you must in itself contain quality content and have a high PageRank for it to impact positively on the PageRank of your website.

If Google's PageRank technology sounds confusing, just try and remember that Google's PageRank is the #1 criterion for calculating the relevancy of any web page in relation to the specified search term. We will come back to link popularity later.

Now, there are supposedly more than 118 factors involved in exactly how Google calculates your search engine rank position (SERP), as mentioned before, Google places more emphasis on PageRank than other engines.

Creating Keywords

It's critical to know exactly why you are building your site and who your site's audience is.

Remember this question? We'll talk now about the first step in using this information: keywords. *Keywords* drive search engines. The idea is that a search engine wants to return a page in response to a search about something that the searcher is looking for. It's doing this by looking at what was entered into the search box (the keywords) and then trying to match those keywords with pages in its database.

A *key phrase* is just a few keywords together. Researchers tell us that very few people just use one word to search any more and are getting more sophisticated and are using three or more keywords.

Imagine you are a potential visitor to your site. What keywords or phrases would you type in to find it? Take a blank piece of paper and write down as many words or phrases as you can that you as a potential visitor would search for to find a site like yours in a search engine.

Here's an example. For a site about ciders in general, you might have:

- Making cider
- Hard cider
- Home brew cider

Notice how I didn't use the single word *cider*. People who are searching on that term might be looking for who-knows-what. At this point, we don't want to be too general.

Try to write five to ten keywords or phrases on your piece of paper. If you're having trouble coming up with keywords, ask your partner, friends, or family members which keywords they would use to find your site.

Now we need to do some research. We need to find out how many people are searching for our keywords and phrases, and other potential keywords that we didn't think of.

What we need now is a tool to tell us this information. The big gun here is something called Wordtracker (www.wordtrackerkeywords.com). It costs just under $10 for a one-day subscription, but the information it gives is worth it. If your site depends on traffic, I recommend this tool.

Another great tool is a free one available from Google: adwords.google.com/select/KeywordToolExternal. I often use this to do my basic research before getting a Wordtracker subscription for a day.

> **TIP**
> The Google keyword tool only tells you how many searches are being made. Another piece of information is how many sites you are competing against. Even if there are a lot of searches for a particular term or phrase, if there are also a lot of competing websites, then getting a high SERP will be challenging. This is where Wordtracker shines. It also gives a factor called the KEI (Keyword Effectiveness Index). Basically, it provides a measure of how effective (rarely used in terms of competition, and useful in terms of number of searches) a particular key phrase will be.

Using any of these tools, enter each of your keywords and phrases and see which ones are being searched on the most (the tools will estimate search traffic). As you do this, you'll also come across key phrases that people are searching on that you didn't think of. Include them too.

The goal is get about five or so key phrases, plus a few more to use in related page content. Here I picked out some phrases that I think might make good keywords to try and use for optimizing:

301,000 apple cider

22,200   hard cider

22,200   cider recipe

14,800   how to cider

NOTE
You might get different results as the terms will change over time.

It's possible to optimize your pages for both single and plural. (This is one type of keyword stemming.) Some engines differentiate between the two. If you depend on traffic for your site, optimize for both.

Next we need to get an idea of the competition. Go to Google and enter in your first key phrase in quotes. Like this: "apple cider" (include the quotes in the search field).

On the right side of the Google search page, you see the number of pages competing for placement (see Figure 8.2).

FIGURE 8.2   Number of Google pages returned on a search.

Not bad, only 2.7 million sites we have to beat. Well, you didn't think this would be easy, did you?

Take your search terms and, for the ones you have narrowed down to, find out what pages are your primary competition. Note that alongside the term and search volume. Make sure you remember to search in quotes, because the search looks for these words as a phrase rather than just anywhere by themselves.

These keywords are going to form the basis for all of your site optimization strategies. Keep your keyword list with you as you read through the rest of these tactics.

I know that's a somewhat labor-intensive process. Tools like Wordtracker automate much of it for you.

Keywords and Domain Name

Engines use your domain name as a factor in the SERP. Now there is a lot of debate here: Some think that branding for the viewers is more important than having a keyword in the URL, it's google.com, not searchengine.com! But, if you can combine both, great! (Notice my domain is www.compass*designs*.net. This will get me a little boost if someone searches for "web *design*," but still retains some branding.)

You can't easily change your domain after you have made your site, so this is why we are thinking about SEO before we have even started on the site design. If we can use a keyword in the domain, go for it, but don't dilute your brand to do so.

Again, this is an area where there is significant disagreement; the current wisdom seems to be coming out that domain name is not so important.

> **NOTE**
> We discuss anchor text—that's the text that appears in the link to your site—when we look at the basic factors that influence SERP. It's astonishingly important. One way that a keyword-based domain can help here is that you can just paste your URL into a page and the keywords will already be there. A lazy man's way of linking perhaps, but not especially effective.

Designing Your Site for Organic Traffic

Ready for the techie stuff? Okay, grab your coffee/beer/herbal chai.

As I mentioned before, designing your site for traffic, both human and search engine spider, is very different than a few years ago. It's now about what is on the page that people can see. No more having a 200 keyword list that is set to the same color as the background at the bottom of the page.

Web Standards and Accessibility

Now, it may seem like I am going off topic here in a chapter about web traffic, but I am going to talk about two things seemingly unrelated to SEO: designing to web standards and accessibility.

Designing a website to *standards* means having a site that will benefit the greatest number of web users while ensuring the long-term viability of the site itself. This means that a site can be viewed in an array of browsers, or other Internet devices such as PDAs.

Specifically, meeting web standards for design essentially means separating content from presentation with Cascading Style Sheets. One advantage of the CSS-based layout is its flexibility—the content can be accessed regardless of the type of browser that is being used. It allows sites to work on many kinds of devices instead of just the personal computer.

Other advantages include

- Smaller file sizes and faster page loads
- Less bandwidth usage
- Your content appears closer to the top of the page
- Faster development and maintenance
- Easier to redesign

It is worth noting that the design principles contained within web standards also lead to sites that are more *usable*. (Along with credibility, usability is a major factor in why viewers return to a site.)

> **NOTE**
> Most content management systems, Joomla included, have challenges when trying to get their sites to validate for web standards and accessibility. The problem is complicated; content is generated dynamically through PHP (for Joomla) so sometimes either the PHP code or the content itself can cause issues. Compass Design, of course, works hard to build valid sites. I even wrote the (original) official Joomla documentation about template design, and Joomlashack specializes in creating fast-loading SEO-friendly templates.

Fortunately, this difficulty has been significantly addressed in Joomla 1.6 with the ability for template designers to completely override the CMS output, as demonstrated by the Beez template described in Chapter 9, "Creating Pure CSS Templates."

Accessibility, sometimes mistakenly called usability, is an attempt for a page to be accessible to all possible viewers. Usually this means such examples as someone who is blind (uses a screen reader) or old (struggles with small fonts/delicate mouse-based navigation). I use these two as examples as they are the ones quoted most often (don't shoot the messenger!).

Okay, so why did I bring those up?

Many of the factors involved in SEO, standards and accessibility overlap. For example, designing a site with CSS makes for leaner, faster pages that will be indexed by search engines more effectively. Another example would be designing a site with accessibility in mind so that it works just as well for someone using a screen reader as it does a search engine spider.

As a piece of roving software, the Google spider is effectively blind and will read your site exactly as someone would in a screen reader. The implication here is you can get the most effective results by designing a site that meets web standards and is also accessible. A significant part of its optimization for search engines will come as a natural consequence. A well-designed site will have a large overlap in the middle of these three areas, and a poorly designed site may have no overlap at all.

The relationship between SEO, standards-based design, and accessibility is an important one. A tutorial is available on this topic at compassdesigns.net.

Basic Things That Influence SERP

First and most important: You need a lot of content, *lots* of it. Before you have even considered site design and such, you should have 100 odd pages of actual content. Yes, there are supposed to be two zeros on the end of that: 100, I mean it. A page of content means about 200-500 words.

Of course, no one does this; I don't! But, if you are serious about getting gobs of traffic, and you do have a lot of rich content to publish, just think how far ahead you will be of poor schmucks like me.

> **THE LEAST YOU NEED TO KNOW**
> You should have some sort of search engine friendly (SEF) URLs enabled. It's thought that search engines don't like dynamically generated pages, and that's the whole point of Joomla. Joomla has a built-in SEF that replaces long URLs with shorter ones without variables. The Alias field seen on menu items is an optional field, but allows you to specifically set the URL for the page. To make it readable, use hyphens between words.

According to the "SEO guys,"[2] here are the most important factors in determining your SERP. (Much of the information here is based on two 2007 studies about ranking in Google from SEOmoz.org and Sistrix.) To be clear in the following discussion,

---

2. Based on a study done at www.seomoz.org.

search terms are the actual words a particular user types into the Google search box. *Keywords* and *key phrases* are our best guess concerning what our target users will type as their search terms and are the words we use heavily on a page that relates to that topic and in the site generally. Real life is such that not every user will search for the exact phrase we came up with, so the following concepts help turn marginal near misses into page hits. Recall that we narrowed our primary list to five or so key phrases that are the keywords we are building into a specific page. We also identified additional keywords and phrases that didn't make the top five cut but should still be considered for expanding the page's content and for the anchor text for incoming links

Search Terms in (Incoming) Anchor Text of Links

The phrasing, terms, order, and length of an incoming link's anchor text is one of the largest factors taken into account by the major search engines for ranking. Specific anchor text links help a site to rank better for that particular term/phrase at the search engines. In other words, it's the actual text that represents the link on a web page. The process of refining the anchor text in third-party site links to your site is sometimes called *offsite optimization*. It's possibly the most important factor in achieving high SERP.

If you want proof of this, search for "miserable failure" in Google and look carefully at the number 1 result. Ponder the implications of that. (It's called Google Bombing.)

Search Terms in Title Tag

This is what appears in the blue bar at the top of your browser, it comes from a tag called <title>. As well as being used as a pure factor in SERP, it also boosts rank in other ways. Some engines use *click-through rates* as a factor. Sites where the title closely matches the content tend to get better click-throughs. (Searchers see it's not a spam site and don't immediately "back" out.) When words in the title are also used as anchor text in a link to the page, you get more benefit.

Joomla easily allows you to manipulate the title of a page—it's the menu item title.

Search Terms in Link URL

With built-in SEF enabled, the title alias will be used to form the URL. If you save an article with the title alias blank, Joomla fills one in for you as it's saved (spaces changed to hyphens).

If your title (and thereby the alias) reflects search terms that relate to the content of the page, the resulting URL also automatically strengthens the SERP.

Search Terms and Keyword Use in Document Text

Your keywords must appear in the actual copy of the page or they become a detriment to your ranking. Supposedly search engines pay more attention to search terms found in the first and last paragraphs. The idea here is that your page is supposed to actually be about what the metatag keywords say it's about!

Usually, the way to go about this is have your keywords firmly in your mind as you write your copy. I don't know about you, but I find this really hard. I prefer a different approach.

There is a simple trick here. Write your quality content, then use a keyword density tool to find the keyword density. Then take the top words and use these as the keywords you might use in a link, or in the keyword metatag. It might seem a little backward, but it's surprisingly effective at creating pages that rank highly in search engines.

There are a number of free tools for checking keyword density. The one I use the most is at www.ranks.nl.

One disadvantage here is linked to the fact that Joomla is dynamic. The code is not very lean; that is, there is a lot of HTML compared to actual copy text. This in turn reduces your keyword density (indirectly). Using CSS instead of tables means leaner code. It's also possible with CSS to have your page *source ordered*. This means that the real content (the middle column to you and me) comes before the side columns and/ or navigation. This also goes back to my previous discussion about the link between SEO and web standards.

> **NOTE**
>
> In the header (the code you can't see but a search engine can), there are a few lines called *metatags*. One of them is for keywords. It's widely recognized that search engines no longer use these to calculate SERP. It *is* still thought that they can be negative. If you have keywords in your tag that are *not* on your page, you can get penalized for it. Some engines also consider the description metatag for ranking text. Personally, I don't bother with them much.
>
> If you do want to use these, it's easy to add keywords to the keywords tag for that page. You just go to the meta info when you are editing the content and plop them in. Joomla also has a button that puts in the section, category, and article title. Note that the global metatags are added as well, those specified for the site in the global configuration. It's good to only have your most important two to three words there and put the rest in the pages.

I am not sure that spending a lot of time on metatags (description and keywords) is efficient. As just mentioned, they are not really used much by search engines so their contribution is negligible.

Accessibility of Document

When we talk about accessibility for SEO, we're talking about avoiding anything on the page that would impede a search engine spider's ability to fully crawl a page. There can be a number of culprits:

- **Bloated templates**—Many template vendors are producing templates that have more and more eye candy, bells, and whistles. Unfortunately, this means that the pages get bigger and bigger, loading more and more JavaScript and CSS files. Page load time has been demonstrated to affect a page's ranking in search engines. As mentioned elsewhere, Joomlashack specializes in fast-loading accessible templates.

- **Splash pages**—Flash and heavily graphic introductions prohibit engines from crawling your site.

- **Frames**—Never use pages with frames. Frames are too complex for the crawlers and too cumbersome to index. Joomla uses something called a wrapper that has the same problems. Avoid it when you can.

- **JavaScript**—Though JavaScript menus are very popular, the ones that are not based on styling Joomla's simple lists of links can disable crawlers from accessing those links. Most, well-indexed websites incorporate text-based links primarily because they are search engine friendly. If necessary, JavaScript should be placed in an externally referenced file. Try using CSS to style your menus; you'll be surprised how good they look.

- **Not utilizing error pages**—Too often webmasters forget about error pages (such as 404 errors). Error pages should always redirect "lost" users to valuable, text-based pages. Placing text links to major site pages is an excellent practice. Remember that search engine links can lead to obsolete pages, and it's better to give those users content instead of a dead end. Visit www.cnet.com/error for an example of a well-utilized error page. You can customize your Joomla site's error page by editing /templates/error.php.

- **Tables used for layout**—This is explained more in Chapter 9, but it's part of the interrelationship between accessibility and SEO. An excellent description is at www.hotdesign.com/seybold/everything.html.

Links to Document from Site-Internal Pages

Almost as useful as the holy grail of external links linking into the site, are internal links. And they certainly are a lot easier to implement. Internal links are easily the most underrated criteria. But, it's important to make sure you are making good use of anchor text to cross-link between pages of the site. A well-linked to document is considered more important than an obscure page, even if the links are coming from within the site itself. The easiest way to ensure proper internal linking is with navigation bars (menus) and sitemaps.

Primary Subject Matter of Site

What your website is about is determined through analysis of the content. It's critical that your content correlates to keywords, anchor text, and so on.

One strange offshoot of this is perhaps it's not worth spending much effort trying to build the page rank of the home page. This strange concept is explained in the idea of Search Engine Theme Pyramids.[3]

A related factor is having a good sitemap. Not only is it good spider food, you can also load it with a lot of quality anchor text for those internal links as well as relevancy text (the text that appears near a link). Also important is the invisible Google sitemap, which is an XML file for use by the Google spider only. There are also some extensions for creating a Google sitemap, though I find it's best to upload a Google sitemap independently.

You can set up sites for the viewers to add their own content, so it's effortless to add a lot of content quickly and easily. Remember, it's a Content Management System, after all.

External Links to Linking Pages

These are the links from other sites to you. Note it's much better to have specific pages linked rather than your home page because of the idea of Search Engine Theme Pyramids. Don't bother with link farms or anything you see advertised for a link. You are much better off finding links from sites that have similar topics as yourself.

---

3. http://www.searchengineworld.com/engine/theme_pyramids.htm.

Link Popularity of Site in Topical Community

The search engine is trying to figure out what your page is about, so it can decide if it's relevant to a user's search. Links from pages with similar topics add credence to your page. Use the `related:` tag in Google—for example, type **related:www.cnn.com**, and it will search for sites related to the topic of www.cnn.com. Then spend some time emailing webmasters and asking for links. Software is available that will do this automatically for you, I would advise against using any of them, however. They are pretty easy to spot and usually get a one-way trip to the trash bin. PR Prowler was made to be able to create personal emails quickly and easily.

Global Link Popularity of Site and also Popularity with Trusted Experts

This means that links from sites that are "important" (that is, have a high SERP) are more valued than those from a lower SERP. A factor worth considering when searching out links: Get the ones from sites with a high page rank first, and not just high page rank but also a high "trust rank." Google has actually trademarked this term, so most people are pretty confident they are using it in their optimization. Trust rank is a site's value in terms of how authoritative it is on a subject/keyword.

Avoid Keyword Spamming

Be careful: Spamming is a negative factor! If you have a keyword density in text or tags so high that the engine decides you are stuffing, your rank will go from #1 to #10,000 in a heartbeat. Want to know the best part? No one actually knows what percent density this is, and it's probably different for different engines! Between you and me, I am not going above 5% to 10% on my pages.

Optimizing within Joomla

Many factors determine search engine page ranking. Rather than tweak minor tags, it's better to leverage Joomla's true power of being a fully fledged Content Management System to gain rank by efficiently adding a lot of quality content. Uh, and don't use Flash. (Okay, I admit I am biased.)

Specific Joomla! Action Items for SEO

Bearing the preceding information in mind, there are a few key steps to take to make sure we are leveraging Joomla for maximum SEO benefit:

1. **Turn on the core Joomla SEF feature.** This turns long dynamically generated URLs into something more readable. For example: http://homebrewcider. simplwebsite.com/index.php?option=com_contact&view=contact&id=2& Itemid=2 is changed to http://homebrewcider.simplwebsite.com/contact-us.

2. **Carefully craft your article titles.** It's possible to make Joomla use an article title as the metatag title (mentioned previously). This means that if we think carefully about the title of the article, including keywords, then the generated page will be well optimized for search engines through the title tag.

3. **Use a lot (within reason) of automatic internal links.** We just saw that internal links are very beneficial. We can use some of the Joomla content linking modules such as Most Popular to create many automated links.

4. **Use a fast-loading template.** Ideally, your home page should be under 40KB to 50KB according to Google. (You can search Google for your domain to see how big Google thinks your site is.)

Advanced SEO Techniques

One of my favorite expressions is "maximum efficiency, minimum effort." It's sometimes known as the 80/20 rule. Do the 20% of things you need to get 80% of the result. What we discussed in the basic section is the 20% effort. If we really want to try and squeeze everything we can from SEO, then there are some more advanced techniques we can try. Remember, we are not being very efficient here. To be honest, your time would be better spent adding pages with content targeted at some new, related search terms, but let's assume you have hired someone to do that, or you are very bored!

Boosting Your Site's Keyword Density

Your site's keyword density is one criterion that search engines will judge your site on when deciding where to rank your page on a per-search-term basis. *Keyword density* refers to the number of times a keyword appears throughout a particular page on your website. We can boost the keyword density of our website in four ways:

- Place keywords in the `<title>` tag.
- Use `<h1>` and `<h2>` tags to emphasize keywords.
- Include keywords in page titles.
- Incorporate keywords into body text.

Let's now take a look at each of these methods in more detail.

> **NOTE**
> As you work through the following sections, make sure you have your top five key-words handy.

Placing Keywords in the `<title>` Tag

Overall, we are aiming for a 10% keyword density per page on your website. That means that for every page on your website, you need to incorporate your top five key-words/phrases to achieve a 10% keyword density.

When a web page is chosen by Google as a match to a search term, the title and first few lines of "readable" text are shown from that website in Google's results. Google also weighs these two pieces of text highly when calculating the relevance of your website.

> **NOTE**
> We are talking about the title of the web page here, which for blog-style pages is set in the menu item, and not to be confused with the title of the article in Joomla, which appears in an `Hx` tag on a multi-article page. But, be aware that for single-article and "read more" pages, Joomla will take the article title and use it in the web page title if you set the Show Meta Title Tag to Yes in the Global or Local Parameters for the article.

> **TIP**
> One of the best ways to check the effectiveness of the phrasing of your keywords is to compare them to those of your competitors. Use Google to search for one of your top five keywords/phrases. Look at how the top five ranked search results word their titles. Are you using your keywords similarly? Maybe you could rearrange a word or two? Analyze these results and make sure your web page titles are the same—if not better—than those of your competitors.

Using `<h1>` and `<h2>` Tags to Emphasize Keywords

Heading tags have been used for years in HTML to improve the formatting of a par-ticular word or sentence on a web page. Heading tags range from `<h1>` (bigger text, signifying more importance) to `<h2>`, `<h3>`, `<h4>`, `<h5>`, and `<h6>` (smaller text, signify-ing least importance).

Heading tags are generally used to emphasize a page or paragraph heading's importance to search engines. Not only is text between heading tags more visually appealing, but if worded correctly it will boost your Google ranking significantly, as Google picks up keywords between heading tags as having a higher relevance than any other text around it.

Here is where things start to get tricky.

Unfortunately, if your template does not modify the default output of Joomla components, some of the most important keywords are output by the Joomla core with CSS class settings that have no effect on communicating importance to a search engine. For example, an article title shown on the default blog layout page is shown in the code as follows:

```
<td class="contentheading" width="100%">Welcome to Joomla!</td>
```

Not only is this not viewed as important to Google, but also, being placed in a table dilutes the text density. Fortunately there is a solution. In Joomla 1.6, for backward compatibility the default output is for the most part unchanged from this example, but there has been a significant improvement in how the template is rendered. The template override feature makes it possible to override the way Joomla outputs the code (for example, see the tableless Beez template in Chapter 9). So, it would be easy for a template designer to create a template that rendered the title as

```
<H1>Welcome to Joomla!</H1>
```

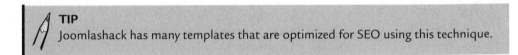

TIP
Joomlashack has many templates that are optimized for SEO using this technique.

Incorporating Keywords into Body Text

We've already seen how to use your keywords in both the title and headings of your web pages. The last thing that we can do to boost keyword density is to include keywords throughout the actual content of your web page. As I've already mentioned, you should aim for a keyword density of 10%—but where do you put your keywords?

Well, it's simple actually. Writing for the Web is generally more succinct than writing prose. Paragraphs tend to have fewer than the typical four to seven sentences, and those sentences tend to be shorter than the usual 25 or so words. Your mileage will vary, but assume the typical paragraph you write for the Web averages about 60 words, and to keep your articles brief and to the point, they average five paragraphs in length. That's 300 words to an article. To achieve a 10% density, there will be an instance of a keyword for every ten words on the page or 30 instances in total. On average this means for a page with five keywords, that each keyword will be used six times in the article or about once per paragraph. But the density takes into account all keywords mixed together and some paragraphs may focus on one topic with many instances or variations of one or two keywords while others will be heavy on other keywords.

My general rule of thumb is to distribute keywords using this ratio:

$$\text{Number of keywords per paragraph} = \frac{\text{Number of paragraphs}}{\text{Number of keywords}}$$

For example, if I have two keywords and four paragraphs on one of my web pages, then I would rephrase my paragraphs to include two keywords per paragraph. Yes, this totals to eight instances of using some variation of those two words (2 keywords x 4 paragraphs). I then subjectively modify this by focusing attention to placing more instances in the first and, to a lesser degree, the last paragraph.

If you use these guides correctly then your content should have an average keyword density of 10%. It is okay (and possibly preferred) to have one paragraph with a keyword density of 13% and another with 7%, just as long as they all average out. When used in combination with the keywords in the title tag and headings on your website, you now have a perfect keyword density setup for Google, which will produce excellent rankings for your web pages.

Keep in mind that first and foremost, your page is for your reader. Too much attention to these keyword distributions will make your content hard to read and look contrived. Web pages are scanned more than they are read. As mentioned at the outset, the easiest approach is to simply write well. Focus on a subject important to your business and defined by a couple of your selected keywords. Write about it clearly and succinctly, using those keywords whenever they help to make your point.

NOTE
Remember that you should choose two or three of your keywords per page and include them in your title tag, page, and paragraph headings, and also the content of your web page. Rearrange and reuse them as needed to form new phrases.

Referral Traffic

This is offsite optimization, and is the meat of SEO. Referral traffic is perhaps one of the most important components of SEM. A link building campaign that refers many sites will generate traffic purely through people following the links. But perhaps even more critical is that the number and quality of links to your site is one of the principal factors search engines use to calculate your SERP. So you get two benefits: pure traffic and also ranking in the search engines.

Google PageRank

Google particularly emphasizes how many sites link to yours. The *most important* criteria for ranking a website is its link popularity, but what exactly is link popularity and how can you get it? Put simply, link popularity represents the number of sites that link back to your website.

But how is this rank calculated? Quite simply, actually. Google's main criteria for the calculation of relevancy for a page is based on the number of websites that link back to that particular site and the relevance and quality of the page doing the linking.

How many sites are currently linking back to your website? If you don't know, it's easy to find out. Just go to google.com and type **link:www.*yoursite.com*** into the search box (replacing *yoursite.com* with the domain name of your website). Note that Google displays only a small percentage of the true backlink set for any given URL. You can get other estimates by doing the same thing at Yahoo! and MSN. When the search results are returned, look at the text in the right-hand side of the blue bar at the top of the page. It should look something like what's shown in Figure 8.3.

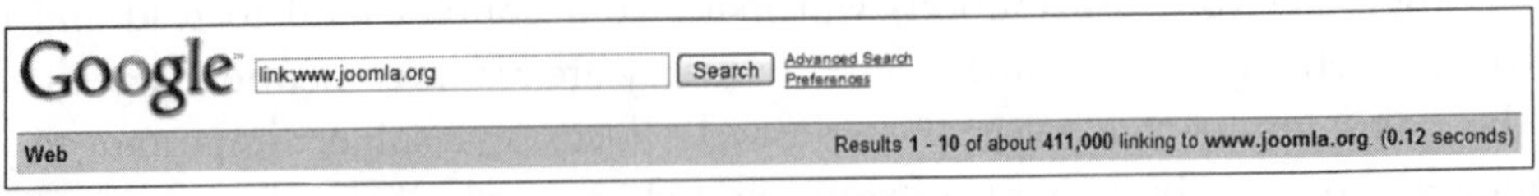

FIGURE 8.3 Number of pages returned in a Google search.

Figure 8.3 shows there are 411,000 websites linking back to this site. If only a handful link back to your website, don't worry—by the end of this section you should be able to increase this number by 5, 10, 20 or even 100 times!

"How many websites should be linking to my site?" I hear you ask. As a general rule of thumb, you want as many sites linking back to your site as those linking back to the site in position #1 for one of your five keywords. Keep in mind that the rate of link growth is very important. Backlinks should be acquired at an even pace, and should not be acquired all at once or within a short time frame. This sets off filters with Google.

Take one of your keywords/phrases that we worked out earlier and search for it on Google. Take the www part of the URL for the first search result of this keyword and find the number of websites that link to that website—this should be your goal for the number of websites linking back to yours.

For example, if one of your keywords was "hard cider" and the first site that came up when you did a search for this keyword was en.wikipedia.org/wiki/Cider, then perform a link popularity check on this site by searching for **link:en.wikipedia.org/wiki/Cider** in Google. Now this is a very coarse measure as it is measuring all links to the page regardless of keyword, as we can see with this example. The Wiki entry is #1 because of its huge "trust rank" in addition to the numerous backlinks to it on a number of topics. As mentioned before, Google is complex, but these steps are a basic method to optimize your site.

When the search results page is displayed, look at the number after "about" in the text on the right-hand side of the blue bar at the top of this page. That's the number of sites linking back to this website, and it's also the number that you should be aiming for to link back to your website.

So how do you go about finding sites to link back to *your* web site? Spy on your competition using a tool like PR Prowler (www.pr-prowler.com). This tells you exactly who is linking to your competition, and how.

As we saw earlier in this chapter, the most valuable links for your site are from another site that is related by topic to yours. So if you have a site about cider, a link from a site about apple trees would be more valuable than one from a site about computers. So the challenge is not a need to find links, but to find links from highly ranked sites that have a theme or topic similar to yours.

So how do we find them? We just saw in the example that you can also use `link:` in the search box to find sites linking to a particular URL. You can also use search engines to find websites that are related to a particular URL. The command to do this is `related:`.

So you can go to Google and type in **related: www.cidery.com**, for example, and that will find many sites that are related by topic to www.cidery.com. You can also use the related command to find out sites that are topically related to your competition.

So let's summarize where we are right now:

1. You find keywords by finding out how many people are searching for a particular keyword and how much competition there is for a keyword by using a tool such as those at tools.seobook.com or freekeywords.wordtracker.com or the Google keyword tool.
2. Succeeding at SEO means you only have to beat your competition. Find out who the competition is by searching with your keywords in Google.
3. Find out how many people are linking to the top results using the `link` command. That's how many links you need to outrank and beat them to the click.
4. Use the `related` command to find topically related sites to yours.

Now these four steps are pretty labor-intensive, but they are critical to achieving high search engine ranking.

It's tedious but absolutely essential to find useful sites to link back to you. It's possible to buy software that does all of this automatically for you. For a long time, I did not use such software, but for a couple years I have used PR Prowler. It's simple and pretty effective; if you are serious about trying to rank for competitive keywords, then you might want to look into something like this. PR Prowler searches for sites related to your keywords, and then figures out what boost they will give you based on their PageRank, how many sites link to them, and how few links they have outgoing (the fewer the better). It then sorts all these choices, ranks them by which sites will give the most benefit, and outputs it as an HTML file. It not only hunts for potential link partners and assesses their value as link partners, but it hunts down pretty much anything for you, whether it is competitor information or joint venture partners, and gives you several methods to contact them. It is the first SEO tool to show the age of any site to help find trusted sites. It finds niche markets with little competition.

Despite the fact the site looks similar to e-book scam sites, you can find out more at www.pr-prowler.com.

Other Link-Building Strategies

As well as holistically inviting up links using the techniques described previously, you can also create links to your site in other ways. Traditionally, this involves submitting your site to all sorts of directories. I do not advocate this any longer as the effect of these directories is diluted, if not detrimental, and usually require more time and cost to set up than the benefit you receive. Definitely make sure you do not pay anyone to "submit your sites to directories"; it's not useful compared to the amount of money you might spend.

However, having just said that there is one circumstance where submitting to directories can be useful. If you know of industry- or trade-specific and/or topic-specific directories related to your website, a submission can be useful. This is because links from a topic-related site are worth more than just a general one.

There are a few easy places where you can submit a Joomla site for free. If you are using a commercial template such as one from Joomlashack, we have our own site showcase (www.joomlashack.com/community/index.php/board,9.0.html). There is also a larger showcase at http://community.joomla.org/showcase/.

Another place to put links to your website is in your signature on a forum. For this to be effective, you need to do a couple of things:

- Find a forum that is related to your website based on its industry or topic.
- Become an active contributing member of that forum.
- Place a link to your website in your signature, making sure you follow forum rules.

The nice thing about this strategy is that the more you contribute the more members of the community will see your link. Plus, search engines sometimes prioritize links from active, focused "'expert" social networking sites, and you have control over the anchor text. It's a situation where everybody wins.

Internal Linking

As previously mentioned internal links are often forgotten when people are developing a link building campaign. The truth is that properly constructed internal links on your site are almost as useful as external links to your site. One tremendous advantage is that you have total control over these internal links. An efficient way to leverage Joomla to automatically produce useful internal links is using the "read more" feature in combination with creating a sitemap.

Joomla! Linked Titles and "Read More"

The great thing about Joomla is that a CMS is designed to add a lot of content very quickly and to create dynamic pages that are automatically linked. So, for example, on your home page you might designate certain articles to be displayed in a blog format, with the option of having a linked title that goes deeper into the site to a page that fully displays the actual article.

You can control whether titles are linked or not in the Article Options of the Article Manager (to set it globally for the whole site) or by setting Advanced Options in the menu item that generates that page or the Advanced Options for a particular article. The same is also true for the "read more" link that is commonly shown on Joomla sites to indicate that a longer article is available.

Linked titles are off by default and the "read more" link is on. Change Linked Titles to Yes and click Save. If we preview the frontend of the site now we see that the titles are now links, and there is also a "read more" link to read the full article. This is shown in Figure 8.4.

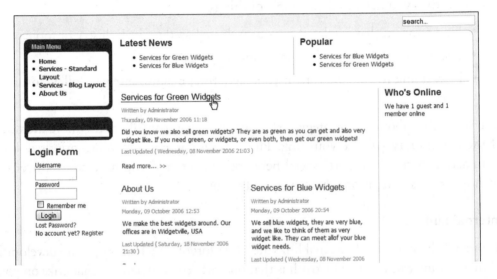

FIGURE 8.4   Frontend view of linked titles and "read more" links.

Notice a couple of important things here. One is that my linked title is beneficial for organic SEO. I carefully chose my article title "Services for Green Widgets" to contain some useful keywords: *services*, *green*, and *widgets*. This means that I have a great internal link to that article. The "read more" link is not nearly so useful. Based on what is in the anchor text here (the part that is the blue link), I am optimizing for the keywords *read* and *more*.

If you want to see how common this kind of linking strategy is, go to Google or Yahoo! and do a search for "click here" or "read more." Astonishingly enough there are about 1.5 billion websites that are trying to optimize their organic traffic for the keywords *click here*. Remember, it's the words in the link, called the anchor text, that search engines use to decide what the page being linked to is about. It's absolutely criti-cal that your anchor text represents that page.

If you want further proof of this, as mentioned previously, do a Google search for "miserable failure." Take a look at the number one search result and you will see the powerful effect of anchor text in search engine optimization. As much as I would like to make a political commentary here, the words *miserable* and *failure* are not anywhere in that site, and this example demonstrates the power of the anchor text in external links!

So how do we solve the problem of "read more"? Fortunately there is an easy solu-tion: You can create a template override that replaces the phrase "Read More" with "Read more about *whatever this title is.*" I actually use this on my site www.compass designs.net. You can see it working in Figure 8.5.

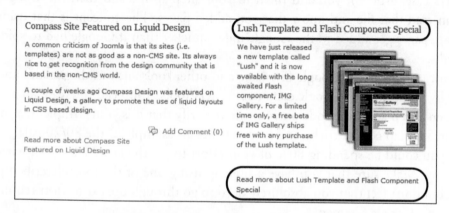

FIGURE 8.5   Expanded "read more" links.

This is the introduction text shown on my home page from two of my blog articles. You'll notice that the title is a link and also the "read more" has been expanded to include the title and that also is a link. Not only does this make sure that search engine spiders quickly index those articles, it also provides two immediate internal links for that article with keywords in the anchor text. The technique to implement template overrides is described in Chapter 9.

NOTE
While we're talking about my blog, it's packed full of great news and tips about Joomla. If you haven't already you should definitely head over and check it out, www.compassdesigns.net.

Sitemaps

A sitemap serves as a hierarchical display with an internal link indexing every page on your site. A sitemap also provides a useful technique to make sure that search engine spiders index your whole website. Depending on your site's structure, a basic sitemap can be created using List Layout pages, a secondary menu, or a sitemap extension available on the Joomla Extension Directory (JED).

Google Sitemap

Recently Google started offering a number of webmaster tools, the first offering was something called Google Sitemaps. The basic idea is that you actually submit a sitemap to Google and then keep a copy of it in your root directory. As you add pages (or in Joomla's case, articles), you add them to your sitemap file and then the Google spider can read that file and know that you added pages. The concept is that using the sitemap, pages get added to the Google index quicker than if Google had to spider all the links.

You can register for Google Sitemaps and other tools such as diagnostics and statistics by going to www.google.com/webmasters/tools. You need to create an account and then also place some code on your site to verify that it is yours. Implementing the Google Sitemap is a bit tricky and is sometimes an example of the 80/20 rule. At this point you could be spending 80% of your effort to get the last 20% out of what you are doing. Make sure that you have a sitemap using one of the tools described previously, but don't feel that you absolutely need to go through the extra effort required to maintain a Google Sitemap.

Pay Per Click Traffic

If you have a website (Joomla or otherwise), and you have a vague interest in getting traffic, then Pay Per Click (PPC) may need to be part of your SEM strategy.

Why is PPC so useful?

If you put an ad in a magazine about your product, you pay the magazine the ad fee and it goes in. At that point you are hoping that the ad is compelling enough to get people to call/email/visit your site. If you get no leads from the ad, though, you still had to pay the magazine the fee.

AdWords is an example of PPC, which means you only have to pay for an ad if somebody clicks on it. The equivalent would be you only have to pay the magazine if you get a sales lead from your advertisement. No magazine in the world is ever going to give you an offer like that; they would go out of business in a heartbeat! On the Web using sophisticated tracking software, this kind of arrangement is possible. The two leading providers are Google and Yahoo! AdWords is actually one of the main ways Google makes its money. (It had to get the $1.3 billion it paid for YouTube somewhere.)

PPC has even more going for it than the manner in which you pay for the ad. It actually draws on three ideas:

- You are advertising to people who are looking for your product or service right now.

- You only pay when they click on your ad, as I just explained.

- Pricing is based in real time; you bid live against other advertisers.

How Google AdWords Works

When you do a search in Google the results are based on organic search, the results based on Google's complicated algorithm, and advertising or AdWords, what Google calls sponsored links. Let's do a search in Google (see Figure 8.6).

Figure 8.6 shows the results of a Google search for everybody's favorite content management system, Joomla. On the left-hand side are the organic search results. We can see in position #10 a great website for commercial Joomla templates. (Okay, I'll admit that's my site!) On the right-hand side, you can see smaller listings that are Google's PPC AdWords. Circled in position #2 is an ad I created for a Joomla manual.

Sometimes people think that the organic search on the left is free and the sponsored links on the right are paid advertising. From your perspective as someone who is trying to market your website this is not true. You have to pay for *both* listings.

To get listed on the left-hand side you do not have to pay for the listing itself, but you have to spend time and effort on both your "on the page" and "off page" SEO. To get listed on the right-hand side involves much less time and effort, but you have to pay for the listing. Either way it's a combination of time, effort, and money from your perspective.

At the end of the day one method for promoting your site might end up being more cost effective than the other. However, the reality is you probably need to do both. In the same way as your retirement plan needs to have a diversified portfolio, so does your search engine marketing strategy need to be balanced.

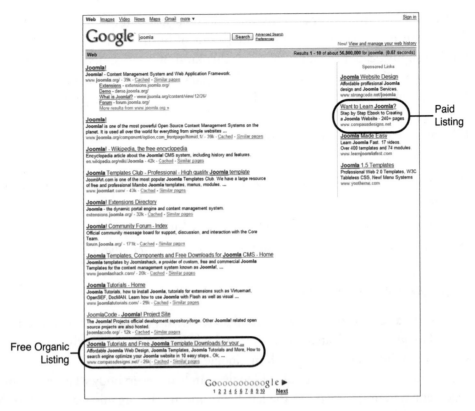

FIGURE 8.6 Paid search results in Google.

At this point, I have given a basic introduction to PPC and some suggestions to convince you why you should be adding it to your marketing strategies. There is not much value to me explaining how to develop a Google AdWords campaign because it's already been done. It's generally accepted that there is one leading guide to AdWords, written by Perry Marshall. You can find out more about it at www.perrymarshall.info. I absolutely recommend it and have a copy myself. I have managed to reduce how much I am paying for my AdWords campaigns by half using his techniques. As you can see in Figure 8.6, I have an ad at position #2 for a very competitive search term and let's just say I'm not paying too much for it!

One strategy I would like to share from the book is Perry's idea of using Google AdWords to test things. Say you are starting a new product and you're struggling between a couple of ideas for a slogan for it. All you have to do is whip up a landing page with some sort of signup form, and then create a Google AdWords campaign that uses the two slogans in the ads. Then all you need to do is insert the free conversion tracking code from Google and you can find hard statistics about which slogan converts your customers better. For $5 or $10 you have implemented sophisticated split testing, something normally only within the reach of big companies and expensive marketing budgets.

Joomla! and AdWords

So far we have been discussing the usefulness of PPC advertising, which you could apply to any website. Where does Joomla come in?

Google AdWords is a powerful way to drive controlled traffic to your website. Getting the traffic there is only half the story, though; you need to know what happens when a prospect gets arrives at your website, so you can have a better picture of whether your advertising money is being well spent. You do this through *conversion tracking*.

When you set up conversion tracking, you can see your conversion rate and thereby your cost per conversion. Figure 8.7 is a great example of why this is critical. This product only costs $19.99, and I am paying over $21 for every sale. I am losing money! Armed with this information, I need to dig out Perry's book and find out how to either lower my bid price or increase my conversion rate. Without this information I would be burning money.

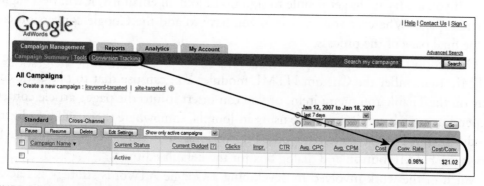

FIGURE 8.7   Google AdWords conversion tracking.

Adding the conversion code is relatively simple on a Joomla website. When you click on conversion tracking, Google gives you some JavaScript code that you need to insert onto your website. The code looks something like this:

```
<!-- Google Code for purchase Conversion Page -->
<script language="JavaScript" type="text/javascript">
<!--
var google_conversion_id = YOURIDEHERE;
var google_conversion_language = "en_US";
var google_conversion_format = "1";
var google_conversion_color = "FFFFFF";
if (1) {
  var google_conversion_value = 1;
}
var google_conversion_label = "purchase";
//-->
</script>
<script language="JavaScript" src="http://www.googleadservices.com/pagead/
conversion.js">
</script>
<noscript>
<img height=1 width=1 border=0 src="http://www.googleadservices.com/pagead/
conversion/YOURIDEHERE/?value=1&label=purchase&script=0">
</noscript>
```

To figure out what page you need to put it on, you'll have to decide which page represents a successful conversion. For an e-commerce store it might be the thank you page. If you are trying to get people to sign up to join an email list, it will be a slightly different page. Whatever your scenario, you have to add the Google conversion code to the final page of the process.

One important thing to remember is that you will need to add to the code as HTML. Remember the Custom HTML module? You can use that to place the code only on the Thank You menu item, or you can insert it into the page's article content. Depending on what editor you are using in Joomla, somewhere there will be a button to edit the raw HTML code, as opposed to working in WYSIWYG mode. Figure 8.8 shows the HTML button and dialog box for the default editor.

Much of the work involved in developing a Google AdWords strategy is relevant to any website. But if you have a Joomla website, it's a website nonetheless. Arm yourself with Perry's book (www.perrymarshall.info) and make sure you are tracking the conversions.

If you are interested in finding out more about how to optimize your Joomla site for organic searches, check out the many articles I have on the subject at compassdesigns.net.

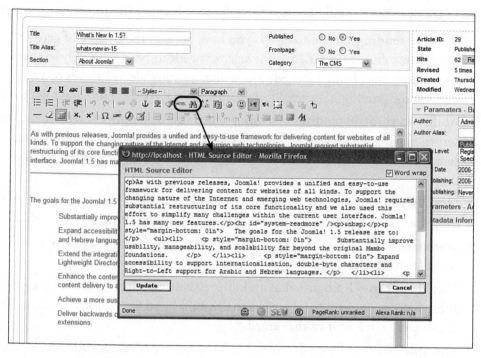

FIGURE 8.8   Button to edit HTML source in JCE.

Email Traffic

A modern website should have many tools that allow two-way communication with your site visitors. A key part of this communication is the use of email newsletters. Many people associate email marketing just with spam, but email can fill many needs, for example:

- Follow up emails from e-commerce purchases
- Communicating with family members on a family website
- Sequential e-books or newsletters about a particular topic
- A news and tips email from a topic niche site

Recently, RSS has become more popular to send information to subscribers, but it has only been really adopted by a few web users. Most still are using their inbox to get information. I actually use an RSS to email system from Feedblitz on my site.

An email newsletter should contain the following features (in no particular order):

- **Reliable sending mechanism**—If you have gone to the trouble of getting visitors to subscribe, your email newsletter needs to be sent reliably so that it's received without being blocked. The ability to schedule in batches or pause and resume sending is a useful feature to help make sure your emails get out.

- **Ability to throttle sending**—Sending email can be resource intensive for your server. Having emails sent in batches with delays after a certain number are sent is called throttling. It also can overcome forced web host email sending caps.

- **Unsubscribe mechanism**—For you email to be legal, it must meet the CAN-SPAM act requirement of having an easy and effective unsubscribe mechanism.

- **Subscribe form**—You need to be able to offer site visitors the ability to subscribe to your email list.

- **Double opt in**—Recognized as an industry best practice, it is advised to ask subscribers to confirm their email subscription by some manner, for example, clicking on a link sent to that email.

- **Multiple targeted lists**—It's useful to have different lists for different topics/purposes.

- **Bounce handling**—Emails might bounce for many reasons. It's important for these to be automatically removed from your list as repeat bounces from a particular server can get you flagged as a spammer (blacklisted) by ISPs.

- **HTML templating**—Current research indicates that HTML emails have a greater response rate than pure text. They also allow easy tracking of "opens."

- **Import/Export subscribers**—As your needs change, you might well need to change your email newsletter system. You'll need to be able to easily import and export your subscriber list. You will also want to have some sort of duplicate handling.

- **Integration into Joomla user database**—Many sites will have registration set up on their Joomla site for many reasons, such as e-commerce, private pages, and paid subscriptions. You will often want to send emails to your Joomla user database.

- **Email statistics**—It's important to be able to track statistics about your newsletters, such as opens and click rates.

This is by no means an exhaustive list, but is what I would consider the minimum to both meet federal legal requirements for email marketing and for an email marketing solution that complements Joomla.

One important consideration that you will need to immediately take into account is how your website is hosted. Most Joomla webmasters have their site on a relatively affordable hosting plan called *virtual hosting* or *shared hosting* for about $10 to $20 per month. This means your site is on a server that is shared between many other sites. Most hosting companies have in place an email sending cap. For example, Bluehost, a popular host, only allows you to send out 200 emails per hour. Obviously, if you have a large list, this will be inadequate. You will either need a dedicated server, with prices from $200 per month, or a hosted email solution.

To a certain extent, this does immediately question the usefulness of Joomla email newsletters. If you have big lists, or hope that you will, you need a dedicated server to make use of them.

Third-Party Hosted Email Solutions

If you are serious about trying to monetize your site, email marketing is a key part. Assuming your plan for this is successful, then you hopefully will grow your list. When this happens, integrated email newsletter extensions are not totally adequate:

- Unless you are running on an expensive dedicated server, sending out thousands of emails in one go will strain your performance. You can throttle the email sending, but with email lists in the thousands, this can take up to a day to send out a single newsletter.

- It's possible to get caught by the CAN-SPAM act by accidentally mixing your subscription and Joomla user databases. If you email somebody who has unsubscribed from your list you can get penalized.

- Following on from the preceding points, hosted email solutions work hard to ensure deliverability. This includes such things as white listing their IPs and providing automatic CAN-SPAM compliance.

- Third-party email providers usually have very good stats analysis, especially if you are dealing with a large volume of emails.

Many hosted email marketing solutions are available, for example, MailChimp or iContact.

Joomla! SEF Extensions

SEF or search engine friendly URLs is a core option for Joomla that modifies the default URL produced by the CMS.

Much of the discussion about SEO revolves around various third-party SEF components. These components allow for advanced manipulation of URLs and metatags. Neither of these was identified as a major factor in any studies I have seen. Turn on the default Joomla SEF, but I am not sure there is much evidence that most of the extra SEO components have much effect.

> **NOTE**
> A while ago on my old blog, I changed back and forth between SEF and non-SEF URLs. I did this to point out that easily readable and memorable URLs like www.compassdesigns.net/downloads are much more important for humans than they are for search engines. Joomla SEF fixes a major usability issue that also has an SEO benefit.
>
> I stand relatively alone in this opinion. (A lot of people disagree with me on this one.) For further reading check out www.alledia.com/blog/joomla-urls/in-defense-of-search-engine-friendly-urls/.

Quick Start SEO for Joomla!

If you are looking for a quick start list of ways you can SEO your site, check out Appendix C, "A Quick Introduction to SEO."

Summary

In this chapter, we went far beyond search engine optimization (SEO) into the broader fields of search engine marketing (SEM). We saw that if you want your website to be successful, it is absolutely critical that you have a balanced marketing plan that addresses four different tactics to get site traffic. Just focusing on only one tactic puts you at a disadvantage to competitors that have a more balanced approach:

- **Organic**—What was traditionally known as SEO, organic marketing is the idea of having your website visible in various search engines when people search using search terms that match a page's keywords.
- **Referral**—Quite simply, the idea of having links from other high-quality sites to yours. A robust SEM plan will have a comprehensive link building strategy.

These can be natural through attracting links to your high-quality content, or can be links in forum signatures or other techniques.

- **Pay Per Click (PPC)**—This strategy involves bidding for placement on search results. Submitting such an ad to a search engine such as Google also means that it appears on its distributed ad network, for example, in Google's case, AdWords. So, your ads will appear both in search results and on content sites.

- **Email**—Building an email subscription list is a key part of a modern SEM plan. It's important to know who your website viewers are and, if appropriate, to capture email addresses so that you can present them with information that might draw them back to your site.

Chapter 9

Creating Pure CSS Templates

In This Chapter

This chapter walks through the steps of creating a Joomla template. Specifically, you will create a template that uses Cascading Style Sheets (CSS) to produce a layout—without using tables. This is a desirable method because it makes the template code easier to validate to World Wide Web Consortium (W3C) standards. It also tends to load faster, is easier to maintain, and performs better in search engines. These issues are discussed in detail later in the chapter. This chapter covers the following topics:

- What is a Joomla template? What functions does a Joomla template perform, and what is the difference between a template that has no content and a template whose content is added to the CMS?

- How does the localhost design process differ from that of a static HTML or XHTML web design process?

- What are the implications of tableless design in Joomla, and what is the relationship between W3C standards, usability, and accessibility?

- What files make up a Joomla template, and what functions do they perform?

- How do you create a source-ordered three-column layout by using CSS rather than tables?

- What are the basic CSS styles that should be used with Joomla, and what are the default styles that the Joomla core uses?

- How do you place and style modules, and what are some new techniques for rounded corners?

- What would be a simple strategy for producing lean CSS menus that mimic the effects of menus developed with JavaScript?

- How do you control when columns are shown and hide them when no content is present?

- What are the proper steps in creating a Joomla 1.6 template?

A DISCLAIMER OR TWO OR THREE

This is probably the most technical chapter in the book. To be successful with this chapter, you need a firm grasp of XHTML and CSS; for example, you need to understand what *float* does and how to clear it.

If you are not sure you have the skills needed to make a Joomla template, I strongly advise grabbing a free template from compassdesigns.net. A good way to learn is to grab one of my free templates and try to reverse engineer it to see how it works.

What Is a Joomla! Template?

A Joomla template is a series of files within the Joomla CMS that control the presentation of content. A Joomla template is not a website; it's also not considered a complete website design. A template is the basic foundational design for viewing a Joomla website. To produce the effect of a "complete" website, the template works hand-in-hand with content stored in Joomla databases. Figure 9.1 shows an example of this.

Part A, shows a template in use with sample content. Part B shows the template as it might look with a raw Joomla installation and little or no content. The template is styled so that when your content is inserted, it automatically inherits the styles from stylesheets defined in the template, such as link styles, menus, navigation, text size, and colors, to name a few.

Fig. A—Joomla Template
with Sample Content

Fig. B—Joomla Template
with Little or No Content

FIGURE 9.1   A template with and without content.

Notice that the images associated with the content (the photos of the people) are not part of the template, but the header is.

Using a template for a CMS, as Joomla does, has a number of advantages:

- Joomla does all the work of placing content within pages. You can add new information to existing blog pages simply by typing a new article. The template and its CSS make sure it appears stylistically consistent with other content on the site.

- There is a complete separation of content and presentation, especially when CSS is used for layout (as opposed to having tables in the `index.php` file). This is one of the main criteria for determining whether a site meets modern web standards. In a standards-compliant site, the HTML tags for tables are reserved for presenting tabular data and not laying out a page into columns.

- You can apply a new template, and hence a completely new look to a website, instantly. This can involve different locations for positioning content and modules, as well as colors and graphics.

THE LEAST YOU NEED TO KNOW

Modern websites separate content from presentation by using templates and CSS. In Joomla, a template controls the presentation of content.

The Localhost Design Process

The web page you see at a Joomla-powered website is not static; it is generated dynamically from content stored in the database. When content in the database is changed, all pages that display that content are instantly changed. The page you see is created through various PHP commands in the template that query the database. Because the template looks like lines of code instead of content, it presents some difficulties in the design phase.

It's common now to use a "what you see is what you get" (WYSIWYG) HTML editor, such as Dreamweaver, so you don't need to code the HTML. However, using such an editor is not possible in the Joomla template design process because WYSIWYG editors cannot display and edit dynamic pages. Therefore, you must code a template and its CSS manually and view the output page from the PHP on a served page that you frequently refresh as you make changes. With a fast enough connection, this could be a web server, but most designers use a local server, or localhost, on their own computer—a piece of software that serves the web pages on your computer, such as the localhost setups described in Chapter 2, "Downloading and Installing Joomla!"

There is no "right way" to create a web page; how you do it depends on your background. Those who are more graphics inclined tend to make an "image" of a page in a graphics program such as Photoshop and then break up the images so that they can be used for the Web (known as *slicing and dicing*). More technology-based designers often jump straight into the CSS and start coding fonts, borders, and backgrounds. However, as just mentioned, as a Joomla template designer, you're limited by the fact that you cannot instantly see the effect of your coding in the same editor. You can therefore use the following modified design process:

1. Have a localhost server loaded with content running in the background to "run" Joomla.

2. Make your edits to the HTML and CSS with an editor and then save your changes to the server.

3. View the pages affected by your edits in a web browser.

4. Return to step 2.

 THE LEAST YOU NEED TO KNOW
When creating a template, you have to have Joomla "running" on a server so you can make changes and refresh the resulting pages to check them.

Localhost Server Options

In Chapter 2, you saw how to install a web server (WampServer) that will run on your computer. To move further along in this chapter, you need to have WampServer installed. If you haven't done so yet, go ahead and install it. I'll wait right here.

> **TIP**
>
> One useful technique for making the design process more efficient is to serve a web page that you are designing and then copy and paste the generated source from your browser into an editor. For example, once the CSS for your layout is set up, you can use a localhost server to serve a page, and then you can view the source of the page. You can then copy and paste the source code into your editor, and then you can easily style the page using CSS, without having to go through the cycle of steps described earlier. When you have completed your editing, you can copy your perfected CSS styles back to the server.

On a hosted web server, you can edit the HTML template and CSS files in the backend while having the frontend open in another tab of your browser. As you save your changes, you can simply refresh the frontend view to see the impact.

With a localhost setup, you have the added convenience of direct access to the files to edit them with the editor of your choice. As you save your changes, without having to close the editor, you can refresh the frontend view in your browser and see the impact.

> **A FREE XHTML EDITOR**
>
> In addition to commercial editors, such as Dreamweaver, some free editors are available. Nvu is a solid choice that has built-in validation and is 100% open source. This means anyone is welcome to download Nvu at no charge (ttp://net2.com/nvu/download.html). You can even download the source code and make special changes, if you want.

> **TIP**
>
> When using Firefox as you're designing a template, you can use three add-in tools that are of particular help: the Web Developer toolbar, Firebug, and ColorZilla.

W3C and Tableless Design

Usability, accessibility, and search engine optimization (SEO) are all phrases used to describe high-quality web pages on the Internet today. In reality, there is a significant amount of overlap between usability, accessibility, and SEO, and a web page that demonstrates the characteristics of one typically does so for all three (see Figure 9.2). The easiest way to achieve these three goals is to use the framework laid out in the W3C web standards.

For example, someone who has poor vision can easily read a site that is structured semantically with HTML or XHTML (the XHTML explains the document's content, not how it looks) through a screen reader. It can also be easily read by a search engine spider. Google is effectively blind in how it reads a website; it's as though it is using a screen reader.

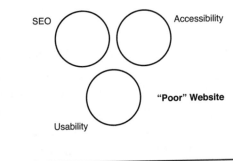

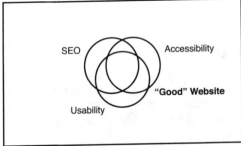

FIGURE 9.2   The overlap between usability, accessibility, and SEO.

Web standards put into place a common set of "rules" for all web browsers to use to display a web page. The main organization pushing these standards is the W3C, whose director, Tim Berners-Lee, is credited with inventing the Web in 1989.

To understand where web standards came from, some history is helpful. Many web pages are actually designed for older browsers. Why? Browsers have continually evolved since the World Wide Web was born. Each generation introduced new features, and the manufacturers came up with different, sometimes proprietary, tags (names) for those features. Each browser tends to have a different syntax, or "dialect," and quirks for implementing the same base HTML language. New browsers have appeared, and some old ones have disappeared (remember Netscape?).

Current W3C standards serve to (hopefully) push manufacturers to release more compliant browsers that read the same language and display pages more consistently so that designers can design to a single common platform.

Another complicating factor is that historically, different browser makers (such as Microsoft) tend to have their browsers interpret HTML/XHTML in slightly different ways. Consequently, web designers must design their websites to support older browsers rather than new ones. Designers and website owners often decide that it's important that a web page appear properly in these "legacy" browsers. The W3C standards outlined for web page code were developed to achieve consistency. A site that incorporates the W3C's web standards has a good foundation for making itself accessible, usable, and optimized for search engines. Think of these as building codes for your house: A website built with them is stronger and safer and coincides with users' expectations. You can check your pages with the W3C's HTML validation service (validator.w3.org). It's easy and free (just make sure you use the correct DOCTYPE when you try to validate your code. At its simplest, a site that meets W3C validation is likely to also use semantic HTML or XHTML and separate its content from presentation by using CSS.

Ask five designers what web standards are, and you will get five different answers. But most agree that web standards are based on using valid code, whether HTML or XHTML (or others), in the manner specified in the latest version of the standards.

Semantically Correct Code

As mentioned earlier, being semantically correct means that the HTML or XHTML tags in a web page describe only content, not presentation. In particular, this means structured organization of H1 tags, H2 tags, and so on and using tables only for tabular data, not for layout. One area where Joomla template designers compromise slightly on being purely semantically correct is the convention of naming the left and right columns of a two- or three-column layout as, well, `left` and `right` instead of the more semantically correct `sidebar` or `sidecolumn`. If these are only position names used in the template's PHP, they are technically correct. If they are also used to define matching classes in the HTML and CSS, it's a forgivable convenience to have everything associated with displaying the page's left column named or classed as `left`. In the examples that follow, you will see that the position of `left` is styled with the class `sidebar` and `right` is `sidebar-2`, which is semantically correct code.

Cascading Style Sheets (CSS)

Closely related to making code semantically correct is using CSS to control the look and layout of a web page. CSS is a simple mechanism for adding style (for example, fonts, colors, spacing) to web documents (see www.w3.org/Style/CSS/). CSS exist parallel to the HTML and XHTML code and let you completely separate content (code) from presentation (CSS). To see this in action, check out CSS Zen Garden (www.csszengarden.com), a site where the same XHTML content is displayed in different and unique ways, just by changing the CSS file. The resulting pages look very different but have exactly the same core content.

Designing Joomla-powered sites currently presents considerable challenges in terms of meeting validation standards. In the first series of Joomla releases, 1.0.X, the code used a significant number of tables to output its pages. This isn't really using CSS for presentation, nor does it produce semantically correct code. This problem is compounded by the fact that many third-party developers of components and modules are still using tables to generate their layouts.

Fortunately, the Joomla core development team recognized this issue with Joomla. In Joomla 1.5, it's possible for template designers to completely override the output of the core (called a *view*) and strip out the tables or customize the layout—in whatever way they want.

Care can still be taken when creating a template to make sure it is accessible (for example, scalable font sizes), usable (clear navigation), and optimized for search engines (source ordered).

THE LEAST YOU NEED TO KNOW
Creating valid templates should be a path, not a goal. The idea is to make your template as accessible as possible for humans and spiders, not to achieve a badge of valid markup.

Creating a Simple Template: 960TemplateTutorialStep1

To understand the contents of a template, let's start by looking at a blank Joomla template.

> **NOTE**
>
> There are two ways you can use this chapter. You can start with new files and type in the code shown here to slowly build the template. This process is time-consuming and prone to error. Instead, you can refer to the supplied templates from www.joomlabook.com. There are four templates, each of which corresponds to the stage of its development at the *end* of the related section in this chapter. Download the sample template that matches the section you are reading, and you can follow along.
>
> You can also follow along by installing these four templates in your localhost, in which case you'll be able to see your edits and tests live on the frontend.

Template File Components

This section reviews the manual process of setting up template files. Normally, you would install the template using the Joomla installer, which takes care of all these steps.

When constructing your own templates, you need to set up several files and folders in a coordinated manner. A template needs to contain various files and folders. These files must be placed in the `/templates/` directory of a Joomla installation, each in a folder designated for that template. If you had two templates installed called Element and Voodoo, your directory would look something like this:

```
/templates/element
/templates/voodoo
```

Note that the directory name for a template must be the same as the name of the template—in this case, `element` and `voodoo`. These names are case-sensitive and shouldn't contain spaces.

Within the directory of a template, there are two key files:

```
/element/templateDetails.xml
/element/index.php
```

These filenames and locations must match exactly because this is how they are called by the Joomla core script.

The first of these is the template XML file:

```
templateDetails.xml
```

This is an XML-format metadata file that tells Joomla what other files are needed when it loads a web page that uses this template. (Note the uppercase *D*.) It also details the author, copyright, and what files make up the template (including any images used). The last use of this file is for unpacking and installing a template when using the extension installer in the administrative backend.

The second key file is the primary template file that generates pages, the `index.php`:

```
index.php
```

This file is the most important in a Joomla template. It lays out the site and tells the Joomla CMS where to put the different components and modules. It is a combination of PHP and HTML/XHTML.

Almost all templates use additional files. It is conventional (although not required by the Joomla core) to name and locate them as shown here for a template called Element:

```
/element/template_thumbnail.png
/element/params.ini
/element/css/template.css
/element/images/logo.png
```

These are just examples. Table 9.1 lists the files commonly found in a template.

TABLE 9.1   Example Core Files Needed for a CSS-Based Template

/templatename/folder/filename	Description
`/element/template_thumbnail.png`	A web browser screenshot of the template (usually reduced to around 140 pixels wide by 90 pixels high). After the template has been installed, this functions as a preview image that is visible in the Joomla administration Template Manager.
`/element/params.ini`	A text file that would store the values of any parameters the template has.
`/element/css/template.css`	The CSS of the template. The folder location is optional, but you have to specify where it is in the `index.php` file. You can call it what you want. Usually, the name shown is used, but you will see later that there are advantages to having other CSS files, too.
`/element/images/logo.png`	Any images that go with the template. Again for organization reasons, most designers put them in an images folder. Here we have an image file called `logo.png` as an example.

templateDetails.xml

The `templateDetails.xml` file acts as a manifest, or packing list, that includes a list of all the files or folders that are part of the template. It also includes information such as the author and copyright. Some of these details are shown in the administrative back-end in the Template Manager. An example of an XML file is shown here:

NOTE

If you are following along and creating the template as you read, at this point, open up a text editor, create a file called `templateDetails.xml`, and make sure it includes the code shown here.

```
<?xml version="1.0" encoding="utf-8"?>
<!DOCTYPE install PUBLIC "-//Joomla! 1.6//DTD template 1.0//EN"
➥"http://www.joomla.org/xml/dtd/1.6/template-install.dtd">
<install version="1.6" type="template">
    <name>960TemplateTutorialStep1</name>
    <creationDate>1/10/10</creationDate>
    <author>Barrie North</author>
    <authorEmail>contact@compassdesigns.net</authorEmail>
    <authorUrl>http://www.compassdesigns.net</authorUrl>
    <copyright>Copyright (C) 2005 - 2010 Barrie North</copyright>
    <license>GPL</license>
    <version>1.6.0</version>
    <description>The first of 4 tutorial templates from
➥Joomla 1.6 - A User's Guide</description>
    <files>
        <filename>index.php</filename>
        <filename>templateDetails.xml</filename>
        <filename>params.ini</filename>
        <folder>images</folder>
        <folder>css</folder>
    </files>
    <positions>
        <position>breadcrumbs</position>
        <position>left</position>
        <position>right</position>
        <position>top</position>
        <position>footer</position>
        <position>debug</position>
    </positions>
```

```
<config>
    <fields name="params">
        <fieldset name="basic">
            <field
                name="colorVariation"
                type="list"
                default="white"
                label="Color Variation"
                description="Base Color of template">
                <option
                    value="blue">blue</option>
                <option
                    value="red">red</option>
            </field>
        </fieldset>
    </fields>
</config>
</install>
```

Let's look at what some of these lines mean:

- **`<install version="1.6" type="template">`**—The contents of the XML document are instructions for the backend installer. The option `type="template"` tells the installer that you are installing a template and that it is for Joomla 1.6.

- **`<name>960TemplateTutorialStep1 </name>`**—This line defines the name of your template. The name you enter here will also be used to create the directory within the templates directory. Therefore, it should not contain any characters that the file system cannot handle, such as spaces. If you're installing manually, you need to create a directory whose name is identical to the template name.

- **`<creationDate>`**—This is the date the template was created. It is a free-form field and can be anything such as May 2005, 08-June-1978, 01/01/2004, and so on.

- **`<author>`**—This is the name of the author of this template—most likely your name.

- **`<copyright>`**—Any copyright information goes in this element.

- **`<authorEmail>`**—This is the email address at which the author of this template can be reached.
- **`<authorUrl>`**—This is the URL of the author's website.
- **`<version>`**—This is the version of the template.
- **`<files></files>`**—This is a list of various files used in the template. The files used in the template are laid out with `<filename>` and `<folder>` tags, like this:

```
<files>
    <filename>index.php</filename>
    <filename>templateDetails.xml</filename>
    <filename>params.ini</filename>
    <folder>images</folder>
    <folder>css</folder>
</files>
```

The "files" sections contain all generic files, such as the PHP source for the template or the thumbnail image for the template preview. Each file listed in this section is enclosed by `<filename> </filename>` tags. You can also include whole folders, such as an image folder, by using the `<folder>` tag.

- **`<positions>`**—This shows the module positions available in the template. It is the list of page locations, such as `top`, `left`, and `right`, defined in the template in which modules can be set to appear, using the Position drop-down of the Module Manager. The position names in this list must precisely match the PHP code that generates content for each listed position inside `index.php`.
- **`<config>`**—This section describes the parameters that can be set in the back-end and passed as global variables to allow advanced template functions, such as changing the color scheme of the template.

index.php

What is actually in an `index.php` file? It is a combination of HTML/XHTML and PHP that determines everything about the layout and presentation of the pages.

> **NOTE**
> If you are following along and creating the template as you read, if you haven't already you should create the template folder in `/templates/960Template TutorialStep1` and then create the `index.php` and `templateDetails.xml` files in that folder.
>
> As we have added the files directly, you need to run the Discovery process to install them. Select Extensions>Extension Manager>Discover.

Let's look at a critical part of achieving valid templates: the DOCTYPE at the top of the `index.php` file. This is the bit of code that goes at the top of every web page. At the top of our page, put this in the template:

```php
<?php
/**
 * @copyright    Copyright (C) 2005 - 2010 Barrie North.
 * @license      GPL
 */

defined('_JEXEC') or die;
?>
<!DOCTYPE html PUBLIC "-//W3C//DTD XHTML 1.0 Transitional//EN"
➥"http://www.w3.org/TR/xhtml1/DTD/xhtml1-transitional.dtd">
```

The first PHP statement simply shows the copyright/license and makes sure the file is not accessed directly for security.

A web page DOCTYPE is one of the fundamental components of how a web page is shown by a browser—how various HTML tags are handled and, more importantly, how the browser interprets CSS. The following observation from alistapart.com should To give you further understanding:

> [Information on W3C's site about DOCTYPEs is] written by geeks for geeks. And when I say geeks, I don't mean ordinary web professionals like you and me. I mean geeks who make the rest of us look like Grandma on the first day She's Got Mail.

You can use several DOCTYPES. Basically, the DOCTYPE tells the browser what version of HTML was used to design the page, whether it has some legacy code or also contains XML, and therefore how to interpret the page. Here the words *strict* and *transitional* start getting floated around (float:left and float:right usually) to indicate whether legacy code was included. Essentially, ever since the Web started, different browsers have had different levels of support for various HTML tags and versions of CSS. For example, Internet Explorer 6 or less won't understand the min-width command to set a minimum page width. To duplicate an effect so that it displays the same in all browsers, you sometimes have to use browser-specific "hacks" in the CSS that make up for shortcomings in each browser's adherence to the published standards.

Strict means the HTML (or XHTML) will be interpreted exactly as dictated by standards. A *transitional* DOCTYPE means that the page will be allowed a few agreed-upon differences from the standards (for example, continued use of discontinued tags).

To complicate things, there is something called "quirks" mode. If the DOCTYPE is wrong, outdated, or not there, the browser goes into quirks mode. This is an attempt to be backward compatible, so Internet Explorer 6, for example, will render the page as if it were Internet Explorer 4.

Unfortunately, people sometimes end up in quirks mode accidentally. It usually happens in two ways:

- They use the DOCTYPE declaration straight from the WC3 web page, and the link ends up as DTD/xhtml1-strict.dtd, which is a relative link on the WC3 server. You need the full path, as shown earlier.

- Microsoft set up Internet Explorer 6 so you could have valid pages but be in quirks mode. This happens when you have an xml declaration put before instead of after the DOCTYPE.

Next is an XML statement (after the DOCTYPE):

```
<html xmlns="http://www.w3.org/1999/xhtml" xml:lang="<?php echo $this-
➥>language; ?>" lang="<?php echo $this->language; ?>" >
```

The information I just gave you about Internet Explorer 6 quirks mode is important. In this chapter, you're designing only for Internet Explorer 6 and later, and you need to make sure that it's running in standards mode to minimize the hacks you have to do later on.

> **NOTE**
>
> Making a page standards compliant, so that you see `valid xhtml` at the bottom of the page, does not require really difficult coding or hard-to-understand tags. It merely means that the code you use follows the rules—it matches the DOCTYPE you said it would. That's it! Nothing else.
>
> Designing your site to standards can on one level be reduced to "saying what you do" and then "doing what you say."
>
> Here are some useful links that will help you understand DOCTYPE and quirks mode:
>
> · www.quirksmode.org/css/quirksmode.html
>
> · www.alistapart.com/stories/doctype
>
> · www.w3.org/QA/2002/04/Web-Quality

Let's look at the structure of the `index.php` file header; you want it to be as minimal as possible but still have enough for a production site. The header information you will use is as follows:

```php
<?php
/**
 * @copyright    Copyright (C) 2005 - 2010 Barrie North.
 * @license      GPL
 */
defined('_JEXEC') or die;
$app = JFactory::getApplication();
?>
<!DOCTYPE html PUBLIC "-//W3C//DTD XHTML 1.0 Transitional//EN"
➥"http://www.w3.org/TR/xhtml1/DTD/xhtml1-transitional.dtd">
<html xmlns="http://www.w3.org/1999/xhtml" xml:lang="<?php echo $this-
➥>language; ?>" lang="<?php echo $this->language; ?>" >
<head>
<jdoc:include type="head" />
<link rel="stylesheet" href="<?php echo $this->baseurl
➥?>/templates/system/css/system.css" type="text/css" />
<link rel="stylesheet" href="<?php echo $this->baseurl
➥?>/templates/system/css/general.css" type="text/css" />
<link rel="stylesheet" href="<?php echo $this->baseurl ?>/templates/<?php
➥echo $this->template ?>/css/template.css" type="text/css" />
</head>
```

What does all this mean?

We already discussed the implications of the DOCTYPE statement in the index.php file. The `<?php echo $this->language; ?>` code pulls the language from the site's language setting in Global Configuration.

`$app = Jfactory::getApplication();` is a variable that allows you to grab various parameters, like the name of the site and use them in the template.

The next line is for including more header information:

```
<jdoc:include type="head" />
```

This code snippet inserts in the generated page (that is, your frontend) all the header information that is set in the Global Configuration. In a default installation, it includes the tags shown here:

```
<meta http-equiv="content-type" content="text/html; charset=utf-8" />
<meta name="robots" content="index, follow" />
<meta name="keywords" content="joomla, Joomla" />
<meta name="rights" content="" />
<meta name="language" content="en-GB" />
<meta name="description" content="Joomla! -
the dynamic portal engine and content management system" />
<meta name="generator" content="Joomla! 1.6 -
Open Source Content Management" />
<title>Home</title>
<link href="/Joomla_1.6/index.php?format=feed&amp;type=rss" rel="alternate"
type="application/rss+xml" title="RSS 2.0" />
<link href="/Joomla_1.6/index.php?format=feed&amp;type=atom"
rel="alternate" type="application/atom+xml" title="Atom 1.0" />
```

Much of this header information is created on-the–fly, specific to the page (article) that someone is viewing. It includes a number of metatags, and any RSS-feed URLs.

The last lines in the header provide links to CSS files for Joomla-generated pages in general and also in this template:

```
<link rel="stylesheet" href="<?php echo $this->baseurl
?>/templates/system/css/system.css" type="text/css" />
<link rel="stylesheet" href="<?php echo $this->baseurl
?>/templates/system/css/general.css" type="text/css" />
<link rel="stylesheet" href="<?php echo $this->baseurl ?>/templates/<?php
echo $this->template ?>/css/template.css" type="text/css" />
```

The first two files, `system.css` and `general.css`, contain some generic Joomla styles. The last one is all the CSS for the template, here called `template.css`. The PHP code `<?php echo $this->template ?>` returns the name of the current template. Writing it in this way rather than writing the actual path makes the code more generic. When you create a new template, you can just copy this line (along with the whole header code) and not worry about editing anything.

The template CSS can include any number of files, such as conditional ones for different browsers and for different media, such as print. For example, the following code detects and adds an additional CSS file that targets the quirks of Internet Explorer 6 (we'll leave it out of our working example here):

```
<!--[if lte IE 6]>
<link href="templates/<?php echo $this->template ?>/css/ieonly.css"
➥rel="stylesheet" type="text/css" />
<![endif]-->
```

The next example is part of a technique for using a template parameter. In this case, a color scheme selected as a parameter in the Template Manager is loading a CSS file that has the same name as the selected color:

```
<link rel="stylesheet" href="<?php echo $this->baseurl ?>/templates/<?php
➥echo $this->template ?>/css/<?php echo $this->params-
➥>get('colorVariation'); ?>.css" type="text/css" />
```

It might generate this:

```
<link rel="stylesheet" href="/templates/960TemplateTutorialStep1/css/red.css"
➥type="text/css" />
```

NOTE
If you want to load the MooTools JavaScript library, commonly used in Joomla functions and extensions, you'll need to load it in the head, adding two lines like this:

```
<?php
/**
 * @copyright    Copyright (C) 2005 - 2010 Barrie North.
 * @license      GPL
```

```
    */
defined('_JEXEC') or die;
JHTML::_('behavior.mootools');
$app = JFactory::getApplication();
?>
```

The Joomla! Page Body

Still in the `index.php` file, now that the `<head>` part of the page is set up, we can move on to the `<body>` tag. Creating your first template will be easy! Ready?

To create the template, all you need to do is use Joomla statements that insert the contents of the mainbody, plus any modules you want:

```
<body>
<?php echo $app->getCfg('sitename');?><br />
<jdoc:include type="modules" name="top" />
<jdoc:include type="modules" name="left" />
<jdoc:include type="modules" name="breadcrumbs" />
<jdoc:include type="component" />
<jdoc:include type="modules" name="right" />
<jdoc:include type="modules" name="footer" />
<jdoc:include type="modules" name="debug" />
</body>
```

The template contains the following, in reasonably logical viewer order:

- The name of the site
- The top modules
- The left modules
- A breadcrumb bar
- The main content
- The right modules
- The footer modules
- A debug module

At this point (if you preview it, make sure it's the default template), the site does not look very awe inspiring (see Figure 9.3). Note I applied the template to the dataset I continued with from Chapter 7, "Expanding Your Content: Articles and Editors."

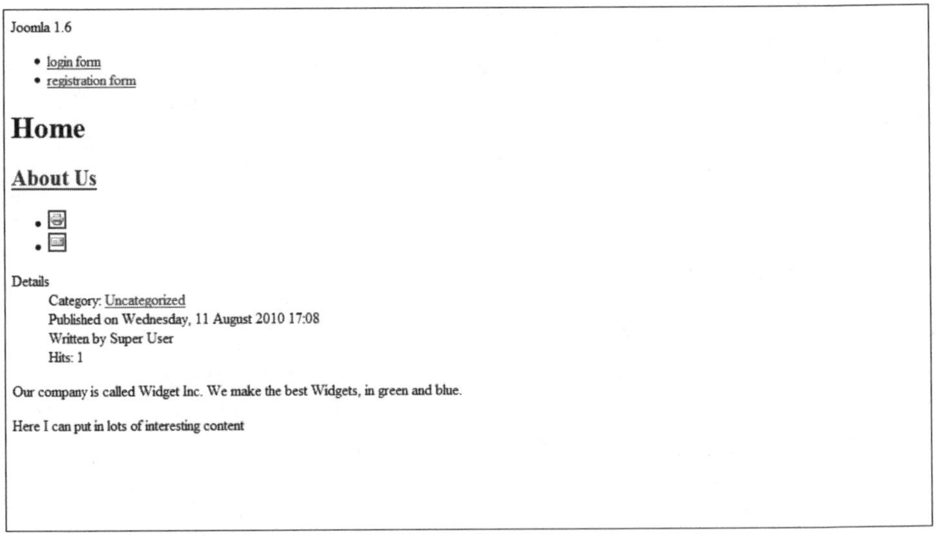

Joomla 1.6

- login form
- registration form

Home

About Us

-

Details

    Category: Uncategorized
    Published on Wednesday, 11 August 2010 17:08
    Written by Super User
    Hits: 1

Our company is called Widget Inc. We make the best Widgets, in green and blue.

Here I can put in lots of interesting content

FIGURE 9.3 An unstyled template.

THE LEAST YOU NEED TO KNOW
The most basic template simply displays the Joomla modules and mainbody (component). In a CSS-based template, layout and design are accomplished by the CSS, not by the template.

You want to come as close to semantic markup as possible. From a web point of view, this means a page can be read by anyone—a browser, a spider, or a screen reader. Semantic layout is the cornerstone of accessibility.

NOTE
What you have with your template so far is really only the *potential* for semantic layout. If you were to go ahead and put random modules in random locations, you would have a mess. An important consideration for CMS sites is that a template is only as good as the population of the content. This often trips up designers who are trying to validate their sites.

Notice that you use the first of a number of commands specific to Joomla to create this output:

```
<body>
<?php echo $app->getCfg('sitename');?><br />
<jdoc:include type="modules" name="top" />
<jdoc:include type="modules" name="left" />
<jdoc:include type="modules" name="breadcrumbs" />
<jdoc:include type="component" />
<jdoc:include type="modules" name="right" />
<jdoc:include type="modules" name="footer" />
<jdoc:include type="modules" name="debug" />
</body>
```

The PHP `echo` statement simply outputs a string from the `configuration.php` file. Here, you use the site name; you could as easily use the following:

```
The name of this site is <?php echo $mainframe->getCfg('sitename');?><br />
The administrator email is <?php echo $mainframe->getCfg('mailfrom');?><br />
This template is in the <?php echo $this->template?> directory<br />
The URL is <?php echo JURI::base();?>
```

The `jdoc` statement inserts various types of XHTML output, from either modules or components.

This line inserts the output from a component. What component it is will be determined by the linked menu item:

```
<jdoc:include type="component" />
```

This line inserts the output for a module location:

```
<jdoc:include type="modules" name="right" />
```

This line generates content for all modules that have their position set to `right`. The content generated for those modules is placed in the page in the order set in the Order column of the Module Manager.

This is the full syntax:

```
<jdoc:include type="modules" name="location" style="option" />
```

We'll look at the various options for styles in the section "Modules in Templates," later in this chapter.

> **960TEMPLATETUTORIALSTEP1**
> At this point, you have a very bare template.
>
> I have created an installable template that is available from www.joomlabook.
> com: `960TemplateTutorialStep1.zip`.
>
> By opening this file, you can install a template that has only two files, `index.php` and
> `templateDetails.xml`. In these files, I removed references to other files to give barebones
> output with no CSS. This is a useful diagnostic template; you can install it and track errors
> that are occurring with a component or module.

Using CSS to Create a Tableless Layout: CSSTemplateTutorialStep2

In this section, you will use pure CSS to make a three-column layout for the Joomla template. You will also be making it a "fixed" layout. There are three main types of web page layouts—fixed, fluid, and jello—and they all refer to how the width of the page is controlled.

A fixed layout has the width set to some fixed value. A fluid layout can grow and shrink to the browser window, and a jello layout is fluid but between some minimum and maximum values.

A few years ago, fluid width templates were all the rage. Accessibility guys loved them, and it was cool to grab the corner of your browser window and see all that content slide around.

But now, I don't make fluid templates, but focus on fixed width templates. I firmly believe they are the best fit on today's Web. Four years ago, many people were still using 800px width screens. The main point of a fluid width was that you could have a web page that looked okay in a 1024px screen, but still could shrink down to the smaller screens still used.

Now, the trend in screens is the opposite. People are getting huge screens; 32% of people browsing Joomlashack.com are doing so with resolutions over 1440px!

With these big screens and a fluid width layout, you get a new problem—readability. Studies have shown that readability onscreen drops off as you go over 960px. So a fluid width will fill that big screen and a) look daft and b) slow down your reading.

A typical design might use tables to lay out the page. Tables are useful as a quick solution in that you just have to set the width of the columns as percentages. However, tables also have several drawbacks. For example, tables have a lot of extra code compared to CSS layouts. This leads to longer load times (which surfers don't like) and poorer performance in search engines. The code can roughly double in size, not just with markup but also with "spacer GIFs," which are 1x1 transparent images placed in each cell of the table to keep the cells from collapsing. Even big companies sometimes fall into the table trap.

There are a couple major problems with a site using tables for layout:

- They are difficult to maintain. To change something, you have to figure out what all the table tags, such as `<tr>` and `<td>`, are doing. With CSS, there are just a few lines to inspect.

- The content cannot be source ordered. Many web surfers do not see web pages on a browser. Those viewing with a text browser or screen reader read the page from the top-left corner to the bottom right. This means that they first view everything in the header and left column (for a three-column layout) before they get to the middle column, where the important stuff is located. A CSS layout, on the other hand, allows for "source-ordered" content, which means the content can be rearranged in the code/source. Perhaps your most important site visitor is Google, and it uses a screen reader for all intents and purposes.

THE LEAST YOU NEED TO KNOW

Modern web design uses CSS rather than tables to position elements. It's difficult to learn but worth the investment. There are many (non-Joomla) resources available to help you.

When it comes to CSS layouts, there has been a trend toward what have been coined *frameworks*. The idea is that a consistent set of CSS is used to create the layout, and then that set is maintained for various issues like browser compatibility. For this template we are going to adopt the 960 grid system developed by Nathan Smith (http://960.gs/). At its most basic, your template might look as shown in Figure 9.4. It's still not very exciting, but let's look at what the different parts are all about.

In Figure 9.4, each column—left, middle, and right—is given its own element and grid size. With the 960 grid system, you merely have to specify with a class how big you want the grid to be. In this example, I am using a 12-column grid, so for the header to run across the full width of 960px, in the `index.php` use:

```
<div id="header" class="container_12">.
```

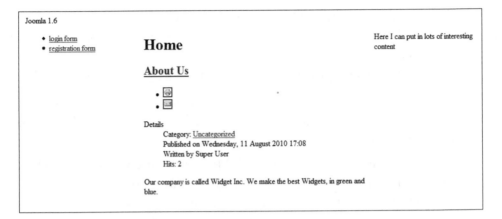

FIGURE 9.4   Basic template layout.

For our three columns, we add grids inside a container like this:

```
<div id="content" class="container_12">
  <div id="" class="grid_3 ">
    <jdoc:include type="modules" name="left" />
  </div>
  <div id="" class="grid_6">
    <jdoc:include type="modules" name="breadcrumbs" />
    <jdoc:include type="component" />
  </div>
  <div id="" class="grid_3">
    <jdoc:include type="modules" name="right" />
  </div>
</div>
```

Notice that there is already some breathing room to the content with a 10px column spacing, commonly called *gutter*. This is all automatically done by the clever 960 CSS grid framework, and all browser issues (yes, we mean you, Internet Explorer) are dealt with.

NOTE
The 960 grid works only in "modern browsers." These are defined as A grade http://developer.yahoo.com/yui/articles/gbs/.

The `<body>` code for `index.php` is as follows:

```
<body>
<div id="header" class="container_12">
  <?php echo $app->getCfg('sitename');?><br />
  <jdoc:include type="modules" name="top" />
</div>
<div id="content" class="container_12">
  <div id="sidebar" class="grid_3 ">
    <jdoc:include type="modules" name="left" />
  </div>
  <div id="maincolumn" class="grid_6">
    <jdoc:include type="modules" name="breadcrumbs" />
    <jdoc:include type="component" />
  </div>
  <div id="sidebar-2" class="grid_3">
    <jdoc:include type="modules" name="right" />
  </div>
</div>
<div id="footer" class="container_12">
  <jdoc:include type="modules" name="footer" />
</div>
<jdoc:include type="modules" name="debug" />
</body>
```

In this example, I renamed the CSS file to `layout.css`. With the 960 grid framework, we will rarely need to touch this file and can compress it as much as possible. The critical parts of the `layout.css` file look like this:

```
.container_12 {
margin-left:auto;
margin-right:auto;
width:960px;
}
.alpha {
margin-left:0 !important;
}
.omega {
margin-right:0 !important;
}
.grid_1,.grid_2,.grid_3,.grid_4,.grid_5,.grid_6,.grid_7,.grid_8,.grid_9,
.grid_10,.grid_11,.grid_12,.grid_12 {
```

```
display:inline;
float:left;
position:relative;
margin-left:10px;
margin-right:10px;
}
.container_12 .grid_1 {
width:60px;
}
.container_12 .grid_2 {
width:140px;
}
.container_12 .grid_3 {
width:220px;
}
.container_12 .grid_4 {
width:300px;
}
.container_12 .grid_5 {
width:380px;
}
.container_12 .grid_6 {
width:460px;
}
.container_12 .grid_7 {
width:540px;
}
.container_12 .grid_8 {
width:620px;
}
.container_12 .grid_9 {
width:700px;
}
.container_12 .grid_10 {
width:780px;
}
.container_12 .grid_11 {
width:860px;
}
.container_12 .grid_12 {
width:940px;
}
```

Quite simply, everything is floated left, and the various grid sizes are set based on their desired width. It's a 12-column grid, so, for example `grid_6` means six columns, which would be 460px—the full width minus the padding. This simple layout is a good one to use for learning about how to use CSS with Joomla because it shows two of the advantages of CSS over table-based layouts: It is less code, and it is easier to maintain.

However, this simple layout is ordered in the code in the sequence in which you see content on the screen. It is not "source ordered" to place the most important content at the beginning of the generated HTML source yet still have the same viewer-ordered appearance onscreen, with the left column displayed before (that is, to the left of) the center column.

Source-ordered layouts perform better for SEO than do layouts where the important content occurs late in the code. From a Joomla site perspective, the important content is that which comes from the mainbody component. For now, to keep the CSS simple, we'll stick with this viewer-ordered layout, and we'll change to source-ordered layout later in the chapter. Many commercial templates, for example, Joomlashack's, develop this source-ordered concept further.

Default CSS

So far, all the CSS has been only about layout, which makes a plain page. So let's add some formatting, placing the CSS in a new file called `typography.css`. Remember to add it to the `index.php` file!

As you begin working on typography with CSS, you should set some overall styles and include a simple *global reset*:

```
/*Compass Design typography css */

* {
    margin:0;
    padding:0;
    }

h1,h2,h3,h4,h5,h6,p,blockquote,form,label,ul,ol,dl,fieldset,address {
    margin: 0.5em 0;
    }

li,dd {
    margin-left:1em;
    }
```

```
fieldset {
    padding:.5em;
    }

body {
    font-size:76%;
    font-family:Verdana, Arial, Helvetica, sans-serif;
    line-height:1.3;
    }
```

The purpose of a global reset is to override the default settings that are different in every browser and get to a clean, consistent starting point, regardless of which browser the page is being displayed on. Everything is given a zero margin and padding, and then all block-level elements are given a bottom and a bottom margin. This helps achieve browser consistency. (The first CSS selector above is called the *star selector*, and it acts as a universal selector even in Internet Explorer 6.) You can read more about the global reset at www.clagnut.com/blog/1287/ and www.leftjustified.net/journal/2004/10/19/global-ws-reset/.

You set the font size to 76% to try to get more consistent font sizes across browsers. All font sizes are then set in ems. Setting `line-height:1.3` helps readability. When you set fonts and line heights in ems, the pages are more accessible because the viewers will be able to resize the fonts to their own preferences, and the pages will reflow and remain readable. This is discussed further at www.thenoodleincident.com/tutorials/typography/template.html.

If you were to add some background colors to the header, sidebars, and content containers, you would see something like what is shown in Figure 9.5.

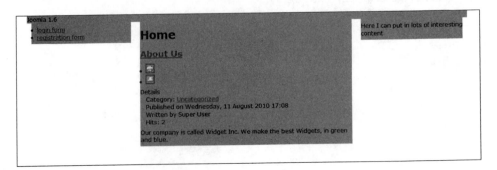

FIGURE 9.5 A basic template with typography.

Notice that the side columns do not reach the footer. This is because they extend only as far as their content; where the space is white on the left and on the right, the side columns don't exist.

If you have a template that has a white background for all three columns, this is no problem. You will use this approach and will have boxes around the modules. If you want equal-height columns that are colored or have boxes, you have to use some technique to give the columns an equal height. One common solution is to use a JavaScript script to calculate and set the heights on the fly.

Modules in Templates

When a module is called in the `index.php` file, there are several options for how it is displayed. The syntax is as follows:

```
<jdoc:include type="modules" name="location" style="option" />
```

The style, which is optional, is defined in `templates/system/html/modules.php`. Currently, the default `modules.php` file contains the following layout options: `table`, `horz`, `xhtml`, `rounded`, and `none`. Let's take a brief glimpse at the lines of code needed for each of these options:

`OPTION="table"` (default display) modules are displayed in a column. The following shows the output from Joomla if we use the `"table"` option. Note the PHP statements would be replaced by actual content:

```
<table cellpadding="0" cellspacing="0" class="moduletable<?php echo $params-
➥>get('moduleclass_sfx'); ?>">
    <?php if ($module->showtitle != 0) : ?>
        <tr>
            <th valign="top">
                <?php echo $module->title; ?>
            </th>
        </tr>
    <?php endif; ?>
        <tr>
            <td>
                <?php echo $module->content; ?>
            </td>
        </tr>
        </table>
```

OPTION="horz" makes the modules appear horizontally. Each module is output in the cell of a wrapper table. The following shows the output from Joomla if we use the "horz" option:

```
<table cellspacing="1" cellpadding="0" border="0" width="100%">
    <tr>
        <td valign="top">
            <?php modChrome_table($module, $params, $attribs); ?>
        </td>
    </tr>
</table>
```

OPTION="xhtml" makes modules appear as simple div elements, with the title in an H3 tag. The following shows the output from Joomla if we use the "xhtml" option:

```
<div class="moduletable<?php echo $params->get('moduleclass_sfx'); ?>">
        <div class="moduletable<?php echo $params->get('moduleclass_sfx'); ?>">
        <?php if ($module->showtitle != 0) : ?>
            <h3><?php echo $module->title; ?></h3>
        <?php endif; ?>
            <?php echo $module->content; ?>
        </div>
```

OPTION="rounded" makes modules appear in a format that allows, for example, stretchable rounded corners. If $style is used, the name of the <div> changes from moduletable to module. The following shows the output from Joomla if we use the "rounded" option:

```
<div class="module<?php echo $params->get('moduleclass_sfx'); ?>">
            <div>
            <div>
            <div>
                <?php if ($module->showtitle != 0) : ?>
                    <h3><?php echo $module->title; ?></h3>
                <?php endif; ?>
                <?php echo $module->content; ?>
            </div>
            </div>
            </div>
    </div>
```

OPTION="none" makes modules appear as raw output containing no element and no title. Here is an example:

```
echo $module->content;
```

As you can see, the CSS options (xhtml and rounded) are much leaner in code, which makes it easier to style the web pages. I don't recommend using the options (suffixes) table (default) or horz unless absolutely needed.

If you examine the modules.php file shown earlier, you will see all these options that exist for modules. It's easy to add your own; this is part of the new templating power of Joomla 1.6.

To develop a template, you can put the module style xhtml on all your modules in index.php:

```
<body>
<div id="header" class="container_12">
  <?php echo $app->getCfg('sitename');?><br />
  <jdoc:include type="modules" name="top" style="xhtml" />
</div>
<div class="clear"></div>
<div id="content" class="container_12">
  <div id="sidebar" class="grid_3 ">
    <jdoc:include type="modules" name="left"style="xhtml"  />
  </div>
  <div id="maincolumn" class="grid_6">
    <jdoc:include type="modules" name="breadcrumbs" style="xhtml" />
    <jdoc:include type="component" />
  </div>
  <div id="sidebar-2" class="grid_3">
    <jdoc:include type="modules" name="right" style="xhtml" />
  </div>
</div>
<div class="clear"></div>
<div id="footer" class="container_12">
  <jdoc:include type="modules" name="footer" style="xhtml" />
</div>
<jdoc:include type="modules" name="debug" />
</body>
```

NOTE
You cannot put these module styles on `<jdoc:include type="component" />` because it is not a module.

THE LEAST YOU NEED TO KNOW
In Joomla 1.6, you can completely customize the output of modules, or you can use the prebuilt output by setting style options for each module position. All these options are referred to as module *chrome*.

Let's remove the background from the layout `divs` and add some CSS to style the modules with a border and a background for the module titles.

We add the following to the typography. Your CSS file should now look like this:

```css
#header{
    font-size:2em;
    }
#footer{
    border-top: 1px solid #999;
    }
a{
    text-decoration:none;
    }
a:hover{
    text-decoration:underline;
    }
h1,.componentheading{
    font-size:1.7em;
    }
h2,.contentheading{
    font-size:1.5em;
    }
h3{
    font-size:1.3em;
    }
h4{
    font-size:1.2em;
    }
```

```
h5{
    font-size:1.1em;
    }
h6{
    font-size:1em;
    font-weight:bold;
    }
#footer,.small,.createdate,.modifydate,.mosimage_caption{
    font:0.8em Arial,Helvetica,sans-serif;
    color:#999;
    }
.moduletable{
    margin-bottom:1em;
    padding:0 10px; /*padding for inside text*/ border:1px #CCC solid;
    }
.moduletable h3{
    background:#666;
    color:#fff;
    padding:0.25em 0;
    text-align:center;
    font-size:1.1em;
    margin:0 -10px 0.5em -10px;
    /*negative padding to pull h3 back out from .moduletable padding*/
ul.actions li{
float:right;
list-style:none;
border:0;}
ul.actions li a img{
border:0;}
```

Here you have added specific style rules for the modules generated with `style="xhtml"`
and therefore generated each with a `<div>` of class `.moduletable` and having the module's
heading displayed in an `<h3>` tag within that `<div>`.

 NOTE
Several of the menus in the default Joomla installation have the menu suffix _menu
in the module properties. To get everything behaving properly, that parameter has
been deleted in this example.

The typography CSS you've created now produces the result shown in Figure 9.6.

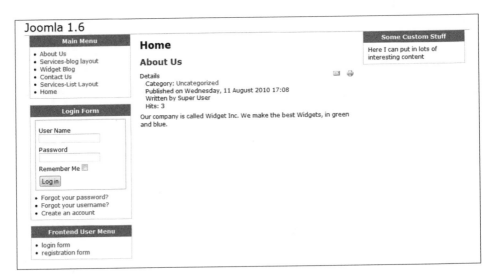

FIGURE 9.6 A basic template with module and title styling.

Menus in Templates

You saw in Chapter 5, "Creating Menus and Navigation," that there are a number of settings for how a menu can be rendered.

Again, using CSS lists rather than tables results in reduced code and easier markup.

One of the other advantages of using CSS for menus is that there is a lot of sample code on various CSS developer sites. Let's look at one of them and see how it can be used.

A web page at maxdesign.com has a selection of more than 30 menus, all using the same underlying code (see www.css.maxdesign.com.au/listamatic/index.htm). It's called the Listamatic. There is a slight difference in the code that you have to change to adapt these menus to Joomla.

These list-based menus use the following general code structure:

```
<div id="navcontainer">
<ul id="navlist">
<li id="active"><a href=" #" id="current">Item one</a></li>
<li><a href="#">Item two</a></li>
<li><a href="#">Item three</a></li>
```

```
<li><a href="#">Item four</a></li>
<li><a href="#">Item five</a></li>
</ul>
</div>
```

This means that there is an enclosing `<div>` called `navcontainer`, and the `<ul>` has an id of `navlist`. To duplicate this effect in Joomla, you need to have some sort of enclosing `<div>`. You can achieve this by using module suffixes. Recall that the output of a module with `style="xhtml"` is as follows:

```
<div class="moduletable">
  <h3>...Module_Title...</h3>
  ...Module_Content...
</div>
```

If you add a module suffix called `menu`, it will get added to the `moduletable` class, like this:

```
<div class="moduletablemenu">
  <h3>...Module_Title...</h3>
  ...Module_Content...
</div>
```

So when choosing a menu from the Listamatic, you would need to replace the `navcontainer` class style in the CSS with `moduletablemenu`.

This use of a module class suffix is useful. It allows different-colored boxes with just a simple change of the module class suffix.

THE LEAST YOU NEED TO KNOW
It's best to always use the `list` option for menu output. You can then make use of many available free resources to obtain the CSS to display a list as a navigation menu.

For your site, say that you want to use List 10 by Mark Newhouse (see www.css.maxdesign.com.au/listamatic/vertical10.htm). Your CSS looks like this:

```
.moduletablemenu{
   padding:0;
   color: #333;
   margin-bottom:1em;
   }
.moduletablemenu h3 {
   background:#666;
   color:#fff;
   padding:0.25em 0;
   text-align:center;
   font-size:1.1em;
   margin:0;
   border-bottom:1px solid #fff;
   }
.moduletablemenu ul{
   list-style: none;
   margin: 0;
   padding: 0;
   }
.moduletablemenu li{
   border-bottom: 1px solid #ccc;
   margin: 0;
   }
.moduletablemenu li a{
   display: block;
   padding: 3px 5px 3px 0.5em;
   border-left: 10px solid #333;
   border-right: 10px solid #9D9D9D;
   background-color:#666;
   color: #fff;
   text-decoration: none;
   }
html>body .moduletablemenu li a {
   width: auto;
   }
.moduletablemenu li a:hover,a#active_menu:link,a#active_menu:visited{
   border-left: 10px solid #1c64d1;
   border-right: 10px solid #5ba3e0;
   background-color: #2586d7;
   color: #fff;
   }
```

You then need to add the module suffix menu (no underscore in this case) to any modules for menus you want styled using this set of CSS rules. This produces a menu like what's shown in Figure 9.7.

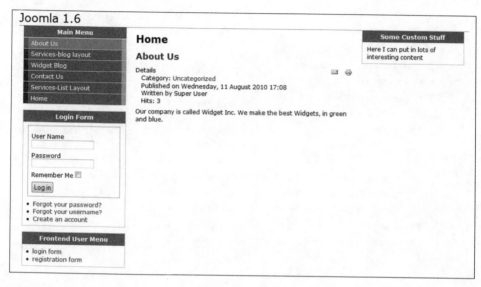

FIGURE 9.7   A basic template with menu styling.

TIP

When trying to get a particular menu to work, create a default Joomla installation and then look at the code that makes up the Main Menu. Copy and paste this code into an HTML editor (such as Dreamweaver). Replace all the links with #, and then you can add CSS rules until you achieve the effect you want. The code for the menu to create the style is as follows:

```
<!DOCTYPE html PUBLIC "-//W3C//DTD XHTML 1.0 Transitional//EN"
"http://www.w3.org/TR/xhtml1/DTD/xhtml1-transitional.dtd">
<html xmlns="http://www.w3.org/1999/xhtml">
<head>
<meta http-equiv="Content-Type" content="text/html;
charset=iso-8859-1" />
<title>Untitled Document</title>
<style type="text/css">
<!--
.moduletablemenu{
```

```
    ...  your menu testing css …


}
-->
</style>
</head>
<body>
<div class="moduletablemenu">
<h3>Main Menu</h3>
<ul class="menu">
    <li id="current" class="active item101"><a href="#">Home</a></li>
    <li class="item2"><a href="#">Joomla! Overview</a></li>
    <li class="item3"><a href="#">What's New in 1.5?</a></li>
    <li class="item4"><a href="#">Joomla! License</a></li>
    <li class="item5"><a href="#">More about Joomla!</a></li>
    <li class="item6"><a href="#">FAQ</a></li>
    <li class="item7"><a href="#">The News</a></li>
    <li class="item8"><a href="#">Web Links</a></li>
    <li class="item9"><a href="#">News Feeds</a></li>
</ul>
</div>
</body>
</html>
```

The CSS is embedded instead of linked to make editing easier. Also note that the class of `active item101` has the 101 determined by the ID of that menu item. It will be different for other menu items.

Hiding Columns

So far, you have a layout such that you always have three columns, regardless of whether there is any content positioned in those columns. From the perspective of a CMS template, this is not very useful. In a static site, the content would never change, but you want to give your site administrators the ability to put content in any column, without having to worry about editing CSS layouts. You want to be able to turn off a column automatically or collapse it if there is no content to display there.

Joomla 1.6 provides an easy way to count the number of modules generating content for a particular position so that you can add some PHP testing of these counts and hide any empty columns or similar unused `<div>` containers and adjust the layout accordingly. This PHP `if` test syntax for modules is as follows:

```
<?php if($this->countModules('condition')) : ?>
   do something
<?php else : ?>
   do something else
<?php endif; ?>
```

There are four possible conditions. For example, let's count the number of modules in Figure 9.7. You could insert this code somewhere in `index.php`:

```
left=<?php echo $this->countModules('left');?><br />
left and right=<?php echo $this->countModules('left and right');?><br />
left or right=<?php echo $this->countModules('left or right');?><br />
left + right=<?php echo $this->countModules('left + right');?>
```

So if we inserted this code into our template, we might get the following results with the sample Joomla content:

- **countModules('left')**—This returns 3 because there are three modules on the left.

- **countModules('left and right')**—This returns 1 because there is a module in the left and right positions. Both tests are true (>0).

- **countModules('left or right')**—This returns 1 because there is a module in the left or right position. Both tests are true (>0).

- **countModules('left + right')**—This returns 4 because it adds together the modules in the left and right positions.

In this situation, you need to use the function that allows you to count the modules present in a specific location (for example, the right column). If there is no content published in the right column, you can adjust the column sizes to fill that space.

There are several ways to do this. You could put the conditional statement in the body to not show the content and then have a different style for the content, based on what columns are there. We are going to take advantage of the grid system and simply pass the sizes of the grid based on some calculations.

In the header, let's define a couple of variables to make sure they have some default value.

```
$leftcolgrid    = "3";
$rightcolgrid   = "3";
```

In the HTML of the template, we can then use these variables to set the `grid` class:

```
<div id="content" class="container_12">
  <div id="sidebar" class="grid_<?php echo $leftcolgrid;?>">
    <jdoc:include type="modules" name="left"style="xhtml"  />
  </div>
  <div id="maincolumn" class="grid_<?php echo
➥(12-$leftcolgrid-$rightcolgrid);?>">
    <jdoc:include type="modules" name="breadcrumbs" style="xhtml" />
    <jdoc:include type="component" />
  </div>
  <div id="sidebar-2" class="grid_<?php echo $rightcolgrid;?>">
    <jdoc:include type="modules" name="right" style="xhtml" />
  </div>
</div>
```

You'll notice we are echoing out the `colgrid` values and then doing a simple calculation to find the main column, as we know they must total 12.

We then can use the `countModules` function to find some value. In our head we insert:

```
<?php
if ($this->countModules('left') == 0):?>
<?php $leftcolgrid = "0";?>
<?php endif; ?>
<?php
if ($this->countModules('right') == 0):?>
<?php $rightcolgrid = "0";?>
<?php endif; ?>
```

Note that we are checking to see whether the left and right positions have zero modules as we have already set the default grid size to 3. We could have also have done this check with a true/false check rather than a numerical value (zero).

TIP
When you try to troubleshoot your conditional statements, you can add a line of code to index.php, like this, to show what the computed value is:

This content column is `<?php echo $(12-$leftcolgrid-$rightcolgrid); ?>`% wide

You are halfway there, but now you have expanded the width of the center column to accommodate any empty (soon to be hidden) side columns.

Hiding Module Code

When creating collapsible columns, it is good practice to set up the modules not to be generated if there is no content there. If you don't do this, the pages will have empty <div>s in them, which can lead to cross-browser issues.

To not generate an empty <div>, you use the following if statement:

```
<?php if($this->countModules('left')) : ?>
   <div id="sidebar" class="grid_<?php echo $leftcolgrid;?>">
     <jdoc:include type="modules" name="left"style="xhtml"  />
   </div>
<?php endif; ?>
```

When you use this code, if there is nothing published in position left, then <div id="sidebar">; also, everything within it will not be included in the generated page.

Using these techniques for the left and right columns, your index.php file now looks as follows:

> **NOTE**
>
> We also need to add an include for the breadcrumbs module, the module that shows the current page and pathway. Note that to have breadcrumbs, the code for that position needs to be included in the index.php file and also breadcrumbs published as a module.

```
<?php
/**
 * @copyright    Copyright (C) 2005 - 2010 Barrie North.
 * @license      GPL
 */
defined('_JEXEC') or die;
$app = JFactory::getApplication();
$leftcolgrid     = "3";
$rightcolgrid    = "3";
?>
<!DOCTYPE html PUBLIC "-//W3C//DTD XHTML 1.0 Transitional//EN"
➥"http://www.w3.org/TR/xhtml1/DTD/xhtml1-transitional.dtd">
```

```
<html xmlns="http://www.w3.org/1999/xhtml" xml:lang="<?php echo $this->language;
➥?>" lang="<?php echo $this->language; ?>" >
<head>
<jdoc:include type="head" />
<link rel="stylesheet" href="<?php echo $this->baseurl
➥?>/templates/system/css/system.css" type="text/css" />
<link rel="stylesheet" href="<?php echo $this->baseurl
➥?>/templates/system/css/general.css" type="text/css" />
<link rel="stylesheet" href="<?php echo $this->baseurl ?>/templates/<?php
➥echo $this->template ?>/css/layout.css" type="text/css" />
<link rel="stylesheet" href="<?php echo $this->baseurl ?>/templates/<?php
➥echo $this->template ?>/css/typography.css" type="text/css" />
<?php
if ($this->countModules('left') == 0):?>
<?php $leftcolgrid    = "0";?>
<?php endif; ?>
<?php
if ($this->countModules('right') == 0):?>
<?php $rightcolgrid   = "0";?>
<?php endif; ?>
</head>
<body>
<div id="header" class="container_12">
  <?php echo $app->getCfg('sitename');?><br />
  <jdoc:include type="modules" name="top" style="xhtml" />
</div>
<div class="clear"></div>
<div id="content" class="container_12">
<?php if($this->countModules('left')) : ?>
  <div id="sidebar" class="grid_<?php echo $leftcolgrid;?>">
    <jdoc:include type="modules" name="left"style="xhtml"  />
  </div>
  <?php endif; ?>
  <div id="maincolumn" class="grid_<?php echo
➥(12-$leftcolgrid-$rightcolgrid);?>">
    <jdoc:include type="modules" name="breadcrumbs" style="xhtml" />
    <jdoc:include type="component" />
  </div>
  <?php if($this->countModules('right')) : ?>
  <div id="sidebar-2" class="grid_<?php echo $rightcolgrid;?>">
    <jdoc:include type="modules" name="right" style="xhtml" />
  </div>
  <?php endif; ?>
</div>
<div class="clear"></div>
```

```
<div id="footer" class="container_12">
  <jdoc:include type="modules" name="footer" style="xhtml" />
</div>
<jdoc:include type="modules" name="debug" />
</body>
</html>
```

THE LEAST YOU NEED TO KNOW

Elements such as columns or module locations can be hidden (or collapsed) when there is no content in them. You can accomplish this by using conditional PHP statements to control whether the code for a column is generated and also that links other content to different CSS styles; you can either modify a class name or load an entire alternative CSS file.

TIP

There are several names associated with modules in Joomla: `banner`, `left`, `right`, `user1`, `footer`, and so on. One important thing to realize is that the names do not necessarily correspond to any particular location. The location of a module is completely controlled by the template designer, as you have seen. It's customary to place a module in a location that is connected to the name, but it is not required.

The basic template created in this section shows some of the fundamental principles of creating a Joomla template.

960TEMPLATETUTORIALSTEP2

You now have a basic but functional template. Some simple typography has been added, but more importantly, you have created a pure CSS layout that has dynamic collapsible columns.

I have created an installable template that is available from www.joomlabook.com: `960TemplateTutorialStep2.zip`.

Now that you have the basics done, you can create a *slightly* more attractive template, using the techniques you have learned.

Making a Real Joomla! 1.6 Template: 960TemplateTutorialStep3

You need to start with a comp. A *comp*, short for *composition*, is a drawing or mockup of a proposed design that will be the basis of the template. In this section, we'll use a design by Dan Cedarholm from his book *Bulletproof Web Design* (see Figure 9.8). I heartily recommend this book, as it's provides an outstanding foundation in some CSS techniques that are useful in creating Joomla templates. We'll use some of these techniques to build this real-word template.

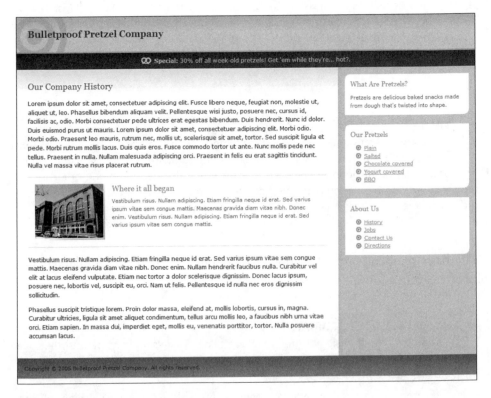

FIGURE 9.8   A design from *Bulletproof Web Design*.

Slicing and Dicing

The next step in the process is slicing. You need to use your graphics program to create small sliced images that can be used in the template. It's important to pay attention to how the elements can resize if needed. (My graphics application of choice is Fireworks because I find it better suited to web design—as opposed to print design—than Photoshop.)

This process could probably fill a whole book by itself. To get a sense of how to slice up a design, you can look at the images folder and see the slices.

Header

The header image has a faint gradient at the top. We put the image in as an untiled background and then assign a matching fill color behind it. That way, the header can scale vertically if you need it to (for example, if the fonts are resized). You also need to change the color of any type to white so that it shows up on the black background.

Here is the CSS we must add to style the header#header {
```
    border-bottom: 3px solid #87B825;
    background: #B4E637 url(../images/header-bg.gif) repeat-x top left;
    }
#header h1 {
    margin: 0;
    padding: 25px;
    font-family: Georgia, serif;
    font-size: 150%;
    color: #374C0E;
    background: url(../images/bulls-eye.gif) no-repeat top left;
    }
```

You did not use a graphical logo here; you use plain text. The reason is mainly because search engines cannot read images. You could do some nifty image replacement, but I will leave that as an exercise for you to do on your own.

The Banner/Message Module

We use our "top" module location from the last template for a message. To give it some styling, we can add

```
#message {
    font-size: 90%;
    color: #cc9;
    text-align: center;
    background: #404530 url(../images/message-bg.gif) repeat-x top left;
    }
#message .moduletable {
padding:1px 10px;
}
```

The header now looks as shown in Figure 9.9.

FIGURE 9.9 Header image background.

Next, you need to implement a technique to show a background on the side columns.

Column Backgrounds

Recall that when you put a color background on the columns, the color did not extend all the way to the footer. This is because the `div` element—in this case, `sidebar` and `sidebar-2`—is only as tall as the content. It does not grow to fill the containing element. This is a weakness of grid-based systems; we would have to use some JavaScript to get a background on the side columns.

There are many scripts out there that calculate the height of columns and make them equal. We'll use one from Dynamic Drive: http://www.dynamicdrive.com/csslayouts/equalcolumns.js.

Note that we must change the columns/elements referred to in the script to match ours. We are also going to add another containing block element, `"maincolbck"` to hold the yellow faded background for the top of the content in the main column.

Our main content code in the `index.php` looks like this:

```
<div id="content" class="container_12">
<div id="maincolbck">
  <?php if($this->countModules('left')) : ?>
  <div id="sidebar" class="grid_<?php echo $leftcolgrid;?>">
    <jdoc:include type="modules" name="left"style="xhtml" />
  </div>
  <?php endif; ?>
  <div id="maincolumn" class="grid_<?php echo
➥(12-$leftcolgrid-$rightcolgrid);?>">
    <jdoc:include type="modules" name="breadcrumbs" style="xhtml" />
    <jdoc:include type="component" />
  </div>
```

```
<?php if($this->countModules('right')) : ?>
<div id="sidebar-2" class="grid_<?php echo $rightcolgrid;?>">
  <jdoc:include type="modules" name="right" style="xhtml" />
</div>
<?php endif; ?>
</div>
<div class="clear">
</div>
```

Let's also put a background onto the footer element while we are adding these. Our added CSS is

```
#content {
    font-size: 95%;
    color: #333;
    line-height: 1.5em;
    background: url(../images/content-bg.gif) repeat-x top left;
    }
#maincolbck {
    background: url(../images/wrap-bg.gif) repeat-y top right;
    }

#footer {
    background: #828377 url(../images/footer-bg.gif) repeat-x top left;
    padding:1px 0;
    }
```

This now gives us a gradient background for the right column:

```
#footer {
    background: #828377 url(../images/footer-bg.gif) repeat-x top left;
    padding:1px 0;
    }
```

> **NOTE**
> As is, the right column background is on a `div` that contains all three columns, so it will be there even if there is no actual content in the right column. It would be easy to make this template a little more robust and flexible to enclose the opening and closing of the `div` with a conditional statement that checks whether there are any modules in the right column.

Flexible Modules

When designing modules, you need to consider whether they will stretch vertically (if more content is in them), horizontally, or both. Here we use the principles of bulletproof design contained in Dan's book. We use a couple of simple background images to create a module background that stretches in both axes. We place one background on the containing div, and the other one for the opposite corner on the h3 header.

As this design does not have a horizontal menu, we also take care of menu styling as we consider the side modules.

Our CSS looks like this:

```css
#sidebar .moduletable,#sidebar-2 .moduletable {
    margin: 10px 0 10px 0;
    padding: 0 0 12px 0;
    font-size: 85%;
    line-height: 1.5em;
    color: #666;
    background: #fff url(../images/box-b.gif) no-repeat bottom right;
    }
#sidebar  h3,#sidebar-2   h3 {
    margin: 0;
    padding: 12px;
    font-family: Georgia, serif;
    font-size: 140%;
    font-weight: normal;
    color: #693;
    background: url(../images/box-t.gif) no-repeat top left;
    }
#sidebar p,#sidebar-2 p,sidebar ul,#sidebar-2 ul {
    margin: 0;
    padding: 0 12px;
    }
sidebar ul li,#sidebar-2 ul li {
    margin: 0 0 0 12px;
    padding: 0 0 0 18px;
    list-style: none;
    background: url(../images/li-bullet.gif) no-repeat 0 3px;
    }
```

Now let's focus on some of the typography.

Typography

The CSS for typography is greatly simplified in Joomla 1.6. Earlier versions of Joomla had unique classes for various parts of the output, such as "contentheading". In Joomla 1.6, the output uses more recognized classes like H1, H2, and so on, and is completely tableless.

Let's style these elements:

```css
h1, h2, h3, h4, h5, h6 {
    font-family: Georgia, serif;
    font-size: 150%;
    color: #663;
    font-weight: normal;
}
h1 {font-size:2em;line-height:1;margin-bottom:0.5em;}
h2 {font-size:1.5em;margin-bottom:0.75em;}
h3 {font-size:1.25em;line-height:1;margin-bottom:1em;}
h4 {font-size:1.1em;line-height:1.25;margin-bottom:1.25em;}
```

We can also add some handy icon treatment for special classes that can be applied to content:

```css
p.info {
    background: #F8FAFC url(../images/info.png) center no-repeat;
    background-position: 15px 50%; /* x-pos y-pos */
    text-align: left;
    padding: 5px 20px 5px 45px;
    border-top: 2px solid #B5D4FE;
    border-bottom: 2px solid #B5D4FE;
}

p.warn {
    background: #FFF7C0 url(../images/warn.png) center no-repeat;
    background-position: 15px 50%; /* x-pos y-pos */
    text-align: left;
    padding: 5px 20px 5px 45px;
    border-top: 2px solid #F7D229;
    border-bottom: 2px solid #F7D229;
}
```

```
p.alert {
    background: #FBEEF1 url(../images/exc.png) center no-repeat;
    background-position: 15px 50%; /* x-pos y-pos */
    text-align: left;
    padding: 5px 20px 5px 45px;
    border-top: 2px solid #FEABB9;
    border-bottom: 2px solid #FEABB9;
}

ul.checklist li {
    list-style:none;
    background: url(../images/tick.png) no-repeat 0 4px;
    line-height: 24px;
    padding-left: 20px;
    }
```

The finished template should look as shown in Figure 9.10.

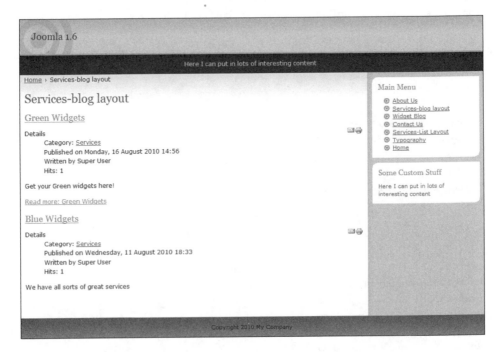

FIGURE 9.10   An advanced template with typography.

THE LEAST YOU NEED TO KNOW
Creating a production Joomla template is more a question of graphical design and
CSS manipulation than some special Joomla knowledge.

960TEMPLATETUTORIALSTEP3
You now have a template based on a comp (or design). Some simple typography
has been added, but more importantly, you have created a pure CSS layout that
has dynamic collapsible columns and slick backgrounds with gradients.

I created an installable template that is available from www.joomlabook.com:
`960TemplateTutorialStep3.zip`.

Summary

This chapter worked through four examples of templates, each time increasing the
complexity and features. Here are the key points we looked at in this chapter:

- Modern websites separate content from presentation by using a technology
  known as Cascading Style Sheets (CSS). In Joomla, a template and its CSS
  files control the presentation of the content.

- When creating a template, it helps to have Joomla "running" on a localhost
  server so you can make changes at the file level with your favorite editor and
  refresh the page output in a browser to see the impact.

- Creating valid templates should be a path, not a goal. The idea is to make a
  template as accessible as possible, for humans and spiders, not to achieve a
  badge for valid markup.

- The most basic template simply loads the Joomla modules and mainbody
  component, preferably in source order. Layout and design are part of the CSS,
  not part of the template.

- Modern web design uses CSS rather than tables to position elements. It's difficult to learn but worth the investment. There are many (non-Joomla) resources
  available to help.

- Joomla consistently outputs specific elements, IDs, and classes in the code of a
  web page. These can be predicted and used to style the design using CSS.

- The output of modules can be completely customized, or you can use the pre-built output options, such as `xhtml`. All these options are called *module chrome*.

- It's best to always use the fully expanded `list` options for menu output. You can then use many free resources on the Web for the CSS that will style and animate your menu.

- Elements such as columns or module locations can be hidden (or collapsed) when there is no content in them. This is done using conditional PHP statements that control whether any code associated with unused modules and their container is included in the generated page; it is also done to link to different CSS styles to adjust the layout accordingly.

- Creating a production Joomla template is more a question of graphical design and CSS manipulation than some special Joomla knowledge.

Chapter 10

Creating a School Site with Joomla!

In This Chapter

School websites tend to be medium to large in size. One of the defining character-istics of Joomla is that it is powerful and flexible, but it can be time-intensive to set up. This chapter provides an extensive guide to creating and setting up a school website using the Joomla CMS. If you are following along and building a site, it's best to start the chapter with a fresh Joomla installation with no content. This chapter covers the following topics:

- Why do you need a school website?
- What features do you need on a school site?
- Where can you get a school template?
- What is the best way to organize the content structure for a school website?
- What is the relationship between categories and the menu?
- How can you best use the Featured Article component?
- What extra functionality can you easily add to the default Joomla installation?

Why Do You Need a School Website?

I started my Internet career as a teacher and the technology coordinator for a small school in Vermont almost ten years ago. One of the things I was responsible for, of course, was the school website. When I think of the time and effort that could have been saved had a CMS such as Joomla been available back then, it makes me realize how lucky schools are today. I wonder how many realize that such an astonishingly powerful tool to build a website is available virtually for free.

A school is an organization that is well suited for having a comprehensive website. Whereas twentieth-century websites were about one-way communication between the website and the readers, in the twenty-first century Web 2.0 world, websites need to be about interaction and two-way communication. What makes a school website interesting is that there are clearly defined stakeholder groups, each with unique needs with respect to communication.

A school website is unique in that there is a clearly defined body of content, and there are a number of different stakeholders that need to get to that content. The key to a successful school website is having different paths to the information, based on the groups. Let's look at these and their needs.

Students

Sometimes students are relegated to being lesser users on a school website. This is a critical mistake—not only because students are the group most invested in the school (it's their education, after all), but they are also the group most likely to adopt web technology.

Students' lives frequently revolve around three areas: academics, athletics, and activities. Students need easy access to these areas of their school site. In addition, the school might want to make sure certain key information—such as guidance help or graduation requirements—is easy to find.

Students are primarily consumers of information on their school website. However, remember that a healthy website should also have mechanisms for interaction.

> **TIP**
> With supervision, students can be prolific contributors to a site, and the cost of that labor is measured in pizzas.

Teachers and Administrators

A school website can make a huge difference in the way a teacher can communicate and educate—from publishing course notes, to homework, to events, and even, for the adventurous (and with appropriate security), class grades.

A big challenge for teachers is that adding the Web to their toolbox can be overwhelming. Always busy, teachers need time and help from IT staff to successfully use their website. Some teachers will be early adopters, and others will probably always struggle, but a commitment to professional development for the teaching staff is critical to implementing a successful school website.

Parents

A school that is able to engage the parents in its community is one where the students are more successful. To that end, a website can be a powerful tool.

The initial goal should be to make a website as sticky and useful as possible for the parents. A principal's blog, email news, calendars of events, and student work are some examples of many things that would keep parents coming back to the site. Ultimately, the goal is to have parents contributing to the site, initially focusing on early adopters and those already involved, such as parent associations.

Potential Students and Their Parents

Many school sites are driven by marketing: They want to attract applicants and retain students. A vibrant website suggests a vibrant and active student community and reinforces a student's decision to enroll and stay the course.

> **THE LEAST YOU NEED TO KNOW**
> A website for a large organization such as a school needs to meet the needs of diverse groups. This can make organizing its content and functions challenging.

What Features Do You Need on a School Site?

With more than 5,000 extensions available on the official Joomla extension site (extensions.joomla.org), it's easy to add everything and the kitchen sink to a website. There are even specialized components for lunch menus! A key consideration for a school website is security, but some extensions are not 100% secure, so you need to be careful about which ones you choose.

What follows is a discussion of potential solutions for common features for a school website. Bear in mind that this list is not a guarantee of security. School webmasters who are using Joomla should subscribe to the security feed at Joomla.org (developer.joomla.org/security.html).

In no particular order, common functionality and extensions for a school website might include the following:

- User registration
- Event calendar
- Downloadable documents
- Staff directory

- Email newsletter
- RSS
- Random images
- Sitemap

We look at these at the end of the chapter, consider options, and then briefly explore a possible solution for each.

Before you get too far ahead of yourself, though, you need to create a fresh Joomla installation with no sample content. The first step is to install a template.

Downloading and Installing a School Template

At www.joomlabook.com, you can grab a free template, called Fresh, that you need for this chapter. This is a relatively simple template with a horizontal menu and three collapsible columns. But more importantly for us in a school setting, the template has a fully standards compliant tableless layout and is highly accessible (see Figure 10.1).

When you have the Fresh template zip file that you need to install into Joomla, go to Extensions>Extension Manager to get to the Extension Manager. (For more on how to install and manage extensions, see Chapter 6, "Extending Joomla!")

Next, you need to browse to the template zip file and click the Upload File and Install button. When you get a message that says "Install Template: Success," you then need to make this template your default template. You do this through the Template Manager.

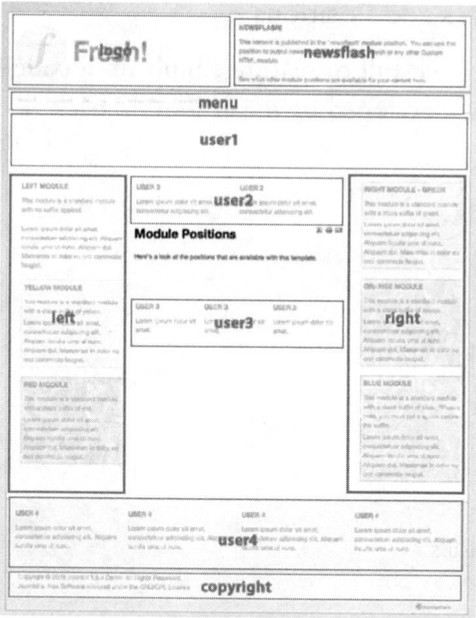

FIGURE 10.1   The Fresh template.

Go to Extensions>Template Manager, select the JS_Fresh template, and click the Make Default button to make this the default template. Viewed in the frontend, your site (empty of content) should look as shown in Figure 10.2.

Wireframe
Joomla
Template
Your Site Slogan

Home

FIGURE 10.2   The Fresh template, empty of content.

Fresh Template Features and Positions

The Fresh template is chock-full of features, built on a code-lean and accessible 960 grid CSS framework first developed by me at Joomlashack:

- Multiple layouts
- 960 grid powered
- Flexible modules
- Suckerfish menu
- SEO-ready template
- Easy SEO-header
- Fast loading
- Source ordered
- W3C valid overrides
- Accessible
- Easy to edit CSS files
- Multibrowser ready

The Fresh template has ten available module positions; we see how to use them shortly:

- **logo**—Reserved for a text or graphic logo
- **newsflash**—High visibility header module
- **menu**—Reserved for horizontal menu
- **user1**—Wide banner position
- **left**—Left vertical column, not reserved
- **right**—Right vertical column, not reserved
- **user2**—Smaller position above main content
- **user3**—Smaller position below main content
- **user4**—Flexible bottom position
- **copyright**—Footer

One powerful feature of this template is that all the userX positions use smart logic to easily adjust the spacing regardless of the number of modules enabled in those positions. Using this strategy, there are actually more than 30 module positions available.

To position the modules (for example, the Main Menu, login, syndicate) in the various template positions, you set the Position parameter in each module. Most of these positions are pretty generic in their potential use. Two, however, were placed with specific locations in mind: The logo module location is really intended for a logo, and the menu module location is intended for horizontal navigation. The newsflash position is a great place for a search box.

Configuring a Logo

The Fresh template offers us three easy options for the logo:

- Use Text
- Use an Image
- Use a Module

All three use a special SEO replacement text feature for SEO. Google sees rich keyword text instead of images. To select which one you want, go to the Fresh template in the Template Manager and choose one in the Logo Type drop-down. We choose Use Text.

We then need to enter values for the Logo Text, Slogan, Logo Grid Size (i.e., width), and Logo Height. The settings I chose can be seen in Figure 10.3.

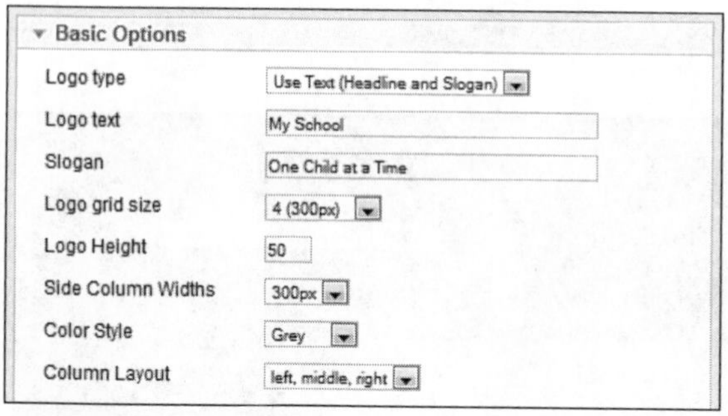

▼ Basic Options	
Logo type	Use Text (Headline and Slogan) ▾
Logo text	My School
Slogan	One Child at a Time
Logo grid size	4 (300px) ▾
Logo Height	50
Side Column Widths	300px ▾
Color Style	Grey ▾
Column Layout	left, middle, right ▾

FIGURE 10.3   Logo options in the Fresh template.

Save your changes.

Configuring the Search Box

If you will use the text search module on your template (for a school site, you really should), you can create a module to go into the newsflash position on the site.

Go to Extensions>Module Manager>New, find the Search module, and select it.

Give the module a title, but make sure the title parameter is set to not show. From the Position parameter drop-down menu, select Newsflash. Click Save and Close. The page should now look as shown in Figure 10.4.

FIGURE 10.4 Configured logo and search modules.

Configuring the Main Horizontal Drop-Down Menu

A website for a large organization such as a school is likely to have many sections, categories, and content articles. This makes it an ideal candidate for drop-down navigation. It's a simple effect in which rolling over a link enables subnavigation (see Figure 10.5).

FIGURE 10.5 A menu drop-down.

Many options exist to achieve this effect using JavaScript. However, there are big problems with using JavaScript in this case. JavaScript links can be difficult to navigate if you are not using a browser or if you have JavaScript turned off. This has big implications for a website's accessibility (viewers using screen readers, for example) and for SEO and search engine spiders.

It might not seem as if a school website needs to worry about SEO, but it does. Schools want their content to be well indexed by search engines so that people, particularly potential students, seeking information can find it easily.

Therefore, instead of using JavaScript, you can use pure CSS to get the same effect. On a screen reader or with JavaScript turned off, these links will look like a simple list of links:

- Academics
  - Science
  - Mathematics
  - Foreign Language
  - History/SS
  - Fine Arts
  - English

THE LEAST YOU NEED TO KNOW

A pure CSS drop-down menu, sometimes called a *suckerfish menu*, is a highly accessible and SEO-friendly way to organize complex navigation.

When Joomla is installed, it starts with the Main Menu and a single home link, as shown in Figure 10.4. However, the default location given for it is not in the right place. You need to move that module into the correct spot for a horizontal menu, as determined by the Fresh template. In this case, it's "menu."

Go to Extensions>Module Manager>Main Menu and change the position to menu. While you're here, you need to set some parameters for your drop-down to work correctly:

- In the Basic Options, set Always Show Submenu Items to Yes.
- Set Show Title to Hide.

- Set End Level to 99 or such (this might change in later beta/revisions/versions).
- In Advanced Options, make sure Menu Class Suffix is blank and set Module Class Suffix to _menu (note the underscore).
- Save and Close.

The menu should now appear at the horizontal position and be prepared for drop-downs. (This template already has the CSS styling rules to implement a multilevel menu.)

Let's now take a detailed look at what is perhaps the most important part of setting up a complex site like this—setting up the site structure, which involves the sections, categories, and navigation.

Organizing Content on a School Website

It is important that you understand some of the basics of how Joomla organizes content and the structure it uses. If necessary, review Chapter 4, "Content Is King: Organizing Your Content."

As mentioned previously, the different groups (students, parents, and teachers) to a certain extent represent different paths to the same core content (academics, athletics, and activities). There will be much more going on in each user group's area, so this structure will form the core of your school website.

As you think about your site design, you should try to use the following principle, which has as its goal to effectively manage a large site with a large number of contributors: Each group/person should have a single main page on the site. So whether it's English teacher Mr. Hardy, the guidance counselor, or the varsity basketball team, we try to have a one-to-one relationship between people/groups and pages.

One of the main reasons to do this is to distribute content generation. This solves two problems: If more people are involved in the content of the site, more people will use the site. Additionally, one person, such as the technology coordinator or webmaster, is not the bottleneck responsible for generating huge amounts of content. So these people take on the role of gatekeepers, as they should be, rather than whole-site creators/maintainers.

The second advantage is that the technology coordinator can start teachers/coaches out small, just one page, and build up their comfort level. Then she can help the early adopters grow the amount of pages they are responsible for on the site.

Using the English department as an example, let's examine how to set up a page. The goal is to have a departmental page that shows the various classes/courses, has a link to that departmental page, and shows some news about the department.

In the drill-down, you want to make sure each course has its own page so that teachers can have meaningful input into what is on pages that relate to them. Thus, the site organization here is as follows:

Category = Academics

Subcategory = English

> Article 1 = A page that will be an article about Freshman English, authored by Mr. Hardy

> Article 2 = A page that will be an article about Sophomore English, authored by Mr. Stevenson

(and so on)

Here's how you set up this single category, subcategory, and the two articles:

1. Go to Content>Category Manager>Add New Category and create a category called Academics. Just give it a title and leave all other fields as is.

2. Go to Content>Category Manager>New and create a category called English—make Academics the parent. Make sure you put in some kind of description in the editor field.

3. Go to Content>Article Manager>Add New Article and create an article called Freshman English—Mr. Hardy and another called Sophomore English—Mr. Stevenson, both in the English subcategory. The Article Manager should look as shown in Figure 10.6 (note the category columns).

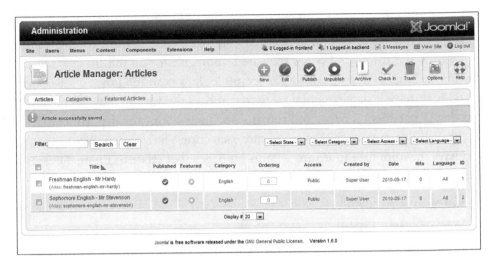

FIGURE 10.6   English Department articles in the Article Manager.

It should be easy to see how this structure can be extended to other parts of the site. Here are two more examples, for athletics and the administration:

Category = Athletics
Subcategory = Basketball
    Article 1 = Ninth Grade Girls
    Article 2 = Tenth Grade Boys
(and so on)

Category = Administration
Subcategory = High School Management Team
    Article 1 = Principal
    Article 2 = Vice Principal
(and so on)

Let's set up the rest of the content categories using the following table:

Category	Subcategories	Articles
Academics	Science	
	Mathematics	
	Foreign Language	
	History/SS	
	Fine Arts	
	English	Freshman English—Mr. Hardy
		Sophomore English—Mr. Stevenson
Athletics	Football	
	Volleyball	
	Track and Field	
	Hockey	
	Basketball	
Activities	Community Outreach	
	Band	
	Student Council	
	Yearbook	
	Chess Club	
Students	Administration	
	Teachers	
	General Info	
	Guidance	
FAQs		

This is a complex organization, but it allows a big site to organize its articles. Key to this example is that a single article is the responsibility of a single individual, whether a teacher or coach.

THE LEAST YOU NEED TO KNOW
There is always more than one way to organize content. It often helps to decide what the articles will be and then build backward into categories.

After you have set up all your categories, the Category Manager should look as shown in Figure 10.7.

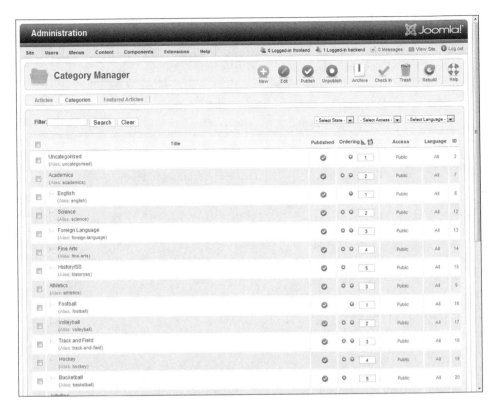

FIGURE 10.7   Completed school categories.

> **NOTE**
> The rationale for some of the category placement might not be immediately obvious, such as the Teachers subcategory in the Students category. But consider who wants to find the information. You could have created a category called Staff, but from a navigation point of view, teachers don't need to find out about themselves—they know who they are! They might want to have that information available for another stakeholder, however. In this case, you can use Students.

This organizational structure was developed based on two factors:

- The goal of having (as far as possible) one person responsible for one page
- Navigation (You'll see how this develops in the next section.)

You now need to create the rest of the horizontal Main Menu.

Creating the Menus

The main horizontal navigation menu for the school site we envisage has links to the categories along the top level and then links to the subcategories as drop-downs. Let's work through an example to see how to set this up.

Going back to the English department, create a link to the Academics categories. Go to Menus>Main Menu>Add New Menu Item.

You want to create a Menu Item that links to the Academics categories and call it Academics. This Menu Item should be a category list layout and generate a page that has a list of all the subcategories in that category. Now you can create Menu Items that drop down under Academics and parallel these categories.

You want to create a Menu Item that links to the English category and call it English. This link should be a category blog layout. When you create this second link, you need to make sure that its parent item is the Academics Menu Item you just created. When you do this, the site shows all the content articles in the English category as a blog—that is, with the introductory text shown and a "read more" link. The Main Menu should now look as shown in Figure 10.8.

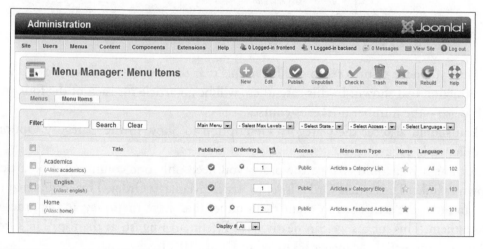

FIGURE 10.8   A submenu item.

It's important that in your Blog Layout Options for the English Menu Item, you have some key settings, as shown in Figure 10.9.

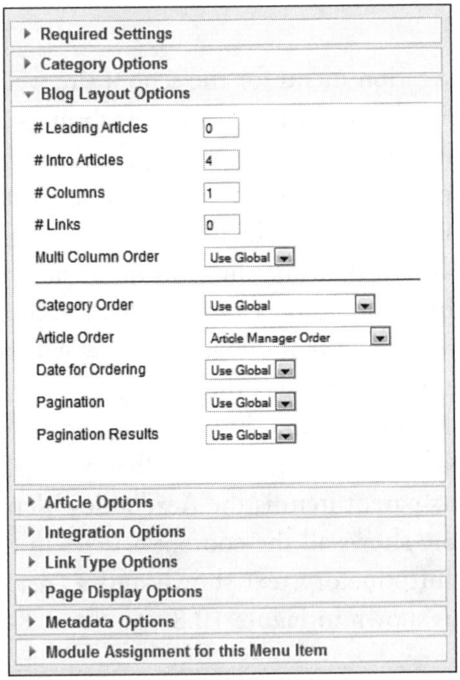

FIGURE 10.9 The English Menu Item's parameters.

Here you have # Intro set to 4. This means that there will be four articles with the introduction text shown. In this case, there will be an article for each of the four years of English—the number of classes/courses.

You should also set the Category Description to Show in the Category Options, here shown in Figure 10.10.

Although you could change the order, you need only one column and no articles shown as links. The Article Order is set to Article Manager Order. This means that the we can order the articles as we want them rather than have them, say, in the order we wrote them. This means we can neatly have Freshman English at the top. The Order column in the Article Manager is circled in Figure 10.11.

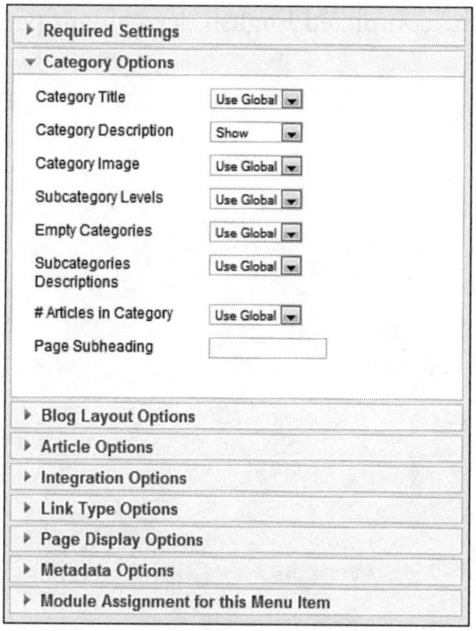

▶ Required Settings

▼ Category Options

Category Title   Use Global ▼

Category Description   Show ▼

Category Image   Use Global ▼

Subcategory Levels   Use Global ▼

Empty Categories   Use Global ▼

Subcategories   Use Global ▼
Descriptions

Articles in Category   Use Global ▼

Page Subheading   [   ]

▶ Blog Layout Options

▶ Article Options

▶ Integration Options

▶ Link Type Options

▶ Page Display Options

▶ Metadata Options

▶ Module Assignment for this Menu Item

FIGURE 10.10   Category Options.

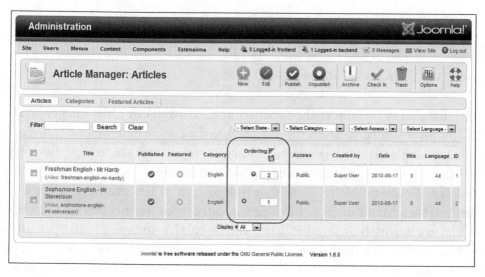

FIGURE 10.11   Ordering articles in the Article Manager.

Figure 10.12 shows the completed English department page.

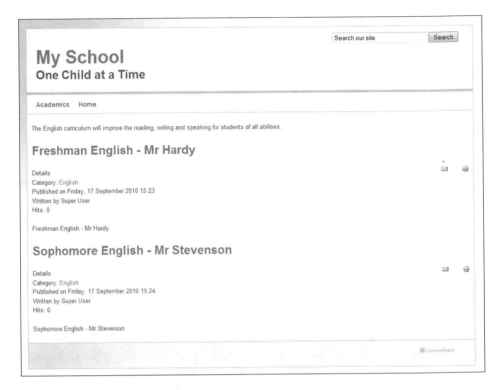

FIGURE 10.12   The English department page.

The first area of text under the department header English is the category description. This gives you content on the page before the course descriptions. The content could be as long or as short as needed. You create the content by editing the category itself: Content>Category Manager>English in this example.

You can also create Menu Items that link to each of the main categories as (list) layouts and then Menu Items (with the main category as parent) that link to the sub-categories as category blog layouts. When you do this it's often easiest to open one, say English, and then click the Save as Copy. This will carry over the various menu option settings we have chosen. After you do this, your Main Menu should look as shown in Figure 10.13.

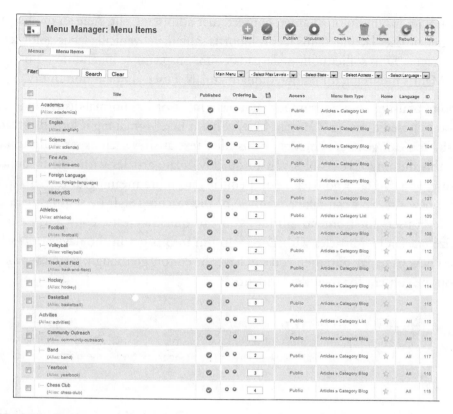

FIGURE 10.13   Development of submenu items in the Main Menu.

THE LEAST YOU NEED TO KNOW

When creating large, complex sites with multilevel menus, it's sometimes easiest if the navigation mirrors the categories.

Building Out Content

Now that you have your categories and links to them in the Main Menu, we need to start adding some content for the articles.

You'll be making use of that standby of web designers everywhere, Lorem Ipsum. You have probably seen this dummy text before; it reads something like this:

> Lorem ipsum dolor sit amet, consectetuer adipiscing elit. Aenean mollis, erat nec ultrices lacinia, tellus lectus lobortis sapien, vel vehicula lacus dolor feugiat magna. Duis sollicitudin malesuada enim. Suspendisse bibendum odio in ante. Mauris mollis auctor enim. Aliquam cursus. Fusce aliquam nonummy dui.

The point of using Lorem Ipsum is that it has a more-or-less normal distribution of letters—as opposed to using "Content here, content here"—making it look like readable English. You can generate chunks of this filler text at sites such as www.lipsum.com. Using this dummy text enables you to quickly create articles with text to build out structure; you can later go back in and edit it into more meaningful text. To quickly create a new site, you can take advantage of the teaching staff by setting them up as editor-level users for frontend editing. You can quickly create, copy and paste, and organize placeholder articles with Lorem Ipsum into pages in the navigation scheme and test how pages lay out; then you can have the editors go though, page-by-page, and develop the content for their departments.

THE LEAST YOU NEED TO KNOW

Using Lorem Ipsum is a useful technique for creating articles that form the structure of a Joomla site so you can check the navigation and page layouts as you go along. The pages/articles can be edited later.

For each subcategory, you need to create an article and add to it some Lorem Ipsum dummy text. Copious use of Save as Copy really helps here. Open an article, just change the category, and click Save as Copy. Rinse and Repeat.

Creating Subnavigation

A website such as a school site will have many articles, and you should have plenty of pathways for site visitors to drill down to that content. To achieve this, you use the left column to place some links of increasing specificity down the page.

The concept is to have the most general links at the top; these are ones that link to other categories in the current section. For example, for the English department, you need to carefully choose what is in the left column, as shown in Figure 10.14.

The top menu, Academics, contains links to all the departments.

The next module shows links to articles that are new in the Academics section. This means, from a hierarchical point of view, these links are the next level down from the Academics menu.

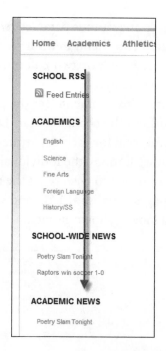

FIGURE 10.14   Eye tracking for an interest-oriented submenu that appears in the left column.

The effect of this for a site visitor is seeing a continuum of information, starting from a broad level and going down to a narrow one (as shown by the arrow). Studies that track eye movement on websites have shown that visitors tend to start in the top left, and the movement of the eye down the page works well with a changing organization from broad to narrow. Using techniques like this is important for usability.

Let's look at each of the modules in turn.

The Academics Submenu

As shown in Figure 10.14, you want to have a submenu at the top of the left column that shows links to all the other sibling categories in that section. For each section you are in, the submenu should change to reflect the section. Fortunately, setting this up is easier than it sounds. All you have to do is create a new menu and copy the Menu Items you need.

Go to Menus>Menu Manager. Create a new menu called Academics.

Looking at the Menu Items, copy all the submenu items (English, Math, and so on) to the new Academics menu using the Batch Process tool at the bottom.

The reason why we copy is so the various parameters/options are duplicated. Note that now we do have to maintain two Menu Items if we want to change something—for example, whether the layout is one or two columns. We could alleviate this by making a menu *alias* rather than a copy.

We then take the module for this submenu, set the position to Left, and then set it to show only sublevel Menu Items by changing Start Level from 0 to 1. You have to use multiple copies of the menu (one for each department) and edit the title for each of those submenus if you want each to say the individual department name instead of a generic title, such as Submenu. You also need to set the module to appear only on the Academics pages and the subpages (English, Math, and so on).

The edited module should look as shown in Figure 10.15.

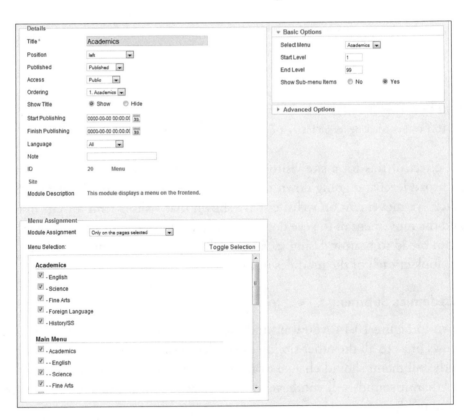

FIGURE 10.15 Module options for a submenu.

You can see the result on the frontend of the site if you navigate to the English department, as shown in Figure 10.16.

Notice how the left column automatically appears and the main column shrinks when you put content there.

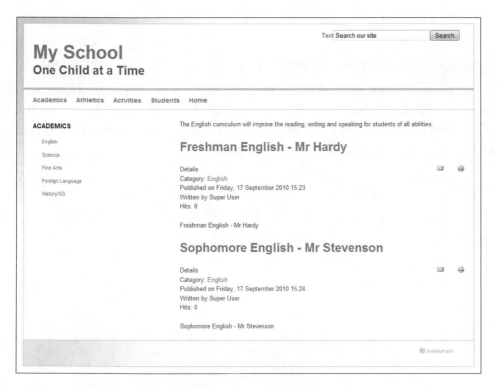

FIGURE 10.16   English department page with left-column submenu.

Creating News Links for a Section

The next step in setting up the left column is to create news links. There are a couple ways to do this, depending on the effect you want.

You could just create a big category called "News" and have all teachers post their news there and display that latest news module on all pages.

Or a more subtle approach would be to create four categories, one for each of the main categories—Academics, Athletics, and so on—and display those individual news items on their own pages. That way all those sports teams results won't overwhelm the English news!

Then, we could have a fifth latest news module that could combine all this news and place it at the bottom. Let's try the second method.

First, we create the four new categories:

- Academic News
- Athletic News
- Activity News
- Admin News (for the "Students" category)

Create a latest news module for the Academic News category (select Extensions>Module Manager>New>Latest News), as shown in Figure 10.17. The module only pulls from the Academic News category and only shows in the Academics area of the site. Make sure the module is assigned only to this category.

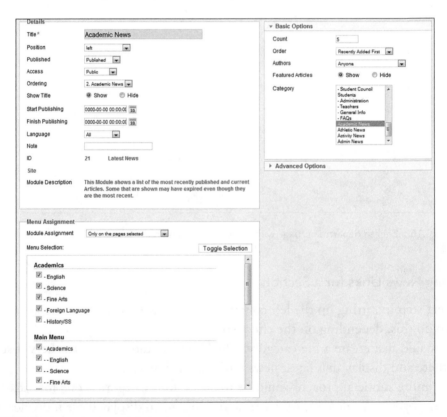

FIGURE 10.17 Latest news module parameters.

Then we can create a last module that shows news from all four categories and shows on all pages. The English department page should now look as shown in Figure 10.18.

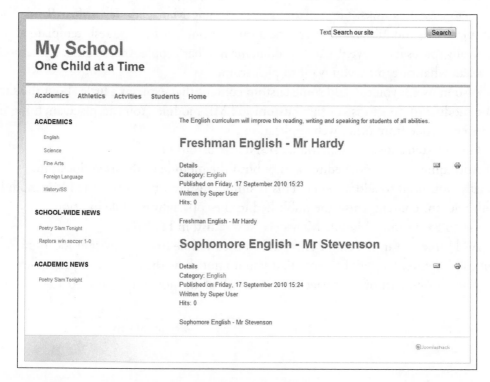

FIGURE 10.18   English department page with latest news modules added.

THE LEAST YOU NEED TO KNOW
Deep sites with many content articles need to provide several opportunities (sub-navigation and links) for site visitors to find that content.

Setting Up the Footer Area

The Fresh template has two locations—user4 and copyright—at the bottom of the page for extra modules.

The school address is something that should be shown on all pages. We can put that in the user4 location with a custom HTML module. Go to Extensions>Module

Manager>New>Custom HTML. Add some text into the editor and publish the module to the user4 location.

Another useful module is Most Read. This shows the most popular content (based on page views) as links. Go to Extensions>Module Manager>New>Most Read. You can place this module in the user4 location and publish it; the Fresh template automatically spaces it out evenly. You could name it What People Are Reading. Remember to select what categories you want to pick from.

Also in user3, you can add some custom content that explains a little about the site. The module to do this is another custom HTML module. You can place anything in here, even code from other web applications.

Go to Extensions>Module Manager>New>Custom HTML.

Add some text into the editor and publish the module to the user4 location. Finally, you need to add a footer. This is simply just another custom HTML module with relevant content, this time published in the copyright module location.

Go to Extensions>Module Manager>New>Custom HTML.

Add some text in the editor and publish the module to the copyright location. You can call it Footer Copyright. Note that you do not show the title for this module.

The bottom part of your page should now look as shown in Figure 10.19.

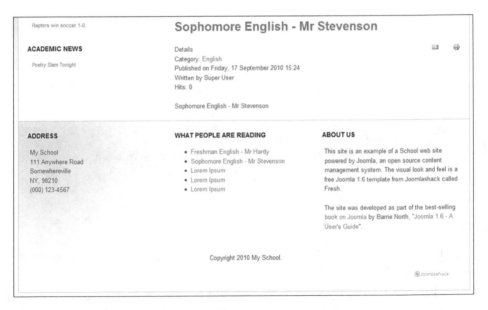

FIGURE 10.19   Setting up the bottom module blocks.

Now you have a site that has robust content organization and a rich network of links for finding that content. Let's move on and do a little more with the home page, which is currently a bit empty.

Setting Up the Home Page

The home page for a school site could follow a portal-type concept. As previously mentioned, there are various stakeholder groups related to a school, so the home page needs to have a little something for everyone.

A school site, as an example of a large organization, is an ideal candidate for using the Featured Article component. As you saw in Chapter 5, "Creating Menus and Navigation," the Featured Article component allows the webmaster to select articles from anywhere on the site and post them to the home page, which allows this person to take the role of content manager rather than content producer.

> **TIP**
> Even though the Featured Article Manager does the work, an organization should still develop a policy about how content will be created and published to the home page.

At this point, you need to create an uncategorized article that will be the first article shown on the home page. We use this as the main welcome content and then we use the Featured Articles Manager to add other articles as desired. Go to Content>Article Manager>New.

Create an article suitable for the home page and make it uncategorized. (You can also add an image.) Also make sure it is published and the Featured option is set to Yes.

Now if you go to the Article Manager, you can pick out a couple articles to appear on the home page, along with your main welcome article.

Go to Content>Article Manager. Publish a couple of the articles to the front page by clicking the icons in the Featured Article column in the Article Manager.

You now need to make sure the articles are in the order in which you want them to appear. You can adjust this in the Featured Article Manager.

Go to Content>Featured Article Manager. Adjust the order by using the up and down arrows until the Welcome to Your High School article (the uncategorized one) is listed first. The Featured Article Manager should look as shown in Figure 10.20.

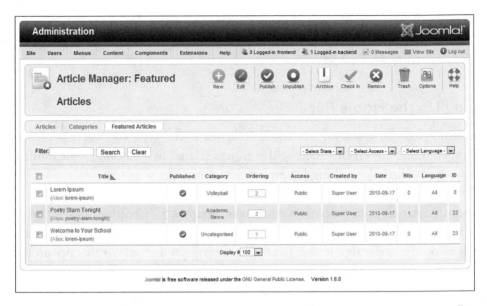

FIGURE 10.20 Featured Article Manager.

Finally, you need to modify the Menu Item parameters. Go to Menus>Main Menu>Home. Under Layout Options, set the following:

Leading = 0

Intro = 4

Columns = 1

Links = 10

Also, set Category Order to Order and Pagination to Hide.

In the Article Options, set Author Name, Created Date, Email, PDF, and Print Icons to Hide. In the Page Display Options, set Show Page Heading to No. The home page should now look as shown in Figure 10.21.

Depending on your needs, you could leave the home page as it is. You will be adding some useful modules to the left and right columns as you explore how to add functionality to the site through core Joomla extensions and third-party add-ons.

THE LEAST YOU NEED TO KNOW

Using the Joomla Featured Article component is an excellent way for a site to manage its home page content when there are several individual contributors.

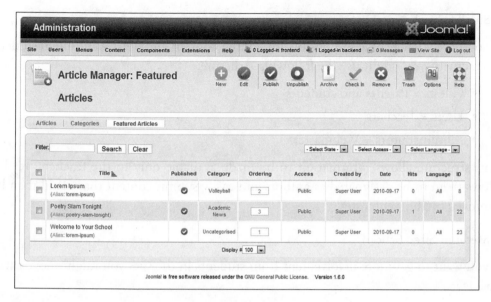

FIGURE 10.21   Completed front page (home page).

Adding Basic Functionality to a School Website

At the beginning of this chapter, you brainstormed a list of possible functionality you would like your site to have. Let's examine each type of functionality for the school website and see what options are available.

User Registration

One of the most powerful features of Joomla is that it allows several layers of permissions. At the most basic, these are as follows:

- Guests
- Users
- Administrators

With Joomla 1.6, you have the potential to create your own custom groups for access to different content and tasks. When setting up you school website, you need to think a little about the needs and size of the school and how you want these user groups to interact with the site. Let's look at a few examples.

A Small School

If you have a few people responsible for adding content and don't want much student interactivity, you might use the following structure:

- Guests = Parents and students
- Users = Teachers
- Administrators = Webmaster

This structure allows information to be made available only to the teachers. It also allows them to be designated as authors and easily submit content that could then be approved by the webmaster.

A Medium-Sized School

If you want to get more involvement from students in the site, you might move them up a level:

- Guests = Parents
- Users = Teachers and students
- Administrators = Webmaster

This structure allows more involvement and interaction, behind a private registered security wall, between the teachers and students. For example, teachers and students could collaborate on assignments and then submit content that could then be approved by the webmaster.

A Large School

If you want to have significant involvement from all stakeholders in the school community, you might use this structure:

- Guests = Public
- Users = Students, teachers, and parents
- Administrators = Webmaster

This structure could be used to leverage the website to increase communication between all the groups. It opens the door for projects such as a student digital portfolio that can be shared privately online with parents, teachers, and peers, as well as involves students and teachers in content creation and editing.

NOTE
To illustrate the differences between the various permissions structures, we have used the size of the school as a delineator. You could just as easily illustrate these structures with an example such as "desire to more fully leverage web technology."

As you can see, you need to make a philosophical decision here, as well as a technical one. For now, add a login module to the home page.

Go to Extensions>Module Manager and check if there is a login module. If there is not, create a login module. Make sure it is in the left column position and set it to be assigned to the Home Menu Item only.

Events Calendar

Many schools are already using Google Apps for Domains. This free service also includes a sophisticated calendar. One of the powerful features of Joomla is the capability to embed code and widgets from third parties to integrate your site with other services. For example, we can embed a Google calendar on the pages of our site.

Downloadable Documents

A school website is likely to need to offer many documents (in PDF format, for example) for easy downloading. Examples might include the following:

- Course descriptions
- Meeting minutes
- Newsletters
- Forms
- Student work (digital portfolio, perhaps)

It's easy to upload these PDF documents through the Media Manager and then link to them in articles.

Staff Directory

For medium-sized or small schools, adding a staff directory is probably most easily achieved through the core Joomla contacts component. First, you need to create contacts and associate them with users. Go to Components>Contacts>Categories>New. Create a category called Staff.

To do the next step, it's easiest if the staff have already registered on the site. You need to create a contact for each one and associate each with the appropriate registered user. You can then create a Menu Item that links to your contacts component.

Go to Menus>Main Menu>New>Contacts>List Contacts in a Directory to create a link to the category you just created; this instantly forms a staff directory (shown in Figure 10.22). It is possible to create a content article to hold this information. But doing it using this user profile has the advantage that the task of creating/editing the profile content is passed onto the staff themselves, reducing the burden on the webmaster to type in everyone's name.

In Figure 10.22, I added two staff members. First I created the users and then the contacts associated with them.

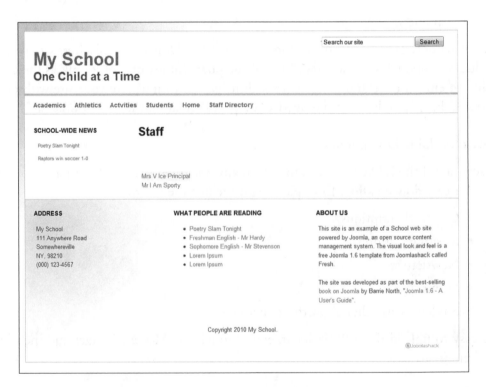

FIGURE 10.22   Default Joomla directory/contacts component.

Email Newsletter

An email newsletter is an important part of a school website. Schools often push out newsletters to stakeholder groups, students, teachers, or parents. Being able to migrate this traditional paper-based communication to email can mean big cost savings for the school.

Although there are a few Joomla extensions that allow bulk emailing, I usually advise using a third-party service. You get higher deliverability and better compliance with the CAN-SPAM act.

My favorite is an extension called iContact. A simple plug-in called JContact integrates iContact with Joomla; you can get it for free at www.compassdesigns.net.

Another good service is MailChimp. It also has an extension that integrates it with Joomla available at extensions.joomla.org.

RSS

A tremendously useful feature of Joomla is its capability to work with RSS.

Joomla has two main RSS features: It can transmit an RSS feed from content within a Joomla website, and it can display RSS feeds received from other places/sites.

In Joomla, the RSS syndication feed is generated from content in the page that is published. To provide content from other categories deeper in the site, a third-party component has to be used. For your purposes, the target audience is probably site visitors who want to use RSS to get the latest news. For that, syndication of the home page only is adequate.

To create an RSS syndication module, go to Extensions>Module Manager> New>Syndicate.

Give the module a name and publish it to the left column, set to publish on all pages.

Displaying an RSS feed provides interesting possibilities for a school website. Imagine a school district with perhaps half a dozen schools in it. Each school and the school district itself could have a website, maybe even powered by Joomla, and each site could provide RSS feeds to be published on the others. For example, one of the school websites might show news from the district's website—all automatically, without any extra effort needed.

Random Image

A school is likely to have many images generated by its community, from photos to student artwork. A great way to share these images is with Joomla's random image module, which randomly displays images taken from a designated directory.

Go to Extensions>Module Manager>New>Random Image. Give the module a name, designate a media folder with images to be displayed, publish it to the right column, and assign it to the Home Menu Item.

Sitemap

A sitemap is an important part of a website, especially a large one such as a school site. Usually a sitemap contains links to all the pages in the website.

Generating a sitemap by hand would be monstrously time-consuming, but again this is where the dynamic nature of a CMS such as Joomla saves the day.

The easiest way to set up a sitemap page is to use a feature of Joomla that loads a module into an article. If, for example, you type within your article the text {`loadposition user1`}, Joomla loads the module currently set to user1 into the main-body area, as part of your article.

To set up a sitemap, follow these steps:

1. Copy the Main Menu module, but put it in a module position unused by the template. I used position-15.

2. Create an uncategorized article and type in content with the text {`loadposition position-15` }.

3. Create a Menu Item called Sitemap that links to the Sitemap article.

Now that you have extended some of the basic functionality, your home page is a much richer experience for the site visitor, as shown in Figure 10.23.

> **THE LEAST YOU NEED TO KNOW**
> Even a site heavily based on content has to have interactive functionality to make the visitor's experience richer. Without interactivity, visitors have little motivation to return.

Extending the School Website Beyond the Basics

Joomlashack.com has a forum especially for school webmasters to meet and swap ideas and get help with problems. (See www.joomlashack.com/community/index.php/board,74.0.html.) Registration is free.

FIGURE 10.23   Home page with login, random images, RSS feeds, and syndicated content.

JOOMLABOOK.COM CHAPTER 10 DEMO SITE
www.joomlabook.com provides a SQL dump of the site created in this chapter. It is an exact copy of what you should have if you followed all the steps in this chapter. You can log in to the administrative backend to see the site framework and the categories and menus. The username/password is admin/joomla.

TURNKEY SCHOOL WEBSITE PACKAGE
A turnkey version of a Joomla (1.5) school website is also available at SimplWeb. It includes fully managed hosting and training and support. You can find out more at www.simplweb.com/schools.

Summary

This chapter looked at using Joomla to develop a large site that has several contributors and that needs to organize its content and extensions to meet multiple needs. Here are the key points we looked at in this chapter:

- A website for a large organization such as a school needs to meet the needs of diverse groups. Organizing its content and functions can therefore be challenging.
- Using a pure CSS drop-down menu is a highly accessible and SEO-friendly way to organize complex navigation.
- There is always more than one way to organize content. It often helps to decide what the articles would be and then build backward into categories.
- When creating larger, more complex sites, it's sometimes easiest if the navigation mirrors the categories.
- Using Lorem Ipsum dummy text is a useful technique for creating articles that form the structure of a Joomla site, so you can check the navigation for it as you go along and delegate content creation to others without being concerned about teaching them your organization scheme (that is, your categories). You can later edit the pages and articles.
- Deep sites that have several content articles need to provide many opportunities (subnavigation and links) for site visitors to find the content.
- Using the Joomla Featured Article component is an excellent way for a site to manage its home page content when there are several individual contributors.
- Even a site that is heavily based on content has to have interactive functionality to make the visitor's experience richer. Without this, visitors have little motivation to return.

Chapter 11

Creating a Restaurant Site with Joomla!

In This Chapter

This chapter looks at the process of creating a small business website, in this case for a restaurant. Starting from a needs analysis, this chapter shows you how to organize possible content all the way through adding photos and considering further extensions. If you are following along and building a site, its best to start the chapter with a fresh Joomla installation with no content. This chapter covers the following topics:

- Why do small businesses such as restaurants need websites?
- What website features does a restaurant need?
- How can I organize my content?
- What's the easiest way to build the content of my site?
- How should I set up the navigation for a restaurant site?
- How should I set up the home page of a restaurant site?
- Where can I get quality photos?
- How can I extend the functionality of my restaurant site?

Why Does a Restaurant Need a Website?

A restaurant is an excellent example of a business that needs a website to communicate its brand and business information. These types of websites are often called *brochure websites* because they function as brochures from an online platform.

The standards for websites are changing. Visitors are becoming increasingly less apt to accept (and repeatedly visit) sites where the content rarely changes, and they want to be able to interact with sites.

A restaurant website example can easily be generalized. A restaurant represents any small business that has relatively fixed content but wants to add enough interactivity to be able to make the site interesting and worth revisiting. For a restaurant, this means regularly updating menus and event information.

Ultimately, the example of a restaurant in this chapter represents a baseline for all small businesses today. The question should not be "Why does a restaurant want a website?" but "How can I make a professional site that's easy to update and very extendable?"

 THE LEAST YOU NEED TO KNOW
A modern business must have a web presence that communicates its brand and information about the company.

Enter the modern CMS.

What Features Does a Restaurant Website Need?

Most restaurants have a number of key facets they need to communicate through their websites. Most visitors look for one of five types of information:

- Menus
- Specials/news
- Hours
- Directions
- Contact information

All five of these types of information can easily be handled with the core default Joomla installation.

Most restaurants have rather small websites, and they are unlikely to need many additional third-party extensions to add functionality. As just discussed, a key function for a restaurant website is the ability to frequently add and change content, such as menus, and to provide PDF printouts of menus. Both of these are core features of Joomla out of the box.

THE LEAST YOU NEED TO KNOW
A default Joomla installation provides the key features needed for a small business site: easily edited content and flexible menu configuration.

One of the most powerful things about Joomla is the ability to easily add functionality as a site grows and needs to be updated.

Several restaurant owners have identified the following "nice to have" extensions they would like to see for their sites:

- **An image gallery**—An important part of a restaurant's branding is the imagery present in its décor and food. Being able to provide an image gallery of these would be a useful tool in projecting that brand onto the Web.

- **Email newsletters**—Any business that has a Web presence needs to include email marketing in its mix of customer communication. For restaurants, this can be a timely way to drive virtual traffic to their sites and foot traffic to the restaurants. Combined with the traditional specials, it's easy to set up customer loyalty programs so that regulars can be emailed offers to return.

- **Google Maps**—Directions are okay, but a map is much better. You'll find that many websites use Google Maps to provide geographic data. This kind of option would improve the visitor (to the site and the restaurant) experience.

As you work to develop a restaurant website in this chapter, you incorporate the basic functionality you need and also learn a little bit about how you could add some of these "nice to have" features.

First, let's find a decent-looking template that a restaurant can use.

Downloading and Installing a Restaurant Template

At www.joomlabook.com (or www.compassdesigns.net), you can grab the free template Ready to Eat that you'll use in this chapter. This is a relatively simple template with a horizontal menu, a single large column, and three equal-height module blocks at the bottom, as shown in Figure 11.1.

FIGURE 11.1 The Ready to Eat template.

After you download this template, you should have a template zip file to install into Joomla:

1. Go to Extensions>Extension Manager to get to the Extension Manager. You learned how extensions are installed and managed in Chapter 6, "Extending Joomla!"

2. Browse to the template zip file and click the Upload and Install button. You get a message that says "Install Template: Success."

3. Go to Extensions>Template Manager to open the Template Manager, select the Ready to Eat template, and click the Default button to make it the default template. Viewed in the frontend, the site (with no content) should look as shown in Figure 11.2.

FIGURE 11.2   The Ready to Eat template, empty of content.

The Ready to Eat template has three main features:

- The header image can be used as the logo header for the site. The image can be easily replaced with any 638×155-pixel image. To do this, you simply replace the file `/templates/js_ready_to_eat/images/header.png` with one of your own.

- The two side images in this template, the fork and knife, are also easy to replace. (Maybe you need chopsticks to fit the restaurant theme!) These are the images: `/templates/js_ready_to_eat/images/fork.png` and `/templates/js_ready_to_eat/images/knife.png`.

- The three bottom columns, which are designed for modules, use some JavaScript to give the containing `<div>` elements equal height.

Now that the template is installed, you can add content. As you have already seen, it's best to first create the categories and then create the menus/navigation that link to them.

Organizing the Content on a Restaurant Website

Your restaurant website will not have many pages. Before going any further, go back and skim Chapter 4, "Content Is King: Organizing Your Content," to revisit the idea that you can organize your articles in more than one way, with categories.

Let's first consider the sitemap, which is shown in Figure 11.3.

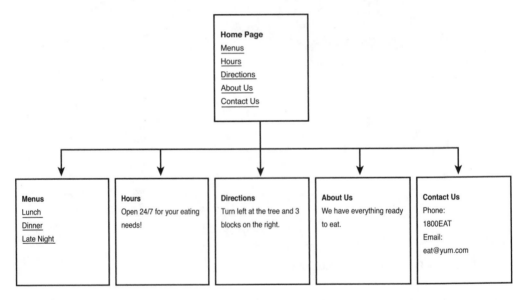

FIGURE 11.3 A simple restaurant sitemap.

As you saw in Chapter 4, there is always more than one way to organize articles. The main things to consider are what the basic content building block of the site will be and what the article is.

As you look at this example for the menus, you need to think about how to structure the site. Consider the following example:

Content Level	Example 1
Article	Lunch menu
	Dinner menu
	Late night menu

The decision comes down to asking, "Will there be any other articles at the menu level or deeper?" For example, if you have lunch menus for different days of the week or a drill-down that provides information about a specific Menu Item (that is, what the chicken salad looks like, not a Joomla Menu Item), then you should plan for that and use a structure that can grow. In this case, you might make "Lunch" a subcategory and have the lunch menus for different days be the articles.

For the purpose of this chapter, you're more interested in a simple structure that's easy to update than in a more complex one that would call for several articles.

With this assumption in mind, you'll build the site with the following structure:

Categories	Articles
Menus	Lunch
	Dinner
	Late Night
Uncategorized	Welcome to My Restaurant (home)
	About Us
	Directions
	Hours
Reviews	Review 1
	Review 2

Consider the following point about this organization: The sitemap in Figure 11.3 doesn't have any specials or reviews included. You will use these categories to hold articles you'll use in modules. This will make more sense in about ten pages.

THE LEAST YOU NEED TO KNOW
A small website does not need a detailed category structure. Often just a single category can be used for all the content articles.

Now you can set up the structure. First, you create your two categories. Go to the Category Manager (by selecting Content>Category Manager) and create categories called Menus and Reviews. After you have created these, the Category Manager should look as shown in Figure 11.4.

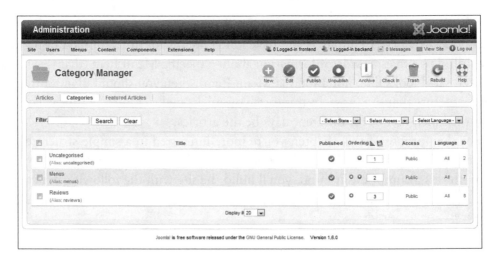

FIGURE 11.4 A simple restaurant category configuration.

Now that your organizational structure is complete, you need to create some articles. The plan here is that the top menu will link directly to articles rather than categories. This means you must create these articles first, so you link to them when you create the links in the Menu Manager.

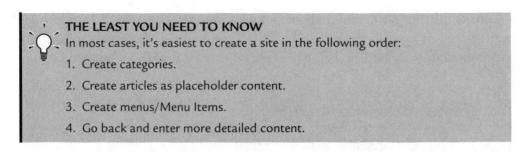

THE LEAST YOU NEED TO KNOW
In most cases, it's easiest to create a site in the following order:

1. Create categories.
2. Create articles as placeholder content.
3. Create menus/Menu Items.
4. Go back and enter more detailed content.

Now that you have your categories, you can start adding some content for your articles.

Building Content Articles with Lorem Ipsum

As in Chapter 10, "Creating a School Site with Joomla!" for this example, you'll use Lorem Ipsum dummy text. As noted in Chapter 10, using this dummy text enables you to quickly create articles with text to build out structure; you can later go back in and edit it into more meaningful text.

Now you can go to the Article Manager and start adding articles, with Lorem Ipsum for each. Then you need to carefully select the correct category for each article. When you're finished, the Article Manager should look as shown in Figure 11.5.

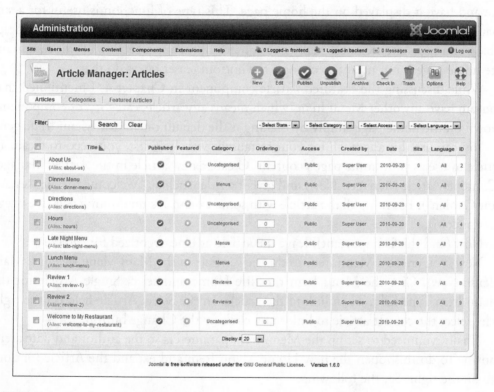

FIGURE 11.5   Simple restaurant filler articles.

Carefully note the categories that the articles are in. In a moment, you will develop meaningful content for these articles. But first, you need to create some menus.

Setting Up the Home Page

If you refer to Figure 11.1, you see that the basic concept for the restaurant site's home page is to have some central content and then three blocks at the bottom. Setting up the main content is easiest, so let's start with that.

Home Page Alternative to the Featured Article Manager

Chapter 4 describes different ways to organize content and how to use Joomla's special Featured Article component that allows you to pull content from anywhere else on the site and have it displayed on the home page. This type of function is useful for a site that might have the main content of the home page change frequently (for example, a blog or a news site). Conceptually, the content of the main section of this restaurant site home page is not meant to change; the bottom teaser boxes do that.

While discussing the Featured Article component in Chapter 4, I mentioned that you can have any other Menu Item (which means any article, category, or component) shown on the home page simply by making it the default one in the Menu Manager.

You can use this approach for your restaurant website. First, you need to create an article to use as your home page's content. Create a new article in the Article Manager (Content>Article Manager>New) and give it a title (such as "Welcome to The Restaurant Garden"). For now, fill the article with some Lorem Ipsum dummy text (see www.lipsum.com).

Now (and this is important), leave the article as Uncategorized for category.

Next, you create a Menu Item to this new article in the Main Menu (Menus>Main Menu>New). Give the Menu Item the title Home and select Single Article for the Menu Item Type field. Then link to the article. In the Select Article field on the right side, select the correct article to link to by clicking the Change button.

Finally, you need to set up the Menu Item parameters so the author and date aren't shown. To do this, open the new Home Menu Item and expand the Article Options tab on the right. Set the following:

- Author Name: Hide
- Created Date and Time: Hide
- Modified Date and Time: Show
- PDF Icon: Hide
- Print Icon: Hide
- Email Icon: Hide

NOTE
You can choose other options here; these are my own personal preferences because I think the home page content should be relatively free of distractions.

Now you have home page content that can easily be updated. The webmaster can just log in and edit live on the home page—or any other page.

Creating Menus

If you look back at Figure 11.1, you can see that the intent is to have a horizontal menu that extends across. Here's how you create it.

If there is already a Menu Item for home, adjust it so that it's a link to a single article and points to our "Welcome to my Restaurant" article. If one is not there, create it.

Create a top-level category blog Menu Item called Menus and submenu single article items that link to the different "time of day" menu articles—lunch, dinner, and so on.

The Main Menu now looks as shown Figure 11.6.

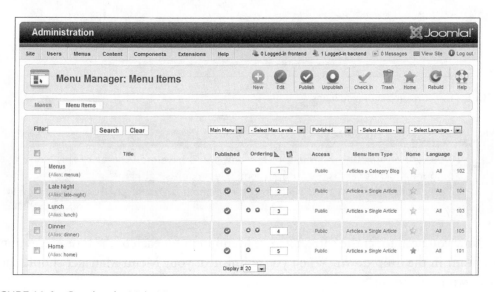

FIGURE 11.6   Creating the Main Menu.

Viewed from the frontend, the site has the top-level parent Menu Items, but the submenu items to the specific time of day restaurant menus are not showing as a drop-down menu. Although your template provides for this functionality, you need to tell Joomla to take advantage of it by adjusting these Menu Items for the lunch menu, dinner menu, and so on to be children of the top Menu Item, Menus.

You can see this drop-down field in the Menu edit screen in Figure 11.7.

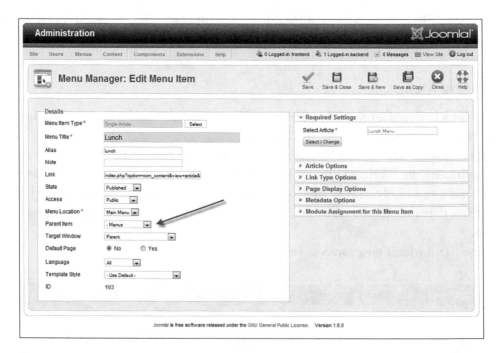

FIGURE 11.7 Creating submenu items.

 NOTE
Using a business other than a restaurant would have made some of this wording (Joomla menus versus restaurant menus) less confusing! Hopefully, the extra concentration you apply here will help you remember the concept better!

Now you need to set the correct parent Menu Item for each of the four Menu Items you want in the drop-down. When you're finished, your Menu Manager should look as shown in Figure 11.8.

When you created the menu, a module was automatically created for it. However, the default position given for it was left. The Ready to Eat template does not have a left position for modules, so you need to move that module into the correct spot for a horizontal menu, as determined by the Ready to Eat template. In this case, it's top. To do this, follow these steps:

1. Go to Extensions>Module Manager>Main Menu and change the Position to top. While you're here, make sure that the menu module's Published attribute is set to Published, make sure that Show Title is set to Hide, and set some parameters for your drop-down to work correctly.

2. In the Basic Options, set Show Submenu Items to Yes, and set the End Level to 2.

3. In the Advanced Options, make sure Menu Class Suffix and Module Class Suffix are both blank.

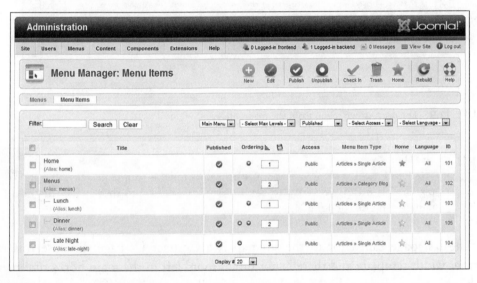

FIGURE 11.8 A completed Main Menu with submenu items.

Creating these submenu items now gives you a drop-down menu, as shown in Figure 11.9.

Look back at your sitemap, where you specified that you wanted to have links in the Main Menu for directions, hours, and "about us" information. You can add these through the Menu Manager by linking to the appropriate articles; each time, you must make sure to select the correct article to link to.

FIGURE 11.9 The drop-down menu from the frontend.

NOTE
The Ready to Eat template has a fixed width for the submenu links, about 170 pixels. This means you have to use words that will fit into that space—the menu names can't be too long.

The last page called for in the sitemap is a Contact Us page. Because this is a narrow-width template and there is not much room left in the main horizontal menu at the top, you can place this Menu Item in a smaller menu in the footer, another module position available in this template.

You now need to create another menu. While in the Menu Manager, click New and create a menu called Footer Menu. Create a single Menu Item in that menu that points to the contact form (Contacts>Single Contact).

NOTE
Because you started with a Joomla installation that had no sample content, you will have to create a contact for this Menu Item to link to. You can find instructions for how to do this in Chapter 4.

You can make it even easier for the webmaster to edit content by providing a front-end login link in the footer so the webmaster can edit without going to the backend:

1. Go to the Footer menu and create a new Menu Item (Menus>Footer Menu>New). Link the Menu Item to the login page (Users Manager>Login Form). Title it Login Form and make sure the Menu Location choice is Footer Menu. Go to the module for that menu and make sure it's published in the correct position (e.g., footer).

2. Go to Extensions>Module Manager, create a new menu module that shows the footer menu, and publish it in the footer position. Make sure that Show Title Parameter is set to No.

The home page of your site should now look as shown in Figure 11.10. Next, you'll add the ubiquitous footer text that you see on most websites.

FIGURE 11.10   The home page with the footer menu.

Creating Footer Content

The Ready to Eat template has a footer location for modules, which you have used already to place the small menu for the Contact Us and Login links. Now you can add some content there.

As described in Chapter 1, "Content Management Systems and an Introduction to Joomla!" a module location is simply a placeholder, or bucket, into which Joomla can drop content (in this case, modules). You can have as many modules as you like in a particular module location. How the modules are presented (vertically, horizontally) is determined by the module style. (This is a rather advanced template concept and is in discussed in Chapter 9, "Creating Pure CSS Templates."

Now you can put some copyright text in the footer. To do this, you need to create a custom HTML module: Go to Extensions>Module Manager>New and select a custom HTML module. The module editing screen shown in Figure 11.11 appears.

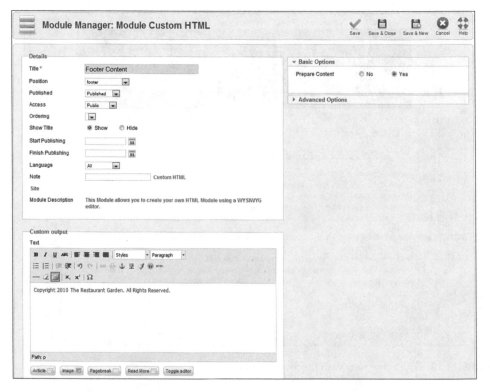

FIGURE 11.11   Creating a custom HTML module.

You can enter a simple copyright statement and make sure it appears in the correct location and that the title is set to not be shown.

When first saved, the module is set to appear in last place. You can adjust this by using the up and down arrows in the Module Manager in the same way you change Menu Item placement in the Menu Manager. (It's handy how all these managers function the same way!)

Last but not least, you need to set up the three blocks of content at the bottom.

Creating Module Teaser Blocks

To create a teaser block, you use modules across two or three columns at the top or bottom of the page. The idea is that the content of the blocks has something compelling in it that will have the site visitor click and go deeper into the site. You frequently see this technique used on websites.

Earlier, when you set up your categories, you created a category that was not part of the navigation structure—reviews. This category will be used in your teaser blocks at the bottom of the home page. To do this, you can use one of the dynamic modules available in Joomla—the newsflash module.

The Newsflash Module

The newsflash module displays a number of articles from a particular category. With every page refresh, it randomly selects new articles to be shown. For a restaurant site, you can use this module for reviews. You can select various reviews, and if someone follows a link, she will see all the ones you have on the site.

To add the module, go to Extensions>Module Manager>New and select the Articles-Newsflash module. On the Module Manager screen, you set up the module parameters as shown in Figure 11.12.

Then set the following:

- Set the position as user2.
- Assign it to all menus so it shows on all pages.
- Set the category as Reviews.
- Select to show the Article Title and Linked Titles.
- Choose to show only one item.

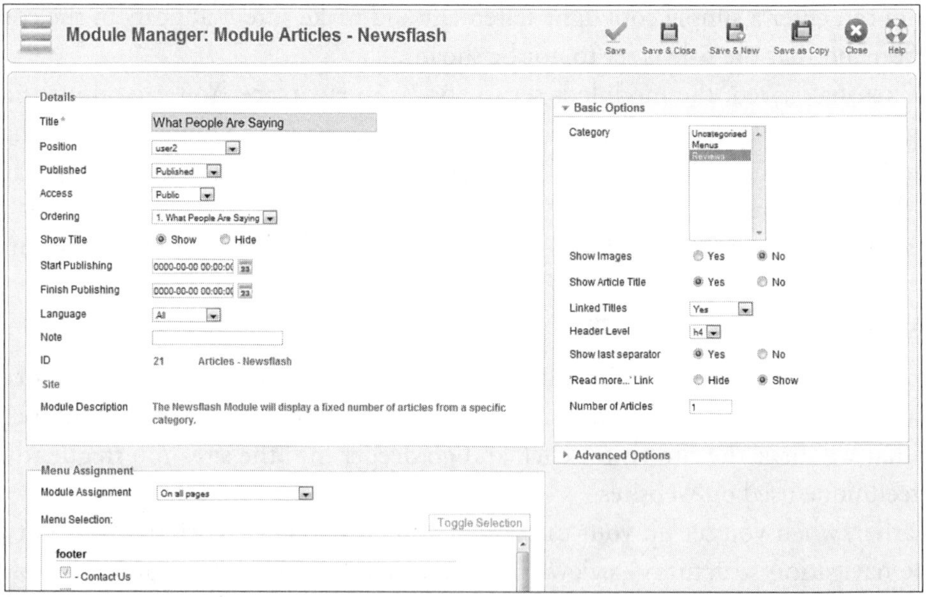

FIGURE 11.12 Setting up the newsflash module.

Viewed from the frontend, your site should now look as shown in Figure 11.13.

Note that the module is stretching across the page. As you add more modules, the template is set up so that Joomla dynamically adds columns as needed and contracts/expands the module content as needed. This collapsible column functionality is a common feature of professional commercial templates—and it is included in this one!

Now let's add some content to help us in search engines.

Using Custom HTML for SEO Content

For a bricks and mortar business like a restaurant, getting found in Google is critical. We can imagine that when people are searching, they'll be typing into Google terms like "Italian restaurant in Boston." Two things to note are that we have the generic type of the business and the locale.

To help us in Google, and particularly in the Google Local search engine, we can add a custom HTML module that appears on all pages with some highly targeted information.

FIGURE 11.13   The newsflash module from the frontend.

Create a custom HTML module and publish it in user3. Include the copy as shown in Figure 11.14.

The site is starting to take shape. It still looks a bit bland, though; you need some images and photos.

Using Stock Imagery

One of the best-kept secrets of web designers is the use of stock photos and imagery in creating websites for clients. There are many websites where you can get royalty-free images to use on a single site. Examples include the following:

- www.dreamstime.com
- www.istockphoto.com
- www.GettyImages.com
- www.sxc.hu

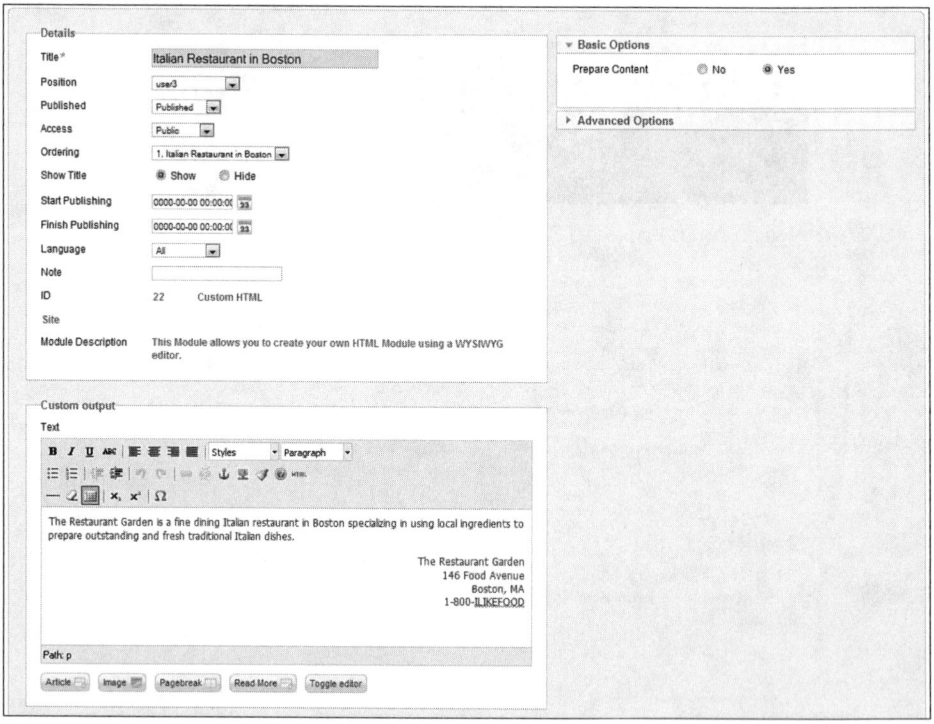

FIGURE 11.14 Search engine optimized business content in a module.

The images you can get from these sites are amazingly affordable, often as low as $1 per image for a high-quality photo, and there are thousands to choose from. Probably 80% to 90% of the images you see on the Web are stock images.

The license terms for these images vary and are typically (depending on the source) characterized as follows:

- You pay once to get an image.
- You don't have to pay each time it's used; that is, the images are royalty free. (Being "used," in this case, means being displayed on a web page, so this is an important license requirement.)
- You can't resell or redistribute them.

For the home page content article, Welcome to Ready to Eat, you can add images in the second and third paragraphs. Remember the following key points:

NOTE
I have downloaded two images: one of a plate of food and another of some drinks and a wine glass. When you download them, they are very big files, so you need to use a graphics editor such as Fireworks, Photoshop, or GIMP to crop them to the size you need.

- Use the Joomla Image button at the bottom to upload and insert the images.
- Remember to set the alignment of the images to left.
- Add some white space/margin. You can do so by adding the class `imagemargin` to the images in the editor in source code mode. (This sets the class for each image to `imagemargin`.)
- Add the class clearing to the second paragraph (which sets the class to `clearing`) in source code mode. This is also in the template's CSS.

THE LEAST YOU NEED TO KNOW
Web designers around the world use stock images to easily add rich graphical content to their sites.

When you add content, some manipulation of the HTML or CSS is usually needed to achieve the result you want. Often, styles can be created in the template CSS and applied within articles by using the Style drop-down in the editor.

You home page should now look as shown in Figure 11.15.
Not bad. Now let's look at some of that extra functionality you want to add.

Extending a Restaurant Website

At the beginning of the chapter, we listed three potential areas in which you can extend the basic functionality of a restaurant website:

- Image gallery
- Email marketing
- Google Maps

Let's look a little more closely at each.

FIGURE 11.15 The final restaurant site home page.

Image Gallery: JPG Flash Rotator 2

An image gallery shows attractive photos or images that the visitor can browse through. For a restaurant website—unlike, say, a photographer's website—the images are shown for effect as a whole rather than there being a need to view specific ones individually. What I mean by that is that a site visitor doesn't specifically need to be able to navigate or zoom the individual images as he or she would with SlideshowPro; instead, the images can just scroll or rotate.

In addition to the built-in Random Image module that displays just a single image, a simple but effective tool for creating an image gallery is the Image Flash Rotator. Image Flash Rotator 2.5 was developed by Joomlashack.com.

You can upload half a dozen images of the same size, and Image Flash Rotator rotates the images with various flash effects, such as fade or swipe. This extension is a module, so you need to place it in a module location (or use {loadposition ...} to place it in an article).

Email Marketing

There are several choices when it comes to marketing a website via email. In Chapter 8, "Getting Traffic to Your Site," we looked at email newsletters as a useful global marketing strategy for any website. Again, I usually advise the use of a third-party application so you get higher deliverability and better compliance with the CAN-SPAM act.

Google Maps

Google Maps provides a great interactive way to give people both clear visual information about the location of your business and dynamic directions to you. It's relatively easy to use: Type your address into Google Maps (maps.google.com), click Link, and then copy the snippet of HTML code that appears to embed a map in your page.

USER'S GUIDE LESSON 11 DEMO
www.joomlabook.com provides an SQL dump that shows what you should have if you followed all the steps shown in this lesson. You can log in to the administrative backend to see the site framework and the categories, subcategories, and menus.

TURNKEY RESTAURANT WEBSITE PACKAGE
A turnkey version of a restaurant website is also available at SimplWeb. It includes fully managed hosting and training and support. You can find out more at www.simplweb.com/restaurant.

Summary

This chapter tackles one of the trickiest parts of creating a Joomla site: how to start with a sitemap and content and organize the content into Joomla's content hierarchy. Here are the key points we looked at in this chapter:

- A modern business must have a web presence that communicates its brand and information about the company.
- A default Joomla installation takes care of the key features in a small business site: easily edited content and flexible menu configuration.

- A small website does not need a detailed category/subcategory structure. Often just a single category can be used for all the content articles.

- In most cases, it's easiest to create a site in the following order:

  1. Create categories.
  2. Create subcategories.
  3. Create articles as placeholder content.
  4. Create menus/Menu Items.
  5. Go back and enter more detailed content.

- Using Lorem Ipsum dummy text is a useful technique for creating articles that will form the structure of a Joomla site so you can check the navigation for it as you go along. You can later edit the page content and articles.

- Web designers use stock images to easily add rich graphical content to their sites.

- When you add content, some manipulation of the HTML or CSS is usually needed to achieve the result you want. Often, styles can be created as classes in the default template's CSS and applied within articles, using the Style drop-down of the article editor.

Chapter 12

Creating a Blog with Joomla!

In This Chapter

It seems as if everyone has a blog these days. Many people still think of blogs as personal diaries, but more and more organizations and companies are using blogs as a way to shape perception of who they are and what they do. If you go to a website today, you will likely find a link to a blog somewhere on the site. It is becoming common now for a website to dedicate a section of the site to the blog.

The ways blogs are used is an important distinction. Originally, a blog was an entire website. In this traditional model, short posts are shown on the home page, along with links to the complete articles. You might find links to other blogs or popular blog posts in a side column. This chapter talks about blogs in a more general sense: as a dynamic communication medium for a person or an organization to interact with stakeholders. This chapter covers the following topics:

- What is a blog?
- Why do you need a blog?
- What features does a blog need?
- How should you organize the content on a blog?
- How can you extend the functionality of a blog?

What Is a Blog?

At the most fundamental level, a blog is a communication medium. Typically, it has frequent brief posts about a particular subject (sometimes the subject is the author). Almost all blogs incorporate some sort of system to allow site visitors to leave comments. This shapes the characteristics of the communication; rather than being one-way communication, as in mere announcements and advertisements, a blog allows two-way communication and aims to engage readers actively.

A second defining characteristic of modern blogs is that they embody a unique communication style. They tend to be most effective when written in an honest first-person voice. A blog that is written as old-school, third-person press releases will die a lonely death. Frequently a blog is written by one person so that the writing voice clearly comes through in the posts.

Another defining characteristic of a blog is frequent posting. It's easy to find heated debate about how often you should post. Some are convinced it needs to be daily; others say weekly. All will agree, though, that you need to make regular posts to build a loyal readership that have consistent expectations about your blog content. Usually blog posts are brief, and only introductory text is shown on the main page, along with a "read more" link.

> **NOTE**
> A blog is *not* TrackBacks, pings, Digg It buttons, blogrolls, permalinks, or Google AdSense. You see all these things on a blog (hopefully not all at once), but these are just features on a blog page, not the blog itself. You can have a successful blog, even be among the top 50 heavyweights, without any of these. As you create a blog, make sure you don't let the trees prevent you from seeing the great potential of the forest.

> **THE LEAST YOU NEED TO KNOW**
> A blog is a modern communication vehicle that is becoming more and more important in today's Web-connected world.

Why Have a Blog?

As blogs become more mainstream, they provide a highly cost-effective medium for organizations to communicate with their stakeholders. They help an organization engage in two-way dialog, which can take many forms. Here are some examples:

- A software company updates users about new developments.
- A nonprofit organization describes new outreach projects.
- A CEO communicates his or her vision to company employees.
- A political candidate rallies his or her base.

Think about this situation: Kryptonite, a popular bike lock manufacturer, had a small lock defect a few years ago. It was possible to open one of the high-end bike locks with a ballpoint pen. Somebody posted the story on the Internet, and it spread from blog to blog. Kryptonite did not, and arguably could not, respond to every blog post, but it also took several days for the company to formulate a plan and post details, even on its own website. Within a few days, the story spread and got picked up by major news outlets. The result was a massive replacement program, followed by a class-action suit against Kryptonite. The interesting point here is that blogs significantly magnified the speed at which the story spread. If Kryptonite had been on its collective toes, it might have used blogs in its response to the issue. Using blogs is a double-edged sword: Blogs can both help and hinder your organization. (Read more about Kryptonite's experience at http://redcouch.typepad.com/weblog/2005/07/kryptonite_argu.html.)

THE LEAST YOU NEED TO KNOW
News and information move faster than ever, in smaller and smaller news cycles. A blog-style page that is easy to update is an important tool for any organization to communicate with its stakeholders.

What Options Are There for Blogging?

There are many places on the Web where you can create a classic single-author sequential blog; some are free, and some are for-a-fee services. Here are a few:

- Blogger (www.blogger.com)
- Typepad (www.typepad.com)
- Wordpress (wordpress.org)
- Movable Type (www.movabletype.com)

The 800-pound gorilla in the room here is Blogger. Part of the Google world, Blogger hosts by far the most blogs. This is probably because it is easy to set up and free.

So why would you want to use Joomla for blogs? Aren't there a number of much easier solutions?

Well, first of all, this is a book about Joomla, not about Blogger, so I want to try to show how you can use Joomla to set up a blog in addition to using it to sell products, build community sites, make your coffee, and so on. But there is another real reason: Blogs are closed systems.

What I mean by that sentence is this: The software that powers many blog sites is basic and straightforward. That's perhaps part of Blogger's huge popularity. But if a time comes when you want to extend the features of your blog site to do more than display articles, you are stuck. Maybe you want to add a forum, a shopping cart for your e-book, or a subscription as part of your blog. You can't add any major functionality in a service like Blogger at this time. This is even true about some of the high-end blog CMS platforms, such as Wordpress. The platform itself is not designed to be extensible, so you can't add anything.

A big theme of this book has been how amazingly extendable Joomla is, with its free (GPL) and commercial extensions. So if Joomla can mimic the basic functions of a blog, it can be a basic foundation on which to build a super-sticky and feature-rich blog site.

What Features Are Needed on a Blog Site?

Let's pause from our headlong rush into joining the blogosphere and consider what essential features are needed for a successful blog site. Each one has solutions that are available within Joomla:

- **Flexible layout**—If you've been to one Blogger blog, you've been to them all. Making yours look different from the other 27 million blogs out there is a good thing.

  Joomla is best-of-breed here. It's recognized as being one of the most "skinnable" open source CMSs available. The feature that controls a Joomla site's look and feel is the *template*. There are many templates available that have a definite blog look to them.

- **Browser-based editing**—You want to get your content on the Web quickly and easily.

- **Automated publishing**—FTWho? You don't want to have to mess with complicated file transfer; you want to click a button and have your posts appear. Text formatting and spell checking are bonuses.

- **Categories**—Part of having a usable site is being able to split your posts into categories that will make them easier to find.

- **Search-engine-optimized URLs**—If you have written a post, you don't want your URL to be www.myblog.com/9823749.html?myleftleg. You want to be able to squeeze every ounce of SEO out of your post. So having a URL that includes keywords about the post is useful when people link to you.

- **Comment systems**—A critical feature, the comment system is the number-one way your site becomes sticky (a measure of how likely a visitor is to return). Bloggers have embraced free-for-all commenting, and it has led to their explosion in popularity. Many corporate sites that have blogs, however, are afraid to tread this path.

- **Syndication feeds**—RSS and ATOM are XML applications that can push your posts onto other RSS readers. Email clients such as Thunderbird come with RSS readers, as do personal portal sites such as Yahoo. Perhaps a more important point is that a website can receive and display RSS, and you can have your posts appear automatically on someone else's website, where (hopefully) they will get even more readership.

- **Email notification**—If you've added a post, wouldn't it be nice if you could notify an email list that you've done so? If you run a web business, you will soon start building a list of emails, and you may want to really put them to use. (This is a whole other subject beyond blogging.)

- **Search**—As a prolific blog poster, your archive will soon be bursting. You need a robust search tool that can help site visitors find your posts. Steve Krug (a usability expert) maintains that some visitors automatically look for a search button as the first thing they do; people are either searchers or browsers.

- **TrackBack**—TrackBacks are complex, but the bottom line is that you read a post, and you comment about it on your blog. You place the URL to the post in yours, and the blog picks up your post and leaves it as a comment in the other's post.

THE LEAST YOU NEED TO KNOW
A blog isn't about widgets and gizmos; it's about the quality of the content. You need a tool that can help you organize and present your blog posts as easily as possible.

Downloading and Installing a Blog Template

At www.compassdesigns.net, you can grab the JS_Optimus template that you'll be using in this chapter. JS_Optimus is a pure CSS-based template design with some nicely integrated SEO features. It's easy to set up. Both a commercial Pro version of Optimus and a free version are available. To follow along with this chapter, you can download the free version, which is shown in Figure 12.1.

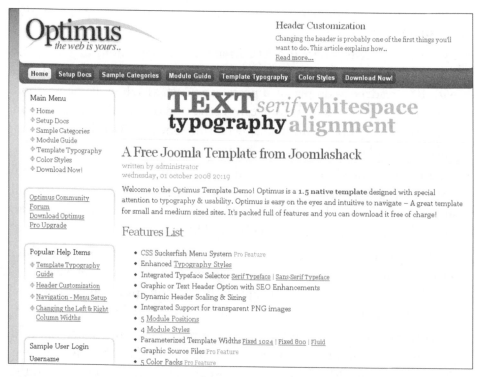

FIGURE 12.1   Screenshot of the Optimus template.

After you download this template, you should have a template zip file to install into Joomla:

1. Go to Extensions>Extension Manager to get to the Extension Manager. You learned how extensions are installed and managed in Chapter 6, "Extending Joomla!"

2. Browse to the template zip file and click the Upload and Install button. You get a message that says, "Template successfully installed."

3. Go to Extensions>Template Manager to open the Template Manager, select the JS_Optimus template, and click the Default button to make it the default template. Viewed in the frontend, the site (with no content) should look as shown in Figure 12.2.

FIGURE 12.2   The Optimus template, empty of content.

Optimus Template Features and Positions

The JS_Optimus template has two main features, along with the usual functionality, such as collapsible columns:

- The logo/header can be either text or a logo. If you select Text in the template parameters, the template shows whatever headline is entered in the template parameter fields. Otherwise, it displays a logo graphic.

- It has the ability to use a pure CSS suckerfish drop-down menu (included in the Pro version).

The Optimus template has eight available module positions.

To position your modules (for example, Main Menu, login, syndicate, polls) in the various template positions, you set the Position parameter in each module. Figure 12.3 shows the available positions on this template:

- **top**—Reserved for a horizontal menu
- **newsflash**—Within the header to the right of logo for rotating quotations; not reserved
- **breadcrumb**—Reserved for the breadcrumb bar
- **left**—Left vertical column; not reserved
- **banner**—Banner position (top of center column); not reserved
- **teaser**—Undefined; not reserved
- **right**—Right vertical column; not reserved
- **footer**—Footer position; reserved for footer information

In addition to these, the Pro version offers six user positions for ads or teasers:

- **user4**—Top-left
- **user5**—Top-center
- **user6**—Top-right
- **user7**—Bottom-left
- **user8**—Bottom-center
- **user9**—Bottom-right

The available positions appear as shown in Figure 12.3.

Most of these positions are generic in their potential use. One, however, was placed with a specific purpose in mind. The top module location is intended for a horizontal navigation bar.

Configuring the Logo

There are two ways you can configure the logo: by setting Header Style to graphic or text in the parameters of the template.

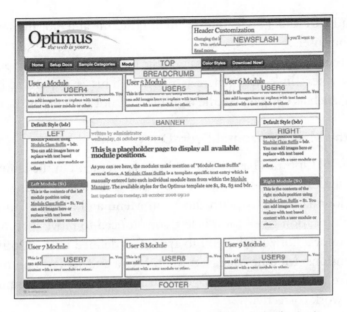

FIGURE 12.3   Template module positions. (Image courtesy of Joomlashack.com.)

Graphic Header

The template includes a logo graphic. All you need to do is create an image in your image editor of choice and set its background color to the same as its container (that is, the header's background) or to transparent so the container background shows through. In the case of the free version of the JS_Optimus template, the background color is white (#FFFFFF). When you have finished creating your header graphic, save it as `logo.png` and take note of its dimensions. Upload it to the `/templates/js_optimus/images/styleX/` folder (where X is the style you are using). The free version of the template uses style 1, so save as `/templates/js_optimus_free/images/style1/logo.png`. Next, log in to the backend as a super administrator and navigate to Extensions>Template Manager, click js_optimus, and in the template parameters enter your logo image width and height values (in pixels). Remember to also fill in Headline and Slogan, as these will be used as attributes for your logo's image tag and visible to search engines.

Text Header

If you don't have access to a graphic image editor or are just looking to save some time, you can set the header to appear as stylized text. To do this, just log in to the backend as a super administrator and navigate to Extensions>Template Manager, click js_optimus, and set Header Style to text. Fill in Headline and Slogan as you want them to appear to your users.

When this template is set to display a graphic logo, it has an SEO-optimized header that will show a text link when there is no CSS. This is important because search engine spiders, such as Google, see the text link and not the graphic header.

Configuring the Main Horizontal Drop-Down Menu

The Pro version of Optimus has a built-in drop-down menu in the template CSS. The free version includes a single-level menu (no suckerfish drop-downs).

An empty Joomla site starts with the Main Menu and a single Home link. However, the default location given for it is left, so you need to move that module into the correct position for a horizontal menu to appear, as defined in the Optimus template.

Go to Extensions>Module Manager>Main Menu and set Position to top.

While you're in the Module Manager, you need to set some parameters for your drop-down to work correctly:

1. In the module parameters, set Show Submenu Items to Yes.
2. Set the title to *not* show.
3. In the advanced parameters, make sure Menu Class Suffix and Module Class Suffix are both blank.

When you configure the menu this way, it moves to the horizontal position and is prepared for drop-downs, as shown in Figure 12.4.

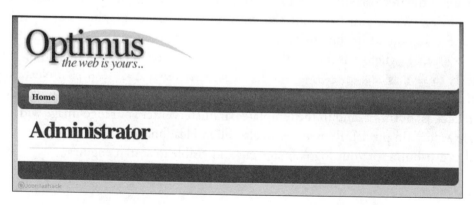

FIGURE 12.4 Configuring the horizontal menu.

At this point, your template is configured and ready to use. Let's now take a detailed look at how to set up the site structure, which with Joomla means the categories and navigation.

Organizing Content on a Blog

It is important that you understand some of the basics of how Joomla organizes content and the structure it uses. If you haven't already, make sure you read through Chapter 5, "Creating Menus and Navigation."

As mentioned in the introduction to this chapter, there are two main types of blog sites: a pure blog site that has little other content than a series of sequential postings and an organization's blog that is part of a larger, more comprehensive site. These two slightly different types of sites need different category hierarchies to organize their articles. Let's look at each of them in turn.

Organizing a Blog Within a Larger Site

A good example of a blog within a larger site is www.joomlashack.com. There are a number of sections for templates, services, and so on and then a Menu Item for the blog posts on the far right in the menu, as shown in Figure 12.5.

FIGURE 12.5   A sample menu in a blog site.

This concept of having the blog as part of a larger site is common; it's most applicable when the blog is supporting the main goal of the site. In this scenario, the category would be the blog, and you could have more subcategories inside it.

Consider the restaurant site example from Chapter 11, "Creating a Restaurant Site with Joomla!" As a business, it's definitely a good candidate for having a rich blog to communicate with site visitors.

You would show all the articles in the blog in the order you wanted, probably by date, most recent first. If you wanted to, you could then have more Menu Items linked to the specific subcategories so people could browse a single category if they wanted.

To do this, you need to create a new menu and in it create Menu Items that link to each category. You can then publish the module for that menu in the location you want. I do this on my own blog, www.compassdesigns.net, as shown in Figure 12.6.

FIGURE 12.6 Using Joomla categories to create a blog-related menu.

The example you work with throughout the rest of this chapter is the kind in which the blog actually *is* the site.

Organizing a Standalone Blog

Standalone blogs have been popularized by tools such as Blogger. The home page shows the most recent blog entries, usually most-recent-first order. An excellent example is www.copyblogger.com, shown in Figure 12.7.

NOTE
I use www.copyblogger.com as an example because it's a really great resource. If you are building a blog, you should have this site on your RSS feed for daily reading.

In the example, you are going to work through in this chapter, you'll make a blog about parenting. (With three boys myself, I can use all the parenting tips I can get!)

In Chapter 11, we discussed organizing categories. We are actually going to use a similar concept here: You will have a category that holds all your blog content; you can call it Parenting Blog. We'll then have subcategories that are different topical areas of the blog posts. The article organization will be as follows:

Category	Subcategories	Articles
Parenting Blog	Parenting	Various blog posts
	Vacations	Various blog posts
	Money	Various blog posts
	Home	Various blog posts
	Family	Various blog posts
	Other Stuff	Various blog posts

FIGURE 12.7   www.copyblogger.com.

To set up this structure, go to Content>Category Manager>New and create a category called Parenting Blog. Next go to Content>Category Manager>New and create the six subcategories shown in the table. Make sure the parent category in each case is the category called Parenting Blog you just created.

It's important to remember that your categories are merely buckets for the webmaster to use for organizing the content. Users might view articles in other ways, such as by date. For blogs, this brings us to an important feature—the ability to use tags as a second, cross-category method to organize content.

About Tagging

If you have been to a blog, you might have seen a box showing several keywords, often in different sizes. These *tags* are a common feature on blogs.

Using a tag is basically another way of organizing the visitor's experience with your content. You have an article, say in the Parenting category, but then add tags such as Bedtime, Reading, and Bath Time (maybe it was a story about getting your kids to bed after bath time). These tags are then shown on the page and present an alternative path to content from the categories that share the same keywords.

In my review of the literature on tags (most of it from bloggers), there seems to be no real consensus as to whether tags are critical to blogs. When used carefully and in moderation, I think they can help, if simply through the benefits they can bring in terms of anchor text internal links (see Chapter 8, "Getting Traffic to Your Site"). I would put them on my "nice to have" list for a Joomla site.

Creating the Menus

You will have two menus for your blog. The first will be a horizontal one across the top, the Main Menu. The second will be links to the categories in a side column.

Creating the Main Menu

For your standalone blog about parenting, configuring the menu will be relatively easy. You just have to pay attention to correct settings for the parameters.

As with the restaurant site in Chapter 11, here you don't really want to use the front page component. You want everything that's posted to the blog section to appear automatically. In the same way as in Lesson 11, here you need to create a new Menu Item that meets your needs, make it the default Menu Item, and then unpublish the Home Menu Item.

Go to Menus>Main Menu>New>Articles>Category Blog Layout, give the layout a name (such as Blog), and link it to the Parenting blog category. You then need to set the following parameters:

- Blog Layout Options:
  - # Leading = 10
  - # Intro = 0
  - # Columns = 1
  - # Links = 10
  - Category Order = Category Manager Order
  - Article Order = Most Recent First
- Article Options:
  - Linked Titles = Yes
  - Show Author = Hide
  - Show Modify Date = Hide
- Page Display Options:
  - Show Page Heading = No

You then need to make the new Menu Item the default and unpublish the old Home Menu Item in the Menu Manager (or you could have edited this original Home Menu Item).

So you can properly see the effect of setting these parameters, add a few content articles using Lorem Ipsum dummy text, as you have done in the last couple chapters. Your home page then looks as shown in Figure 12.8.

If you look around most blogs, you usually find a few other links in the Main Menu. In this case, you should add the standard About Us and Contact Us links. The About Us page is a simple uncategorized article. You'll make that first.

Go to Content>Article Manager>New and create an uncategorized article called About Me. Create a Menu Item for that article. Next, go to Menus>Main Menu>New>Articles>Single Article Layout, name the layout About Me, and link it to the article you just created.

Now create the Contact Us form. As you saw in Chapters 10 and 11, installing with no sample content means that you have to create the Contact category and the contact first. (Flip back to Chapter 11 to see how to do this.)

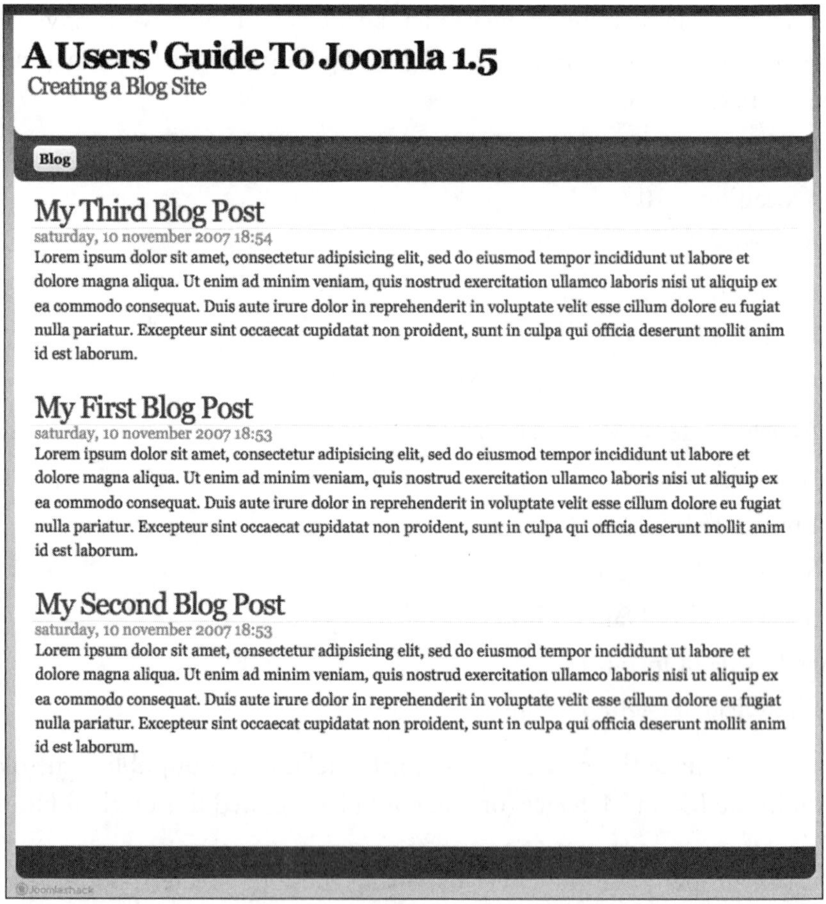

A Users' Guide To Joomla 1.5
Creating a Blog Site

Blog

My Third Blog Post
saturday, 10 november 2007 18:54

Lorem ipsum dolor sit amet, consectetur adipisicing elit, sed do eiusmod tempor incididunt ut labore et dolore magna aliqua. Ut enim ad minim veniam, quis nostrud exercitation ullamco laboris nisi ut aliquip ex ea commodo consequat. Duis aute irure dolor in reprehenderit in voluptate velit esse cillum dolore eu fugiat nulla pariatur. Excepteur sint occaecat cupidatat non proident, sunt in culpa qui officia deserunt mollit anim id est laborum.

My First Blog Post
saturday, 10 november 2007 18:53

Lorem ipsum dolor sit amet, consectetur adipisicing elit, sed do eiusmod tempor incididunt ut labore et dolore magna aliqua. Ut enim ad minim veniam, quis nostrud exercitation ullamco laboris nisi ut aliquip ex ea commodo consequat. Duis aute irure dolor in reprehenderit in voluptate velit esse cillum dolore eu fugiat nulla pariatur. Excepteur sint occaecat cupidatat non proident, sunt in culpa qui officia deserunt mollit anim id est laborum.

My Second Blog Post
saturday, 10 november 2007 18:53

Lorem ipsum dolor sit amet, consectetur adipisicing elit, sed do eiusmod tempor incididunt ut labore et dolore magna aliqua. Ut enim ad minim veniam, quis nostrud exercitation ullamco laboris nisi ut aliquip ex ea commodo consequat. Duis aute irure dolor in reprehenderit in voluptate velit esse cillum dolore eu fugiat nulla pariatur. Excepteur sint occaecat cupidatat non proident, sunt in culpa qui officia deserunt mollit anim id est laborum.

FIGURE 12.8   Initial posts showing on the home page.

To create a link to the contact, go to Menus>Main Menu>New>Contacts>Single Contact Layout, name it Contact Us, and link it to the contact just created.

Now you need to create that side menu.

Creating a Submenu for Categories

To create the side menu, you need to create a whole new menu.

Go to Menus>Menu Manager>New and name your menu Blog Categories. Remember, when you create this menu, Joomla won't automatically create a module for it, so you'll need to create one.

You then need to add the Menu Items for this menu. Go to Menus>Blog Categories>New>Articles>Category Blog Layout, name the layout Family (to correspond to the exact name of the category), and link it to the Family category. Give it the same parameter settings as the home page link:

- Blog Layout Options:
  - # Leading = 10
  - # Intro = 0
  - # Columns = 1
  - # Links = 10
  - Category Order = Category Manager Order
  - Article Order = Most Recent First
- Article Options:
  - Title Linkable = Yes
  - Author Name = Hide
  - Modified Date = Hide
  - PDF/Email/Print Icons = Hide
- Page Display Options:
  - Show Page Heading = No

Do the same thing for each of the other categories.

TIP
A quick way to do this is to copy the original Menu Item. That way, you don't have to keep setting those parameters; you can simply change the name and the category it links to.

You now need to publish your module for the menu in the correct location.

Go to Extensions>Module Manager>Blog Categories. Set it to be enabled (published) and position it in the left column. Your page should now look as shown in Figure 12.9.

While you are adding modules, you need to create some more modules for some of the other functionality you want.

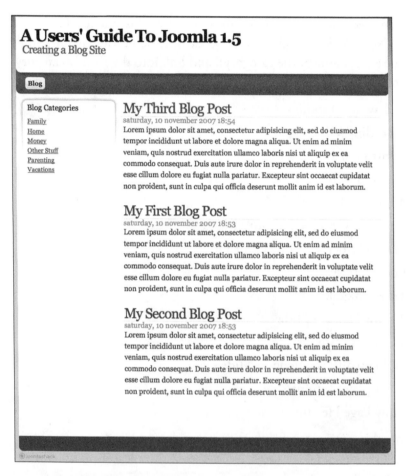

FIGURE 12.9 The home page with the category submenu.

Adding Dynamic Modules

Joomla has many features that allow you to automatically generate page content that is continuously updated. You will add to the left column three modules that do this and that are commonly found in blogs.

TIP

As discussed in Chapter 8, having many internal links is useful. It not only helps visitors drill down to the content they want to view, it also helps with SEO.

For your blog, you are going to use three default Joomla modules:

- Latest news
- Most read
- Related items

To see the full effect of these modules, you need to add some more content. You also need to enter some metadata for the article.

Create the following articles with Lorem Ipsum dummy text and enter the metadata keywords indicated here:

Category	Article Title	Keywords
Family	Family 1	1,2,3
Home	Home 1	2,3,4
Money	Money 1	3,4,5
Parenting	Parenting 1	4,5,6
Vacations	Vacations 1	5,6,7
Other Stuff	Other Stuff 1	6,7,8

After you do this, the Article Manager should look as shown in Figure 12.10.

You need to carefully add the metadata because the related items module uses this information to figure out what to show. As discussed in Chapter 8, it is best to add two to six *specific* keywords for any article.

TIP
Don't add the same keyword to everything; otherwise, the related items module will just list the whole site!

Next, you're going to create the three modules, starting with the latest news module.

Adding the Latest News Module

Go to Extensions>Module Manager>New and select the latest news module. To make it specific to a blog, call it Latest Blog Posts, leave all the other parameters as they are, and place it in the left column. Make sure it is assigned to all menus (meaning it will appear on all pages).

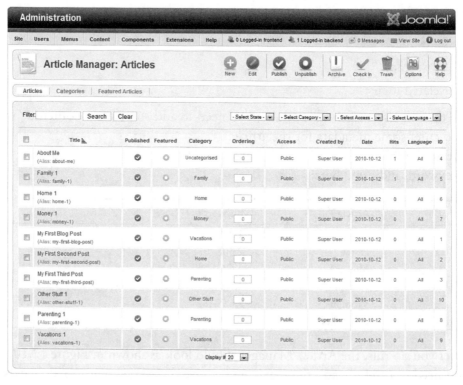

FIGURE 12.10   Building out the articles in the Article Manager.

Adding the Most Read Content Module

Go to Extensions>Module Manager>New and select the most read module. To make it specific to your blog, you can call it Popular Blog Posts, leave all the other parameters as they are, and place it in the left column. Make sure it is assigned to all menus.

Adding the Related Items Module

Go to Extensions>Module Manager>New and select the related items module. To make it specific to a blog, you can call it Related Posts, leave all the other parameters as they are, and place it in the left module location. Make sure it is assigned to all menus.

THE LEAST YOU NEED TO KNOW

Joomla has some powerful features, such as dynamically showing links to more articles in your site. Using this feature is a great way to draw visitors into your content.

Adding Static Modules

As well as including modules that are continuously updated (by Joomla), many blogs include content that is to be more static. Examples include footers and blogrolls (lists of links to other blogs).

Adding a Footer

In this example, you want to put some copyright text in the footer. To do this, you need to create a custom HTML module.

Go to Extensions>Module Manager>New and select a custom HTML module. Then enter a simple copyright statement and make sure it appears in the correct location and that the title is set to not be shown.

Adding a Blogroll

The basic premise of a blogroll is that an easy way to get links to your blog is to link to other blogs. This builds an informal web of linking between a group of blogs. In Joomla, a blogroll is created using a simple custom HTML module that contains links to other blogs.

To create a blogroll, go to Extensions > Module Manager > New and select a custom HTML module. Enter a name (such as Blogroll) and enable in the left column. In the editor area, enter in the URLs of the sites you want to link to. After you add these modules, when you navigate to a particular article, you should see a screen like the one shown in Figure 12.11.

Here you see the latest blog posts and the most popular blog posts in the left column. You also have a mechanism for people to browse deeper into the site with the related items module.

> **NOTE**
>
> A common concept in blogging is the idea of *classic content*. As you write articles, you will likely find that some articles prove to be popular. People will link to them and comment on them, and those articles will form the backbone of your blog. It's important for visitors to be able to find them quickly and easily, hence the use of the most read module on all pages.

Now you need to start adding some of the basic functionality that will increase the stickiness of your blog.

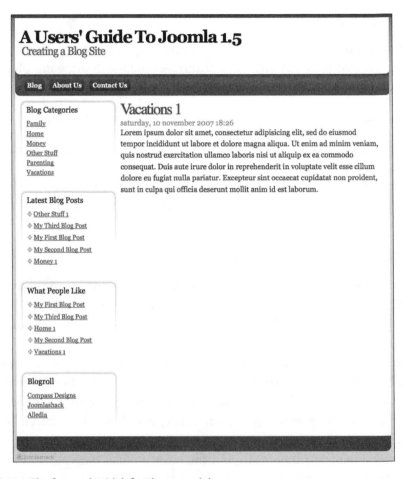

FIGURE 12.11   The frontend, with left column modules.

Adding Basic Functionality to a Blog

The beginning of this chapter lists a number of features that would be nice to have in your blog. Let's look at each one and explore the opportunities to add them to Joomla.

Flexible Layout

Installing the Optimus template demonstrated the flexibility you have in building a blog with Joomla. Thousands of templates are available for Joomla, both free and commercial.

Browser-Based Editing

It's easy to add content to a Joomla site through the backend. You saw in Chapter 7, "Expanding Your Content: Articles and Editors," that you can add a login and user menu to the frontend of the site to make it even easier.

Automated Publishing

Joomla has a nice bit of functionality hidden away in its date parameters for an article: You can actually set the publishing date for an article in the future. This is particularly useful for a blog for which readers have come to expect daily posts. Heading out on a vacation? Just write your blog posts ahead of time and set them to be published every day while you are away.

Categories

As you saw earlier in this chapter, you can already set up a blog into themed categories for your articles, and you can create a subnavigation module that links to those categories.

Search Engine–Friendly URLs

With the default installation of Joomla, the URLs given are difficult to understand. Consider this example:

```
index.php?option=com_content&view=article&catid=2:vacations&id=9:vacations-
1&Itemid=4
```

Joomla can turn them into search engine–friendly (SEF) URLs. (In Chapter 8, I suggest that SEF URLs might have less to do with search engines and more to do with being human friendly—which I like to call HUF.)

If you turn on the basic SEF (go to Site>Global Configuration and set Search Engine Friendly URLs to Yes), Joomla turns the earlier link into this:

```
/index.php/vacations/12-vacations-1
```

This is in the format of *index.php/[menuitem]/category/article*. Note if you have Menu Items in the navigation, they'll be prepended to the URL.

If your web host is running on Linux (for example, Apache), you can take advantage of mod_rewrite and get URLs like this:

```
Vacations/vacations-1
```

Comment Systems

As mentioned earlier, enabling site visitors to leave comments is essential for blogs. Several comment extensions are available for Joomla at extensions.joomla.org.

Syndication Feeds

More and more people are starting to use RSS as a means of gathering updates from their favorite blogs. Many RSS readers exist, and people take the feeds of the blogs they like to read and pull them into a single place—the RSS reader they like to use. For users to access your blog this way, you need the ability to actually produce RSS feeds of your content.

Joomla 1.6 can produce RSS feeds out of the box. All you have to do is create a syndication module and enable/publish it on a page. Joomla then creates an RSS syndication feed of that page. So if it's published on the home page, the feed will be of that page. If it's on an interior page, the feed will be of that page (say, the Family category on your site).

To create a syndication module, go to Extensions>Module Manager>New and select a syndication module. Assign it to the home page only.

You now see an RSS link in the left column.

Ideally, you want to offer this RSS feed link on all the pages in the site. But if you set it to publish on all pages in the module parameters, the feeds will be different on each page. Joomla changes them dynamically.

There are a couple ways around this. The first is to create a custom HTML module with the RSS feed link (from the home page) and then to publish that across all pages. Another trick is to use the third-party service called FeedBurner in conjunction with the Joomla RSS. I pioneered this in 2006 on my own blog and have had a lot of success with it. Figure 12.12 shows the FeedBurner icon, which you have probably seen before.

FIGURE 12.12   The FeedBurner icon.

Using FeedBurner is relatively simple: You go to www.feedburner.com and enter the URL of your website. FeedBurner should auto-detect the feed; if it doesn't, you can enter the feed URL exactly. FeedBurner then produces a feed of your feed. That might seem a bit redundant, but here is why you do it:

- You can now get an HTML snippet from FeedBurner (in the Publicize tab) from which you can create a custom HTML module to publish across the site.

- You can add the FeedBurner Feedcount feature (which shows the number of subscribers).

- You can get global details and stats about who is subscribing to your feed (see Figure 12.13).

- Most usefully, you can take advantage of an email subscription service called FeedBlitz.

FIGURE 12.13   FeedBurner stats.

The site you have been developing in this chapter is running on a localhost, so FeedBurner would not be able to find it. So that you can see how it works, you can create a custom HTML module from the source of the home page. If you view the home page source, you see the following code:

```
<div class="moduletable">
<h3>Get the RSS feed!</h3>
<a href="?option=com_content&amp;view=section&amp;format=feed&amp;
id=1&amp;type=rss&amp;Itemid=4">
<img src="images/M_images/livemarks.png" alt="" align="top" border="0" />
<span>Feed Entries</span>
</a>
</div>
```

Joomla creates the `<div>` tag. You need to copy everything inside that tag and paste it into a custom HTML module. After you have done that, you can unpublish the real Joomla syndication module. You now have a feed link on all the pages of your site.

> **NOTE**
> Unpublishing does not disable the feed generator in Joomla; the link within the code you copied is just accessing it directly and identifying the content to feed. All you did was hide the Joomla version of the module from the page display and replace it with a static custom HTML module you can show on every page. This link works as long as your home page Menu Item from which it was created continues to exist and display new content.

Email Notification

Pushing out blog posts via email through an opt-in list is a great way to build readership. RSS technology is still relatively new, and many people still prefer email as their subscription vehicle.

FeedBurner offers a service called FeedBlitz that allows people to subscribe to an email list of updates created from a feed. When new posts are made, subscribers automatically get an email containing the post. This is a great way of building readership and traffic. It can even supply posts via Skype! I use this on my blog as an alternative to a traditional email newsletter.

To set up FeedBlitz, go to www.feedblitz.com and create an account and then a subscription. You can then create a custom HTML Joomla module with the simple signup form or an icon from FeedBlitz.

If you look closely at the www.copyblogger.com blog used as an example earlier, you see that it uses both FeedBurner and FeedBlitz.

Search

Joomla has a robust search function built into the core. To use it, you need to create a search module. You simply go to Extensions>Module Manager>New and select a search module. Give it a suitable title and then enable/publish it in the left column.

Social Bookmarking

You might have noticed that I have not mentioned *social bookmarking*, which is a popular blog topic these days. I would not go so far as to say that there are no benefits to be found in social bookmarking sites such as Digg or delicious, but I don't think it's as critical as people make it out to be—for several reasons.

First is information overload. It's common to see blogs with a whole row of social bookmark tags. I think that these are going the way that banner ads have gone over the last few years: Site visitors have developed a blind spot for them.

Second, if people want to bookmark your site with one of these other sites, they can do it on their own; they don't need your insistent icon, asking them to do so.

Finally, according to Digg itself, 94% of Digg users are male. 88% of Digg users are in the 18- to 39-year age range, and 52% of them are "IT professionals, developers, or engineers." That's a very narrow demographic. Unless you have a blog that is targeted at this demographic, none of the ensuing traffic you might get will do much good anyway. It's unfocussed, untargeted, and will not convert very well. But if you feel you need it, take a look at JBookmarks and similar social bookmarking services in the Joomla Extensions Directory (JED) at extensions.joomla.org, under Communities and then Social Bookmarking.

You now have a basic blog site ready, to which you can add a lot of high-quality articles and blog posts. Your home page now looks as shown in Figure 12.14.

THE LEAST YOU NEED TO KNOW
Comments and syndication are critical features of a blog.

Extending a Blog Website Beyond the Basics

One of the main reasons to power a blog site using Joomla is so you can use it as a foundation for other efforts. A classic example might be authors or consultants who want to offer further products or services.

As described in the following paragraphs, there are a couple obvious features with which you might want to extend your site.

Forums

Comments are fine for enabling visitor interactivity on blog posts, but a forum is a great mechanism for a community to come around the topic of a website. It allows a site visitor to initiate conversation. An excellent choice for a forum is Kunena, formally known as Fireboard.

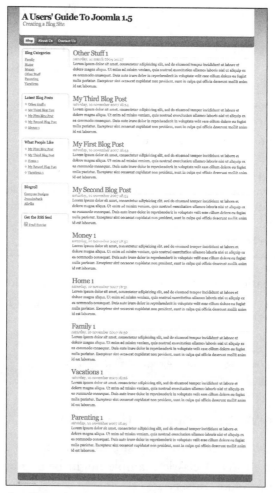

FIGURE 12.14 The completed blog site.

E-commerce

A couple Joomla-based e-commerce solutions are a recent offering from ijoomla.com called DigiStore and the popular VirtueMart. In addition, you can use a third-party application such as E-junkie or Magento.

USER'S GUIDE LESSON 12 SQL DUMP

www.joomlabook.com provides a SQL dump that shows what you should have if you followed all the steps in this lesson. You can log in to the administrative back-end to see the site framework and the sections, categories, and menus.

Summary

This chapter looked at how Joomla can be used to create a basic blog that can be extended as a site grows. Here are the key points we looked at in this chapter:

- A blog is a modern communication vehicle that is becoming more important in today's Web-connected world.

- News and information move faster than ever and in smaller and smaller news cycles. A blog that is easy to update is an important tool for an organization to use in communicating with its stakeholders.

- A blog isn't about widgets and gizmos; it's about the quality of the content. You need a tool that can help you organize and present your blog posts easily.

- How you organize your sections and categories depends on what type of blog you have. Whether part of a more comprehensive site or a standalone blog site, a blog can have all the posts organized in categories under a single place of the site.

- Joomla has some powerful features that dynamically show links to more articles in your site, based on newness, popularity, or related topics. Using Joomla to create blogs is a great way to draw visitors to your content.

- Comments and syndication are critical features of a blog.

APPENDIX A
Getting Help

Community Forums

One of the great things about Joomla, as with many other open source projects, is the enormous community that surrounds the project. Many people measure the Joomla community in terms of the activity of forums related to Joomla. The main Joomla forums are at forum.joomla.org, and many others, including the following, exist:

- www.joomlapolis.com
- www.joomlashack.com
- www.joomlabook.com

 NOTE
This list doesn't include country-specific Joomla sites. Many countries have their own Joomla-sanctioned sites with forums. For example, in Germany, you will find www.joomla.de.

Most of these forums are for commercial products, but they are great resources for getting help, whatever your Joomla needs. Before you ask a question, be sure to search the archives to see if you can find an answer. If you can't turn up any information on your problem, make sure you clearly communicate your problem and be patient as you wait for answers.

Help Sites

A number of websites provide good (original) guides and tutorials about Joomla. (I say *original* because there are many sites that tend to jump on the Joomla bandwagon, put up a couple tutorials, and then cover the site in ads.)

The following are some good-quality Joomla help sites:

- docs.joomla.org (for end users)
- developer.joomla.org (for developers)
- www.compassdesigns.net
- www.howtojoomla.net

Getting Help from Google

The Joomla community is vast, and it's likely that if you're experiencing a problem, someone else has also encountered that problem. Try searching Google with a phrase that describes your issue or, even better, the error you are getting (if any). For the most specific results, remember to enclose the phrase in quotes.

APPENDIX B
A Guide to Joomla! 1.6 ACL

One of the most talked-about features of Joomla 1.6 is the new Access Control Levels or ACL.

With the previous version of Joomla (1.5), if you wanted to give only a group of people, say a particular department in a company, the ability to edit a specific part of your site, you had to install a third-party extension.

Now the ability to give these permissions is in the default core of Joomla 1.6. Some examples of what ACL could do might be

- Give a single user permissions to edit a single article. (Joomla 1.5 could do this.)
- Give only two, or a group of people, permission to edit a single article. (Joomla 1.5 couldn't this.)
- Allow a user permissions to add and edit articles, but only in one category.
- Have three groups of users that are each associated with a single (or multiple) category they can edit articles in.
- Create customized permission in the backend for different administrator groups.
- Give specific users, or groups, permissions to administer specific extensions.

These are relatively easy examples, but the possibilities are virtually limitless. Unfortunately, with that amount of flexibility, setting up complex scenarios can be complicated, and the current interface is not that easy to use or understand.

There are three concepts involved in understanding ACL:

1. **Groups**—Each user can be a member of one or more groups. Various permissions can be assigned to a group. The default groups are public, registered, author, editor, publisher, manager, administrator, and super administrator.

2. **Permissions**—These set what a group can do. They can apply to content or extensions. The core permissions are

   - Site login—The ability to log in to the front of the website
   - Admin login—The ability to log in to the backend of the website
   - Admin—Administrative (root) privileges, such as changing Global Configuration
   - Manage—Ability to change settings on extensions
   - Create—Ability to create new content
   - Delete—Ability to delete (trash) content
   - Edit—Ability to edit existing content that is not necessarily your own
   - Edit state—Ability to change state between published, unpublished, trash

3. **Access Level**—This determines what a group can see. By default, there are three access levels: public, registered, or special. You can add any number of access levels. It's probably useful to match the groups you make to new custom access levels to keep things clearer (though you don't have to).

When working with ACL, it's best to keep things as simple as possible. It can get overly complicated very quickly. Starting with access rules to content is a good way to try out the system, and then you can move on to more advanced features like access to components.

For a more detailed (and more current) guide to ACL, see http://docs.joomla.org/ACL_Tutorial_for_Joomla_1.6.

APPENDIX C
A Quick Introduction to SEO

This appendix provides a much shorter version of Chapter 8, "Getting Traffic to Your Site." Use the information in this appendix if you already have a site ranked and want to see what you can implement to get your ranking higher.

Much of the information here is based on two 2007 studies about ranking in Google from SEOmoz.org (www.seomoz.org/article/search-ranking-factors) and Sistrix (www.free-seo-news.com/newsletter265.htm).

Keyword Use in Title Tag

The number one factor in ranking a page on search engines is the *title tag*. These are the words in the source of a page in `<title>` and appear in the title bar of your browser.

Choose the title of an article very carefully. Joomla uses the title of the article in the title tag (what appears in the title bar).

Anchor Text of Inbound Link

Anchor text appears underlined and in blue (unless it's been styled) for a link from one web page to another.

Try to get some inbound links to your article using the keywords you want to be ranked for. Two ways to do this are through online press services such as PRweb.com or simply by networking.

Global Link Popularity of Site (PageRank)

How many pages are linking to your page is called *link popularity*, or in Google, *PageRank*.

The more sites that link to you, the better. Joomla is a CMS that helps you add content quickly. Create one quality content page per day. Quality content is the most important factor to getting inbound links. For a site that performs well, you eventually need 200-odd pages of content. This is the important point: *Quick SEO is dead!* The only way to perform well in SEO now is to have a rich content site.

Age of Site

When was theare domain of the site registered?

There's nothing you can do about this, but there is evidence that suggests that how long you have your domain registered makes a difference (spam sites are not registered for long). Go and extend your domain registration for a couple of years.

Link Popularity Within the Site

This is the number of links to the page from inside your own domain.

It's critical that you link to articles from within your site using the right anchor text. Make sure that you

- Use the Linked Titles setting under Article Options.
- Make good used of the Most Read Content, Articles – Related Articles, and Latest News modules.
- Have a sitemap component linked to directly from your home page.

Topical Relevance of Inbound Links and Popularity of Linking Site

It's important that you get quality inbound links. This means they have to be from a site that is topically related to yours and one that has a high PageRank. It's worth submitting once to directories (then forget about it).

- Type **related:www.yoursite.com** into Google and contact the top 20 returns for links.

Link Popularity of Site in Topic Community

Make sure you have a blog on your site and network with others in your topical community. Make sure you frequently link to other blogs in your topical community as well.

Keyword Use in Body Text

You need to make sure you have a high keyword density of the phrase you are optimizing for in the content of the page. Still important, the German study from Sistrix identified some interesting results:

- Place targeted keywords in the first and last paragraphs. There is a simple trick here—write your quality content and then use the tool of your choice to find the keyword density. *Then*, take the top three words and add them to the meta keywords in the parameters part of the page (in Joomla admin). This is somewhat backward perhaps, but it optimizes a page for what you actually wrote, rather than making you write a page optimized for certain words (which I always find difficult).

- Keywords in H2–H6 headline tags seem to have an influence on the rankings, while keywords in H1 headline tags seem to be getting less valuable. Modify the output of the core content component through a template override file.

- Using keywords in bold or strong tags has a slight effect; the same goes for img alt tags and filenames.

NOTE
The two SEO studies identified some other factors of measured/estimated influence on search results that had some impact, but not as much as those described here.

File Size

The file size doesn't seem to influence the ranking of a web page on Google, although smaller sites tend to have slightly higher rankings. Optimize those images!

Clean URL

Although keywords in the filename (URL) don't seem to have a positive effect (based on the German study), a URL with few parameters (?id=123, and so on) is important. Turn on Joomla SEF, but don't worry too much about it.

Utilize Your Error Pages

Too often, companies forget about error pages (such as 404 errors). Error pages should always redirect "lost" users to valuable, text-based pages. Placing text links to major site pages is an excellent practice. Visit www.cnet.com/error for an example of a well-utilized error page. To make the error page fit with the rest of the theme of your site, create an uncategorized article and then copy the source as viewed on a web page, and put that into the 404 file.

What's Not Here?

You'll see much of the discussion about SEO revolving around various SEF components. These components allow for advanced manipulation of URLs and metatags. Neither of these was identified as a major factor in either SEO analysis. Joomla's default SEF does a good job at removing extra URL parameters. Once turned on, you can concentrate on the much more important factors influencing your search engine rank, such as quality content and link building campaigns.

If you are more interested in Joomla SEO, I have many articles at compassdesigns. net. Just do a site search for SEO in Google!

APPENDIX D
Installing WampServer

WampServer is a complete package that includes PHP, Apache, and MySQL for Windows and allows you to run a website from your "local" desktop/laptop computer running the Windows operating system.

WampServer is free to use (via the GPL), but you can make a donation on the developer's site. You can obtain a copy of WampServer from www.wampserver.com/en/. Figure D.1 shows this page.

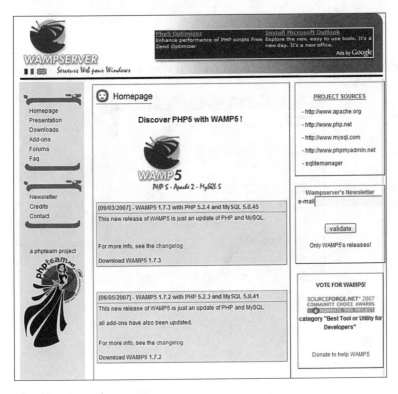

FIGURE D.1   The WampServer home page.

Clicking the Download link takes you to the download page (www.wampserver. com/en/download.php), from which you can download the latest version of WampServer.

After you download WampServer, when you run the download package, the Setup Wizard appears (see Figure D.2).

FIGURE D.2   The beginning of the WampServer installation.

On the next wizard screen (see Figure D.3), you accept the license.

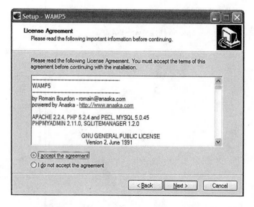

FIGURE D.3   Accepting the WampServer license.

You now need to select the installation folder (see Figure D.4).

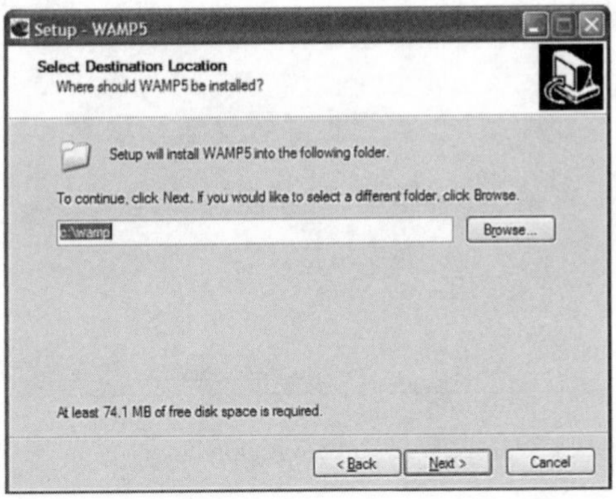

FIGURE D.4   Selecting the installation folder.

Next, you must choose the Start Menu link name (see Figure D.5).

FIGURE D.5   Selecting the Start Menu link name.

You now have an option to have WampServer start automatically (see Figure D.6). I usually don't enable this, preferring to run it manually.

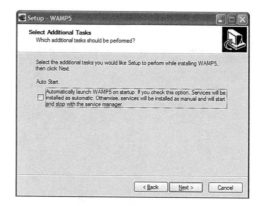

FIGURE D.6   The option to start WampServer automatically.

The wizard now shows the settings you have chosen (see Figure D.7), and you're ready to install.

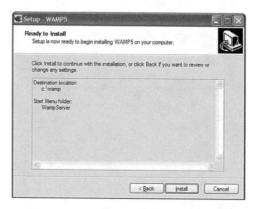

FIGURE D.7   Installation options.

You need to choose a folder that will be the location for all the sites you want to work on (see Figure D.8). I usually just accept the default: \www\.

FIGURE D.8   The website folder.

WampServer is now installed on your computer. Next, you are taken through a series of screens to set up WampServer. First, you need to decide what to call the SMTP server for email (see Figure D.9). On a test Joomla site, this really doesn't matter, so you can leave it as is.

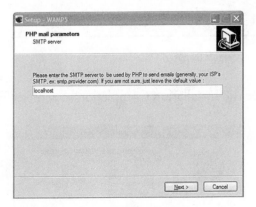

FIGURE D.9   SMTP server name selection.

The default email address is next (see Figure D.10). Again, for local test Joomla sites, this isn't used, so you can leave it as the default.

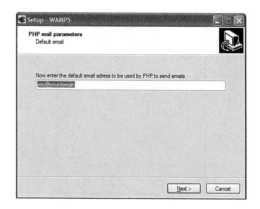

FIGURE D.10   The default PHP email address.

You should now see a dialog box that asks what browser you want to use. Figure D.11 shows the default browser, Firefox, being accepted.

FIGURE D.11   Choosing the default browser.

You should now see the Installation Completion screen (see Figure D.12).

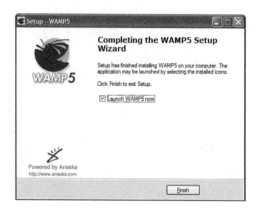

FIGURE D.12   Installation complete.

When you run WampServer, you see a small icon in your system tray (the row of small icons in the lower-right portion of your screen).

If you left-click the icon, you see the option Start All Services, as shown in Figure D.13.

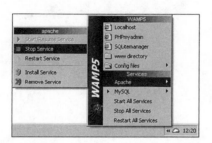

FIGURE D.13   Clicking the WampServer icon.

You now see the icon turn red, then yellow, and then white, indicating that the two services, Apache and PHP, are starting (see Figure D.14).

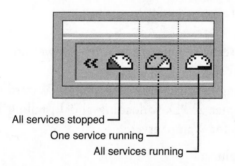

All services stopped ⎯
One service running ⎯
All services running ⎯

FIGURE D.14   The three stages of starting services.

If the icon does not go all the way to white, there has been an error. The most common problem is a conflict with Skype. If you use Skype (and who doesn't?!), you need to quit it first and then start WampServer. Then you can start Skype back up.

When you have WampServer running, you have a folder (for example, c:\wamp\www) that is your web folder. Anything you put here, such as a Joomla installation, will be accessible as a website. It's best to put a site into a new folder (for example, c:\wamp5\www\mysite).

If you click the WampServer icon, you open the main WampServer server as a web page, as shown in Figure D.15.

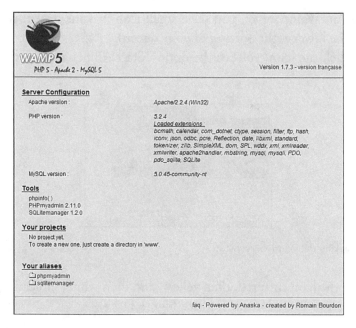

FIGURE D.15   The root level of WampServer.

In the Your Projects section, you see any folders or websites you have created. If you click one, you go to that site.

When you're installing Joomla, on the Installation Wizard page about the database configuration (see Chapter 2, "Downloading and Installing Joomla!"), you need to provide the SQL details for WampServer:

- Host name = localhost
- User name = root
- Password = [none/blank]
- Database name = [Put anything you like here]

WampServer will then be able to create a database for the Joomla site you are installing.

Index

Your purchase of **Joomla!™ 1.6: A User's Guide** includes access to a free online edition for 45 days through the Safari Books Online subscription service. Nearly every Prentice Hall book is available online through Safari Books Online, along with more than 5,000 other technical books and videos from publishers such as Addison-Wesley Professional, Cisco Press, Exam Cram, IBM Press, O'Reilly, Que, and Sams.

SAFARI BOOKS ONLINE allows you to search for a specific answer, cut and paste code, download chapters, and stay current with emerging technologies.

Activate your FREE Online Edition at
www.informit.com/safarifree

STEP 1: Enter the coupon code: TAOVNCB.

STEP 2: New Safari users, complete the brief registration form.
Safari subscribers, just log in.

If you have difficulty registering on Safari or accessing the online edition,
please e-mail customer-service@safaribooksonline.com